Competition and Coercion
Blacks in the American economy, 1865–1914

THIS BOOK IS DEDICATED TO MY PARENTS
JESS AND DORIS HIGGS
WHO BY THEIR OWN EXAMPLES TAUGHT ME
THE THINGS THAT MATTER MOST

Competition and Coercion

Blacks in the American economy
1865–1914

ROBERT HIGGS
UNIVERSITY OF WASHINGTON

HOOVER INSTITUTION PUBLICATION P 163

CAMBRIDGE UNIVERSITY PRESS

CAMBRIDGE

LONDON · NEW YORK · MELBOURNE

Published by the Syndics of the Cambridge University Press
The Pitt Building, Trumpington Street, Cambridge CB2 1RP
Bentley House, 200 Euston Road, London NW1 2DB
32 East 57th Street, New York, NY 10022, USA
296 Beaconsfield Parade, Middle Park, Melbourne 3206, Australia

© Cambridge University Press 1977

First published 1977

Typeset, printed, and bound in the United States of America
by Vail-Ballou Press, Inc., Binghamton, New York

Library of Congress Cataloging in Publication Data
Higgs, Robert.

Competition and coercion.

(Hoover Institution publications; P163)

Bibliography: p.

Includes index.

1. Afro-Americans – Economic conditions. I. Title.

II. Series: Stanford University. Hoover Institution on War, Revolution, and Peace.
Publications; P163.

E185.8.H6   331.6′3′96073   76-9178
ISBN 0 521 21120 4

Hoover Institution Publication P163

Contents

Tables

Preface

The title of this book expresses its central theme: economic competition and racial coercion as joint determinants of the material condition of America's blacks during the first half century after their emancipation. Racial coercion has received extensive scholarly attention, but important competitive processes remain largely overlooked. I seek to redress the balance, to show that competitive forces profoundly influenced black economic life, indeed, that competition played an important part in protecting blacks from the racial coercion to which they were peculiarly vulnerable. Lest this be mistaken for economics run rampant I must warn the reader that my interpretation attaches fundamental importance to political and legal forces in the shaping of black economic development: the exclusion of blacks from effective participation in politics and from the equal protection of the law had both direct and indirect effects that retarded their economic progress. To say that their progress was retarded, however, is not to say that no progress occurred. I have devoted considerable attention to documenting and crudely quantifying the substantial economic gains realized by the black population during the half century after 1865.

My objectives are limited, and no one should mistake the present volume for a comprehensive economic history of black Americans in the post-Civil War era. For example, although I discuss the relation between the postbellum credit system of the South and black economic progress, I make no attempt to resolve the many open questions about the business methods of the merchant creditors, the extent of their monopoly power, or their role in the land tenure system of the rural South. Similarly, my discussions of crop choice and farm size fall considerably short of the sophistication one can expect to find in the journal literature. In some sections I have perhaps generalized with too little micro-level evidence to satisfy historians; in other sections I have relied on evidence that economists may consider anecdotal. On a few occasions, considering a question too important to ignore but too unimportant to detain me for long, I have simply stated my considered opinion. These limitations notwithstanding, I hope that the book still serves its intended purposes: to reorganize the present conceptualization and redirect the future study of black economic history in the postemancipation era, to raise new questions, to suggest new answers to old questions, to assert that some of the old questions are misleadingly framed or not worth pursuing at all.

In writing this book I was forced to make a difficult choice. The exposition could have taken the form preferred by economists, replete with mathematical notation, formally specified models, and the apparatus of econometrics. The alternative was to employ simple English. For several reasons I have chosen the latter, relegating to an appendix the technical analyses I could not resist. Not the least of my reasons for selecting this style of exposition is a hope that historians and students will read the book. And perhaps, should any of my fellow economists give it a try, they will discover – to turn Willard Gibbs on his head – that English is a language, too.

Several scholars helped me by challenging my interpretations, suggesting further questions, pointing out errors, and guiding me to neglected literature. George D. Green tried persistently, over a period of almost a year, to make me address broader and more complex issues; he was always critical but always constructive, possessing a rare and beautiful combination of scholarly talents. Stanley L. Engerman, Gavin Wright, Stephen DeCanio, and Edward F. Meeker read a preliminary draft and made many helpful suggestions. I only wish I were capable of meeting their exacting standards.

I benefited also from the support of several institutions. The Department of Economics at the University of Washington provided a variety of services ranging from funds for computer time and xeroxing to the active encouragement of the chairman, Douglass C. North. At Oxford, Max Hartwell was instrumental in securing me a position as a visiting fellow of Nuffield College during 1971–1972. Nuffield generously provided me an office, equipment, and access to the Oxford University computer center as well as a stimulating environment for research. During 1973–1974 I was the recipient of a National Fellowship at the Hoover Institution on War, Revolution and Peace at Stanford University. There I was able to write and to pursue my studies free from the usual competing demands of university life. I wish to acknowledge not only the financial support of the Hoover Institution but also the intellectually stimulating and helpful people who made my stay at Stanford so enjoyable and productive.

Finally, the reader should know that my text was written in 1974. Only a few publications appearing after mid-1974 have been cited. Black economic history is now a lively field of research, and new findings are constantly appearing; but to complete a book an author must draw the line somewhere. In any event, nothing I have seen recently would lead me to alter the basic conclusions of my text.

June 10, 1976   ROBERT HIGGS

"Race" and "racial discrimination":
A prefatory note on usage

This book deals with the economic history of the "black race" in the United States from 1865 to 1914. What defined this group? Evidently the persons who constituted it were not all literally black; in fact their skin color ranged from black through various shades of brown to red, yellow, and even white. Moreover, any claim that they belonged to a biologically unique class has, in the judgment of modern scientists, a questionable validity at best. Current scientific interpretations maintain "that races are neither discrete nor stable units but rather that they are plastic, changing, integral parts of a whole which is itself changing . . . [and] that racial differences involve the relative frequency of genes and characteristics rather than absolute and mutually exclusive distinctions."[1] All these facts are interesting, and no doubt important for some purposes, but they have little bearing on the present study. For the "blacks" of the post-Civil War era were culturally defined as those persons believed to possess some African ancestry, no matter how remote. More concretely, as W. E. B. Du Bois expressed it back in the days of segregated railway cars, "the black man is a person who must ride 'Jim Crow' in Georgia."[2] Contemporaries had little difficulty with the concept of race, and all but lunatics and small children satisfactorily distinguished the "blacks" from the "whites." The present study follows their own usage. To do otherwise would create burdensome and unnecessary expositional problems.

An additional clarification concerns "racial discrimination." Popular literature and common discourse have come to employ this expression quite loosely, frequently to denote what should properly be described simply as "racial difference." The present study adopts a strict usage: racial discrimination occurs when a black individual and a white individual receive different treatment under conditions that are identical in every other respect. To illustrate, suppose two workers, one white and one black, are employed in the same shop, at the same task, working with the same tools and materials. One produces more output and receives a correspondingly greater wage. In this case the employer is not said to practice racial discrimination. If the two workers under identical conditions produce identical outputs but receive different wages, then the employer is said to practice racial discrimination in the payment of wages. Of course, where a racial difference exists without any racial discrimination, the difference itself may well be traceable to racial discrimination elsewhere, for example, in a worker's admission to apprenticeship or other opportunities for increasing his productivity. Nevertheless, instances of racial difference and racial discrimination must be kept analytically distinct. Otherwise it is virtually impossible to identify the fundamental influences responsible for racial inequalities in such variables as employment, wages, and incomes.

1

Approaching the facts

Emancipation is one fact, and effective liberty is another. Man does not have all his rights and privileges, he does not have free exercise of his faculties and skills by the simple consequence of the abolition of slavery. Old attitudes survive the proclamation of liberty, and old interests persist through the changes brought about by a new regime. After slavery has disappeared from the law, the former rulers seem to want to preserve slavery in fact.

La Tribune de la Nouvelle Orleans, 1865

In black economic history, as in any history, the facts do not speak for themselves. They require selection, classification, and interpretation, and for these purposes the investigator must employ a model. That any attempt at causal analysis must make use of a model, either explicitly or implicitly, is generally admitted. That explicit models are preferable to implicit ones is a long-standing precept of economists and a principle increasingly affirmed by historians. But recognition of the need for an explicit model is only a starting point. Real difficulty arises in choosing an appropriate model. The economic historian, generally a consumer rather than a producer of models, can look to the economic theorist for assistance. The historian may not find exactly what he needs in the existing corpus of economic theory, but it is nevertheless a good place to begin the search for an appropriate model.

Economic development without racial discrimination

The appropriateness of a model depends largely, of course, on the questions at issue. What are the central questions of black economic history? In many respects they are simply the familiar questions of general economic history as they apply to the blacks. Of obvious interest are such matters as the growth of the population, the pattern of migration, the occupational distribution of the labor force, the level and structure of earnings, the rate of property accumulation, and changes in levels of living. The existing body of economic theory has much to say about these subjects, and therefore it provides a useful – indeed an indispensable – point of departure for analysis.

Though the economic experience of black Americans has been

shaped in a profound way by forces associated with race, it is essential
to consider how other forces have operated as well. To see these other
influences in isolation one must consider a world that never really
existed, a wholly hypothetical construction, yet one that is still revealing. This world might have existed had American slavery taken a racially neutral form, had it involved men of all races on the same terms.
To perceive the implications of this counterfactual construction, it will
serve best to eliminate the racial element entirely. Imagine then that
no blacks ever came to America, that the labor force during the two
and a half centuries before 1865 consisted of free whites and enslaved
whites. Otherwise everything was the same.

At the conclusion of the Civil War in 1865, important features of the
situation would have been that almost all the freedmen lived in the
devastated South; they possessed relatively few skills, and those were
applicable mainly in agricultural production; they were predominantly
illiterate and endowed with very little experience in independent management; they were trained in docility and deference to the master
class, with a history of extreme dependence; they owned no property
except the clothes on their backs. But in the summer of 1865 they were
no longer the legal property of their masters. What would the economic
evolution of such people have been in the subsequent half century?
The following sketch is a plausible hypothetical history.

In all likelihood the first occurrence would have been an extended
celebration and vacation from labor. One could scarcely expect anything else from people previously bound to labor for life, now sud-
denly liberated. But certainly this vacation from labor could not have
lasted long; for a group devoid of property could not have expected to
survive long on the charity of their former masters, especially when
those erstwhile masters, having just suffered an enormous loss of wealth
by wartime destruction and the uncompensated emancipation, were in
neither the condition nor the mood to offer much charity. Rather
quickly then, some arrangement would have been made to bring together the only resource of the freedmen, their labor, with the land,
capital, and managerial skills of the former master class, so that all
parties could reestablish production and generate incomes.

Just what forms those arrangements might have taken is, like the
whole story, conjectural. But in one way or another the freedmen
would have entered into employment under the direction of those who
controlled the resources essential for making their labor productive.
Whether they worked for fixed wages, for a share of a crop, or under
some other arrangement to compensate them for their labor services,
the freedmen would have gone to work. And because, typically, they
had little more than muscle to offer, their rewards in the labor market

would have been relatively low, though still conceivably above the real compensation they had received as slaves.

Once at work and earning incomes, the freedmen would have begun to consider the means by which they could improve their material condition. They would have perceived several: migration to areas of superior opportunities; education and training; and accumulation of productive property. One might reasonably have expected that, to some extent, they would move to the cities and to the northern and western parts of the United States. Short moves would probably have been most common, for the freedmen possessed few resources for financing transportation and meeting other costs of moving, and they lacked information about more distant opportunities. So their departure from the countryside and from the South would have begun slowly but, over time, the knowledge of the success of the early migrants would have filtered back and stimulated a more rapid emigration from the rural South, where the relative abundance of unskilled laborers made their remuneration lower than elsewhere. Similarly the people's poverty would have seriously impeded their pursuit of education and training. But again, as some became educated and trained, their incomes would have risen and they would have been better able to finance further advances for their children. Property accumulation, too, would have begun slowly, because people with very low incomes cannot divert much from current consumption and still survive. But accumulation would have fed upon itself, and before long some freedmen – the lucky or especially talented ones – would have begun to amass small fortunes; the second generation, building from its modest inheritances, would have accumulated even more. All these actions would, of course, have been impeded by the legacies of slavery: illiteracy and inexperience in the independent management of their own affairs. But the incentives would have been fairly clear, and many would have responded in ways that advanced their material welfare.

Working in concert with all of this – the migration to better opportunities, the acquisition of economically valuable skills, and the accumulation of property – would have been the increasing difficulty of identifying the freedmen, the even greater difficulty of identifying their sons, the virtual impossibility of identifying their grandsons. Intermarriage with the offspring of the old masters could hardly have been checked, although many a proud old family would have tried hard to prevent it. Moreover, even where "pure stocks" persisted, there simply would have been no distinguishing mark. The grandson of the slave would have looked like the grandson of the master, and he would have acted no differently. Some freedmen would have concealed their background, a simple deception as the "poor free" element of the old master class had never differed much from the slaves anyhow. Above everything would have been the central fact that the freedmen and their descendants were gradually being incorporated, through intermarriage as well as socially and economically, into the overall society.[1]

Racial prejudice, hostility, and discrimination

The preceding hypothetical sketch has a measure of plausibility and, more importantly, it does suggest certain actual events during the first 50 years after the emancipation: black people did migrate to areas of greater opportunity; they did acquire education and training; and they did accumulate property; all of which contributed toward an increase in their incomes and an improvement in their level of living. Insofar as these events occurred, standard economic models adequately explain them; they represent nothing more than investments of various sorts that yielded a positive return, as expected by those undertaking them.[2]

But, having recognized the usefulness of an all-white counterfactual perspective for understanding the actual world of white and black, one must also recognize the severe limitations of this perspective. In the hypothetical world the freedmen and their descendants made their investments, raised their incomes, and merged into the wider society socially and through intermarriage. After a time, perhaps several generations, they lost any distinct identity attaching to them by virtue of their having been or being descended from slaves. Countless real Americans did slough off their identification with a disadvantaged ethnic group in American history. But the black Americans did not. Neither did they ever close the economic gap separating them from others, as many immigrant groups did. Even the infamous "poor whites," so often compared unfavorably with the blacks in the immediate postbellum period, ultimately climbed upward and merged into the wider society. Evidently race made a difference. And any really useful model of black economic history must incorporate the essential racial element that has set the black experience apart from the experience of virtually every other submerged group in American history. The crucial difference can be traced to slavery.

American slavery applied only to blacks, and this fact is supremely important in understanding how black people fared *after* emancipation. During the period of slavery, especially during its last three decades, the whites elaborated an extensive set of beliefs about the blacks. That human bondage existed side by side with the Christian religion and with an ideology of "all men created equal" apparently prompted these beliefs. The whites could not banish completely the guilt that surrounded slavery, but they tried hard and, by fashioning an elaborate justification from various ethical, political, economic, and biological components, they succeeded at least in keeping their feelings of guilt well below the surface most of the time.[3]

Black slavery, so the story went, was a "positive good" because the blacks were inherently inferior. The whites stood in the position of "natural" superiors. But they recognized an obligation to the blacks like that of an adult toward a child, an obligation to protect and care for the simple needs of a simple people. They recognized, too, that the blacks could offer useful services in return, generally the performance of arduous field labor in the production of the Southern staple crops. With whites and blacks occupying their preordained social and economic spheres, society would be not only prosperous but happy, for everyone would recognize and fill his proper "place." Finding biblical, even "scientific," support for these beliefs was not difficult for people committed to them in any event.

After the Civil War, *DeBow's Review,* a leading organ of Southern opinion, opened its pages to a proslavery theorist, George Fitzhugh, who expounded the philosophy of race relations most widely accepted in the South:

We should treat them [the blacks] as mere grown-up children, entitled like children, or apprentices, to the protection of guardians or masters, and bound to obey those put above them, in place of parents, just as children are so bound. Little legal regulation is needed to induce white men to work. But a great deal of severe legislation will be required to compel negroes to labor as much as they should do, in order not to become a charge upon the whites. We must have a black code. . . . Mere law cannot sufficiently govern negroes. . . . They need masters of some sort, as well to protect as to govern them. And masters they will have, or soon perish and disappear from the face of the earth.[4]

And again:

Nature never intended, and never will permit the races to live together, except as masters and slaves, so that the superior race, commanding the labor of the inferior race, shall at the same time be compelled to provide for, and take care of that race. We do not mean by slavery such as that which has been recently abolished, but some form of subordination of the inferior race that shall compel them to labor, whilst it protects their rights and provides for their wants.[5]

Evidently white Southerners intended to preserve the privileged position of their race regardless of the emancipation.

To say that American slavery was a system of carefully justified racial discrimination is to utter the obvious, but an important and not-so-obvious implication is that under slavery racial discrimination acquired a value that transcended the economic gains it made possible for the master class. Long before 1865 the whites had acquired what Gary Becker has called a "taste for discrimination," and that taste, being a fundamental part of their views about proper social life, was certain to persist long after the institution that nurtured it had disappeared. To possess a taste for discrimination is to value racial discrimination enough to pay for its exercise if it cannot be practiced freely. Becker has used this insightful conceptualization of the taste for discrimination to construct an elaborate model of the market system in a world of discrimination.[6]

In Becker's model the taste for discrimination can be indulged in various ways: white workers can refuse to work in company with blacks unless they receive a wage premium, even though this increase in their supply price involves a reduction in the quantity of their labor services demanded; white employers can refuse to hire black workers unless the blacks agree to accept a lower wage than the white workers, even though this policy reduces the quantity of black labor services supplied to discriminating employers; and white customers can refuse to purchase from black sellers unless the price of the good is discounted, even though this price reduction involves a reduction in the quantity of goods supplied. That these forms of discrimination may entail losses for the whites does not necessarily mean that they will not persist. The losses involved may, under certain conditions, simply reflect the price paid for the whites' gratification of their taste for discrimination, for them a Good Thing.[7]

Like any other Good Thing, however, discrimination is subject to the law of demand: the more costly is discrimination for the whites, the less will they discriminate, other things being the same. When some of the whites do not value the exercise of discrimination and cannot be kept from acting accordingly, discrimination can be particularly costly for the whites who do discriminate. White workers, for example, may find themselves priced out of the labor market if they insist on a wage premium that nondiscriminating employers do not consider warranted by their productivity; and discriminating employers, who do pay the higher wage to white workers, will find their costs of production above those of their nondiscriminating competitors, and hence their survival in the industry will be jeopardized. There is, therefore, a fundamental inconsistency between purely economic competition and purely racial discrimination. In the long run, under competitive conditions where not all employers value discrimination, it is unlikely to persist.

This is an ingenious model and one that provides important insights into the workings of discrimination in a market economy. As Becker has said, "no one has shown how thousands of firms and millions of workers are able to conspire successfully against minorities."[8] In some instances this model has provided a compelling interpretation of observed racial equalities under conditions of extreme racial prejudice and hostility.[9] Yet Becker's model has its limitations, and they are quite severe in some contexts, including the American South in the years from 1865 to 1914. The main difficulty arises because the model applies only to market transactions, while racial discrimination in the postbellum South was much more pervasive; discrimination *outside* the market sector had an important influence in determining the opportunities open to blacks *inside* the market sector. A purely individualistic, competitive, economic model cannot incorporate some of the key variables in the larger interdependent system of which the market is but a part.

Moreover, when Becker's book is read in conjunction with some of the documents of postbellum Southern history, one gets the uneasy feeling that the model applies more to a kind of tea-party discrimination than to the blood and steel of the Southern racial scene. Witness the report of Colonel Samuel Thomas, a federal military officer, writing from the South in 1865:

[T]hey [the Southern whites] are yet unable to conceive of the negro as possessing any rights at all. Men who are honorable in their dealings with their white neighbors will cheat a negro without feeling a single twinge of their honor. To kill a negro they do not deem murder; to debauch a negro woman they do not think fornication; to take the property away from a negro they do not consider robbery. The people boast that when they get freedmen affairs in their own hands, to use their own classic expression, "the niggers will catch hell." The reason of all this is simple and manifest. The whites esteem the blacks their property by natural right, and however much they may admit that the individual relations of masters and slaves have been destroyed by the war and by the President's emancipation proclamation, they still have an ingrained feeling that the blacks at large belong to the whites at large, and whenever opportunity serves they treat the colored people just as their profit, caprice, or passion may dictate.[10]

Can a model of purely individualistic, competitive, economic discrimination really say much about such a situation?

Economic development with racial discrimination

Becker himself recognizes the limitations of his model. In the introduction to the second edition of his pioneering book, he says that "the most important and pervasive influence . . . clearly has been government action," and he mentions "the restrictions legislated against Negroes in various southern states." "Our ignorance of the scope and incidence of collective action against minorities," he concludes, "is perhaps the most important remaining gap in the analysis of the economic position of minorities."[11]

In fact, during the period 1865–1914, the legislation of the Southern states probably mattered less than the refusal of the whites who controlled the legal machinery to provide equal protection to the blacks. This allowed a reign of "private" lawlessness, intimidation, and violence that had pervasive effects on the economic behavior of the blacks. By virtue of the public sector's complicity in these actions, "private" coercion and persecution were indirectly aspects of what Becker calls "collective discrimination"; but he has not chosen to incorporate such elements into his analysis. To do so would complicate the model considerably, but perhaps an inelegant analysis of a central problem would be more valuable than a rigorous analysis of a peripheral issue.

In the postbellum South a black was expected to behave in a distinctive fashion. Blacks in their dealing with whites must be subservient, agreeable, and good humored; a black who actively disagreed with a white on even a trivial matter opened the door to verbal abuse, threats, and physical violence. Failure to observe the racial etiquette might bring swift and harsh retribution. Plantation managers who could only curse or dismiss recalcitrant white workers sometimes resorted to whipping the blacks. Blacks who appeared too "uppity" – insufficiently deferential – in the eyes of the whites occasionally fell victim to horrible punishments at the hands of white mobs or gangs of roughnecks out to prove their manhood and protect the moral order of their communities. The racial atrocities of the Reconstruction period are well known; that widespread racial intimidation persisted well into the twentieth century is equally a fact. As late as 1912, L. C. Gray noted that

usually negroes [on plantations] are so densely ignorant that they know little of their rights under the law. There are thousands who have no idea how to obtain legal redress. It is easy to impose on such credulity to effect a practically coerced service. The mere moral prestige of the white and the fear of physical violence, rarely employed, but always a potentiality, are often sufficient.[12]

It would only distort the facts a little to say that whites never received punishment for crimes against blacks.

When black people came into contact with governmental authorities, they could usually expect discriminatory treatment – less so during Reconstruction, almost certainly afterwards. Police dealt more harshly with the black man. At the hands of white judges and juries in the law courts, blacks were more likely to be convicted, and they often received longer sentences or greater fines than similar white offenders. White public school officials allocated fewer resources to black than to white children. In politics blacks might be excluded altogether. Clearly, in the exercise of personal, political, and property rights the two races fared quite differently. While black people could hardly be excluded from the consumption of market goods and services – though segregation regulations did sometimes restrict their consumption of certain goods and services[13] – their consumption of governmental services and protection might be squeezed quite thin, at times to the vanishing point. With few exceptions, the whites sought to indulge their taste for discrimination, a taste for "keeping the nigger in his place." And governmental officials were privileged to occupy positions from which discrimination might be exercised at little or no cost to them. It is hardly surprising if actual effective discrimination were more rampant in the public sector than in the market.[14]

How then did the whites' taste for discrimination, nurtured under the slave regime, affect the economic history of black Americans after the emancipation? In its broad outlines, much of the sketch of the hypothetical white freedmen presented above applies as well to the actual black freedmen. But at almost every step the earlier statement must be altered by a qualifying clause that expresses the influence of racial discrimination. Thus, black freedmen did recognize the critical importance of education, *but* white school officials systematically constricted their access to the public school system. Blacks did respond to opportunities in other regions, *but* their reception in the North and the West was often hostile, and white trade unions in those regions excluded them from opportunities in many nonagricultural occupations. Blacks did accumulate property, *but* the actions of white police and law courts attenuated their property rights by refusing to provide them with the equal protection of the laws. Consequently, although blacks did make considerable progress in raising their productivity and hence their incomes and levels of living in the half century after emancipation, they did not progress as rapidly as they could have in the absence of the whites' taste for and exercise of racial discrimination. And above all – and most unlike the hypothetical white freedmen – they did not merge into the broader society through intermarriage, the proscription of which remained tightly enforced. Except for the few both able and willing to "pass" into the white society, the blacks remained easily identified, open targets for those who wished to discriminate against them.[15]

Investment under discrimination and attenuated property rights

The influence of discrimination on black economic development can be shown in a more rigorous fashion by considering the investment process in somewhat greater detail. When an individual diverts income from current consumption into uses that promise to increase his income in the future, he makes an investment. Many kinds of investment are not ordinarily labeled as such. For example, the man who bears the costs of transferring his family to an area of higher wages makes an investment in migration. The man who sends his children to school instead of to the cotton field invests in their education. Of course the acquisition of land, tools, and buildings has always been recognized as investment.

In considering the desirability of an investment, individuals form expectations concerning the costs, the returns, and the future periods when costs and returns will accrue. Since values differ according to the periods of waiting they require, the investor must translate future values into present values to evaluate his opportunities properly. The economic theorist idealizes the decision process by supposing that the investor calculates the net present value of an investment;[16] whenever this exceeds zero the investment is expected to be profitable and should be undertaken if the investor is to maximize his wealth. Of course, individuals rarely perform such an elaborate calculation, but the theory does express what they usually consider the common sense of an investment decision. Thus, a man will usually regard as unwarranted the expense of moving 500 miles to realize a one percent increase in wages. Nor will he pay as much for a fruit tree that will not yield any fruit for five years as he will for one bearing now. He will not send his children to school if the costs, measured by the sacrifice in the family's level of living, are "too high." Individuals may seldom calculate present values, but they do ask "is it worth it?" Strictly speaking, the answer "it is worth it" and the answer "net present value exceeds zero" are equivalent.

An essential feature of the investment decision, however, is that no one really knows the future. Hence, the returns and costs in future periods are merely "expected" and not certain. Future conditions may turn out differently from those projected; and if they do, it will then be too late for the initial investment decision to be affected. When tomorrow comes, today's investment is already committed. The investor protects himself against the riskiness of the future by discounting in his expectations the values that may later accrue. The returns and costs of the present value formula are themselves the answers to probabilistic problems in every period except the initial one, which is the (known) present. For example, a farmer expects his mule's services next year to be worth a $25 rental, but the mule may die. If the probability is $4/5$ that the mule will survive through the next season, then the expected value of his services next year is: $4/5$ ($25) + $1/5$ (0) = $20. In this example the risk is natural, but other risks arise from the way property rights are defined and enforced.

So far the discussion of the investment decision has implicitly assumed that whatever net returns do accrue from an investment, the investor can actually appropriate them; the assumption has been that secure private property rights prevail. For the typical black investor of the period 1865–1914, this assumption is somewhat at variance with the facts. The black man could expect a higher risk to surround his investments because the agencies charged with enforcing property rights, the police and the law courts, did not offer him equal protection. For the black man the future was always more uncertain than for the white man. Hence, to adjust for this greater risk, he discounted future returns more heavily. Moreover, if he could expect to encounter effective discrimination in the marketplace, the stream of projected returns would be reduced, or the projected costs increased, or the rate of interest higher, as compared with the levels applicable to a white investor. All these differences worked to reduce the present value of investment by blacks and therefore to discourage them from investing as much as whites, other things being the same. In plain language, black people were tempted to migrate, to become educated, and to accumulate property less than similar white people because they could not expect the same results – all of which worked to preserve the *status quo* of their economic condition.

Summary: A scenario for black economic history, 1865–1914

Black economic history in the half century after emancipation makes sense only when interpreted as an interplay of two systems of behavior: a competitive economic system and a coercive racial system. Black people participated actively in the market economy as workers, investors, and consumers, but they acted under more constraints than the white participants in market activities. Denied equal protection of person and property, effectively excluded from governmental decision making after Reconstruction, bullied and abused in their attempts to consume some of the same goods and services as the whites, exposed to horrible risks, black people continued to seek improvement in their material condition, responding to new opportunities along the same avenues as the whites. Investments in migration, in education and training, and in tangible property were the roads to advancement for this racially oppressed people. That they actively grasped these opportunities is clear testimony to their hope for a better future and their willingness to make sacrifices to obtain it; that their advance was less than spectacular is easy to understand. To swim in the sea of a dynamic and highly competitive economic system was difficult enough without the weight of racial discrimination forever pulling downward.

2

The people

"They cannot take care of themselves," it is said; "they can neither take care of their children, nor manage themselves in sickness, nor bring themselves to sanitary laws and habits, now that the benevolent eye of the slave-owner is withdrawn. It is a mere matter of time; they must die out in the end." It is really quite surprising how seriously this is said, when it is so directly contrary to fact. . . . It is patent to the eye that they are not a people who have the least intention of dying out. . . . They are an inevitable fact, and it is incumbent on every well-wisher of America to make the best of them, instead of supposing that heaven will remove the difficulty.

Sir George Campbell, 1879

In the spring of 1865 about five million blacks lived in the United States, some 90 percent of them just set free by the force of Northern arms. Tens of thousands of them were destitute, without homes or any source of material support. Many were refugees from battle zones, transients living at the mercy of their fellows and Northern troops; others huddled in makeshift camps scattered throughout the Southern countryside and outside the larger towns. Wherever they gathered, hunger and disease attended them, and epidemics of smallpox, typhoid fever, and dysentery ran rampant, sweeping away thousands. Infant mortality rose to unprecedented heights. On the plantations, where the bulk of the black population remained, conditions were somewhat better but still menacing. Even where Northern invasions had not penetrated, the breakdown of the Southern monetary system and the creaking inefficiency of the shattered transport network disrupted the supply of food and clothing. In some areas, especially in Texas, plundering by roving bands of desperadoes made the situation even more difficult.[1]

Under such conditions the most immediate concern of black people was mere survival, and it is hardly surprising that many whites predicted a speedy demise of the freedmen. The editor of the Natchez *Democrat* declared in January 1866:

The child is already born who will behold the last negro in the State of Mississippi. With no one to provide for the aged and the young, the sick and the helpless incompetent to provide for themselves, and brought unprepared into competition with the superior intelligence, tact, and muscle of free white labor, they must surely and speedily perish.[2]

In much the same spirit an old Virginia planter made the forecast: "Less than a hundred years of freedom will see the race practically exterminated [sic]."[3]

In the first year after the war such expectations seemed to have some basis in fact but, as the reorganization of the Southern economy proceeded, the prospect of black extinction quickly faded. After two or three years most people recognized that, far from disappearing, the black population was again increasing rapidly. The census of 1870 showed that the number of blacks had grown by 10 percent during the 1860s. This enumeration, however, was particularly defective, and census officials later estimated that the actual increase was 21 percent, hardly lower than the rate of increase that had prevailed during the 1850s. In the 1870s the black population grew by an estimated 22 percent.[4]

In 1890 another serious undercount of blacks by the census led some observers to revive the question of race extinction.[5] While this was hardly a real issue, it was true that the rate of increase declined after 1880. (The rate of natural increase was also slowing for whites, but immigration served partially to offset this retardation.) By 1915 the black population had reached about 10 million, having approximately doubled during the first half century of freedom. Because the white population was growing faster, the black population declined relatively: in 1860 one American in every seven was black, by 1910 less than one in nine (see Table 2.1).

Fertility, mortality, and natural increase

Despite the serious underenumerations of 1870 and 1890, the census reports document the growth of the black population reasonably well. The levels of fertility and mortality that combined to produce the observed growth, however, are difficult to determine. Enumerations of deaths in the censuses of 1850–1900 were so defective that they are worthless. Only a small and unrepresentative fraction of the black population lived in the death registration area, and births were not registered at all before 1915. To circumvent the barriers of deficient data, demographers have made use of sophisticated analytical devices: stable or quasi-stable population theory and model life tables. These permit the estimation of fertility and mortality rates based on data describing the age–sex distribution of the population, which are available in the census reports. Unfortunately, the basic data are inaccurate or incomplete to a varying extent from one census to another, and therefore modifications, corrections, and additional assumptions are required as

Table 2.1. *Black population, 1860–1910*

Year	Number (millions) (1) [a]	% change during previous decade (2) [a]	Black population as % of total population (3)
1860	4.4	22	14
1870	5.4	21	14
1880	6.6	22	13
1890	7.8	18	12
1900	8.8	14	12
1910	9.8	11	11

[a] Columns (1) and (2) disagree slightly because of rounding. Estimates of black population by Coale and Rives imply that the figures in column (1) are understated by 9–14 percent. No doubt the census data are too low, but in view of the highly arbitrary and implausible assumptions employed by Coale and Rives in their statistical reconstructions, no one need accept their conclusions as reliable. Moreover, the growth rates implied by the series of Coale and Rives differ little from those implied by the data in column (1). See Ansley J. Coale and Norfleet W. Rives, Jr., "A Statistical Reconstruction of the Black Population of the United States, 1880–1970: Estimates of True Numbers By Age and Sex, Birth Rates, and Total Fertility," *Population Index* 39 (1973): 21.
Source: U. S. Bureau of the Census, *Negro Population, 1790–1915* (Washington, 1918), p. 29.

part of the estimation procedure. Various demographers have made these adjustments in various ways, and hence their resulting estimates disagree, sometimes by rather wide margins. Nevertheless, some points of agreement have emerged from this research. In examining the conclusions that the demographers have reached concerning vital rates, it is well to maintain a critical stance and to consider whether their findings are consistent with what is known about the economic and social history of the black population.

Demographers agree that black fertility declined rapidly after 1880. A variety of evidence points toward this conclusion. For example, the child–woman ratio, defined as the number of children under 5 years of age per 1,000 women 15 to 44 years of age, declined steadily from 760 in 1880 to 519 in 1910, a reduction of about one-third.[6] This decline is so great that one can scarcely doubt the direction of the trend. Though the child–woman ratio is a common surrogate measure of fertility, it has limitations because it varies with changes in the accuracy of age–sex reporting from one census to another, and with changes in mortality among women and children. Reynolds Farley has estimated a better index of fertility, the gross reproduction rate. This shows the number of daughters an average woman would bear if she lived through the childbearing period and if fertility rates did not change. According to Farley's estimates, the gross reproduction rate declined by about a third between 1880 and 1910 (see Table 2.2). Farley also determined that "the decline in Negro fertility rates resulted from changes in the size of families. Once, many black women had extremely large families – that is, ten or more children. Over time, this changed as small families and childlessness became common."[7]

An economic model of reproductive behavior provides a useful framework for analyzing the long-term decline in black fertility. Suppose that people consider the decision to produce an additional child in the same way that they evaluate an investment in migration or education or physical property. In this view a child is a durable good yielding a stream of returns and requiring a stream of costs over a lengthy period of time. The returns may be tangible; that is, after some minimum age, the child becomes economically useful and therefore capable of earning an income that the parents can appropriate. Or the returns may be psychic, the parents obtaining direct satisfaction from rearing the child. One can imagine a monetary value being attached to such psychic returns even if the parents do not consciously conceptualize the strength of their parental gratifications in pecuniary terms. Set against the material and psychic returns of an additional child are the costs of rearing the child: food, clothing, shelter, and medical care for the child require direct outlays; moreover, an additional cost must be counted if caring for the child requires resources – primarily parental time and labor ser-

Table 2.2. *Estimates of the gross reproduction rate for blacks, 1880–1910*

Year	Uncorrected for undercount		Corrected for undercount	
	Assumes higher childhood mortality	Assumes lower childhood mortality	Assumes higher childhood mortality	Assumes lower childhood mortality
1880	3.21	2.73	3.55	2.90
1890	2.46	2.08	2.70	2.28
1900	2.42	2.08	2.65	2.28
1910	2.18	1.82	2.39	2.00

Source: Reynolds Farley, *Growth of the Black Population: A Study of Demographic Trends* (Chicago, 1970), p. 55.

vices – that could be productively employed elsewhere. If the mother's childrearing activities require her to withdraw from productive employment, then the earnings foregone constitute a true cost of rearing the child. Considering both direct and indirect, tangible and intangible returns and costs, potential parents can form expectations about the distribution of returns and costs over time and compute the net present value of an additional child. Of course no one really calculates with such precision but, as always, an explicit analytical model of behavior serves to highlight some major considerations that do enter into actual decision making. Many parents certainly do evaluate the desirability of additional children by considering the associated costs and returns at least in a rough-and-ready way. Strictly speaking, to say "another child is desirable" and to say "the net present value of another child is positive" are equivalent. Obviously, actual reproductive behavior is more complicated than this model – partly because conception is less controllable than the model assumes – but an investment theory of childrearing furnishes a useful starting point for analysis.[8]

The usefulness of conceptualizing reproductive decisions as investment decisions comes from the testable hypotheses that such a view implies. For example, urban people would be expected to desire smaller families than rural people because (1) direct costs of childrearing, particularly the costs of food and shelter, are higher in cities, (2) mothers occupied at home sacrifice more valuable employment opportunities in cities, and (3) children generate smaller tangible returns in cities. Hence the testable hypothesis: rural fertility exceeds urban fertility at any point in time. And a closely related hypothesis: a relative shift of population into cities over time results in a reduction of aggregate fertility, other things being the same.

The urbanization hypothesis is easily tested and found to be consistent with the facts. Table 2.3 shows that urban residence was indeed associated with greatly reduced fertility. (The data do not directly measure fertility, of course, and a part of the urban–rural difference in the child–woman ratios is attributable to higher infant and child mortality in the cities; differences in the age–sex compositions of urban and rural populations may also bias the comparison.) In the South, where almost 90 percent of all blacks lived in 1910, the child–woman ratio for the population in places of less than 25,000 – mainly a rural population – exceeded the ratio for the population in larger places by almost 150 percent. Table 2.3 shows large regional differences in fertility, but these may also reflect urban–rural differences, at least in part, because the population in places of less than 25,000 was more dispersed throughout the countryside in the South than it was in the other regions, where small cities were relatively more abundant. Changes in the broad re-

Table 2.3. *Children under 5 per 1,000 women 15–44, by race, region, and urban– rural location, 1910*

Area	Black	White
In cities of 25,000 or more		
United States	239	368
South	248	360
North	225	378
West	207	282
Outside cities of 25,000 or more		
United States	596	552
South	609	665
North	383	494
West	270	530

Source: U.S. Bureau of the Census, *Negro Population, 1790–1915* (Washington, 1918), p. 290.

gional distribution of the population, it might be noted, cannot add to the explanation of secular change in fertility because the distribution of the black population between the South and the non-South was virtually constant during the period 1880–1910. The relation between the steady net migration of blacks into cities and the large reduction in their fertility during the period 1865–1914 requires further study, but no doubt urbanization played some part in prompting changes in reproductive behavior. To identify an association between urbanization and declining fertility, however, is not necessarily to discover the precise reason for a change in family behavior. For example, urban residents were generally better educated and more widely informed than rural people, and their lower fertility may have reflected their wider knowledge of alternatives to investment in children.

Some simple calculations are useful in exploring the strength of the association between urbanization and declining fertility.[9] These computations suggest that urbanization can directly account for only a minor part of the observed decline in aggregate fertility during the period 1880–1910. It is possible that some of the decline in "rural" fertility was associated with shifts of population within the class of places with populations of less than 25,000 toward the towns and out of the countryside. However, it seems clear that urbanization, no matter how liberally conceived, cannot directly account for more than a quarter of the decline in aggregate fertility. This is not to be despised; a partial understanding is better than no understanding at all. But the bulk of the change in fertility remains obscure.

Why did both rural and urban fertilities decline so greatly? Many conjectures might be offered. For example, fertility could have been linked to mortality. With declining mortality – a condition that probably prevailed, as shown below – parents would have required fewer births to achieve the same desired number of children surviving to adulthood, and hence would have reduced their fertility. Also, conceivably the decline in fertility represented a gradual adjustment away from the unrestrained fertility behavior inherited from the slave regime and toward a more calculating kind of family planning. Still another possibility is that the progressive spread of venereal disease through the black population resulted in an involuntary reduction of fertility.[10] But these are only conjectures. Clearly the declining fertility of the black population after 1880 requires a good deal of further study.

Changes in the mortality of the black population during the period 1865–1914 are even less adequately documented than changes in fertility. Again, in the absence of death registration data for the great majority of the population, alternative kinds of evidence must be employed in making estimates, and information on the changing age structure of the population provides the basis for the estimates. Although the inferences made about mortality differ according to the assumptions employed in manipulating the data, one thing seems quite clear: at least from 1900 forward, the trend of black mortality was downward. Knowledge of the trend before 1900 is more speculative, but it appears likely that some improvement in life expectancy did occur in the late nineteenth century.

Indirect evidence of a reduction in black mortality appears in the age composition of total deaths in the death registration area early in the twentieth century:

Of the total deaths at all ages, the proportion occurring in the ages under 25 years has tended to decline during the period [1900–1915]. Among males the proportion in the adult ages 25 to 44 years increased from 227 per 1,000 in 1900 to 277 per 1,000 in 1915; the proportion in the ages 45 to 64 increased from 169 to 229; and the proportion in the ages 65 to 84 from 77 to 121. Similar increases are shown for females. These changes indicate marked improvement as regards mortality.[11]

Unfortunately, this evidence applies only to the black population in the North and in large Southern cities. The bulk of the black population, inhabiting the rural South, is almost wholly unrepresented in the pre-1915 area of death registration.

Jack Eblen has developed estimates of mortality by decade intervals for the entire period 1810–1900.[12] Unfortunately, despite the demographic sophistication that appears to underlie them, these estimates are difficult to believe. Eblen's figures show that over the entire period of 90 years the black expectation of life at birth ranged between 33 and 34 years, and that the crude death rate changed between 30 and 31 deaths per 1,000 population. Such remarkable demographic stability sits uneasily beside the great economic and social changes experienced by the black population during the latter half of the nineteenth century. Indeed it appears that Eblen's procedures for adjusting and smoothing the census data have produced a stability in art that was unknown to nature. That the black crude death rate was the same – to the third significant digit – in the 1850s as in the 1860s is almost beyond comprehension in view of the many contemporary descriptions of unusually high mortality during the mid-1860s.[13]

Another set of estimates has been made by Edward Meeker for selected years in the period 1850–1910.[14] Employing quasi-stable population analysis and model life tables, Meeker has estimated the expectation of life at birth for the black population in 1850, 1860, 1880, 1900, and 1910. The basic data input is again the age structure of the population as reported by the census (with, as usual, some adjustments). Meeker's estimates show a decline in the expectation of life between the prewar years and 1880 and a substantial increase during the period 1880–1910. According to his figures, the expectation of life at birth increased by about six years during the three decades after 1880; by 1910 the reduction in life expectancy sustained sometime between 1860 and 1880 – the exact trend within that interval remaining unknown – had been more than recouped. The expectation of life at birth on the eve of World War I was about 33.[15] Meeker emphasizes that true mortality conditions must have improved even more than these figures indicate, because the steady shift of black population into urban (i.e., less healthy) areas tended to offset gains occurring in either urban or rural areas considered separately. The overall pattern of these findings – decline in the period including the war and its immediate aftermath, improvement thereafter with especially large gains in the early twentieth century – seems quite plausible and consistent with evidence on improvement in the average level of living of the black population in the late nineteenth and early twentieth centuries (see Chapter 5 below).

From an examination of the internal consistency of various estimated vital rates, it appears probable that mortality declined significantly after 1880. Suppose that the crude death rate in the 1870s was, as Meeker's estimates suggest, about 33 deaths per 1,000 population. Given that the rate of natural increase was about 20, it follows that the crude birth rate was about 53, which is plausible. (The rate of natural increase is the crude birth rate minus the crude death rate: $20 = 53 -$

33.) By 1910 the rate of natural increase had fallen to about 10. Assuming, as a variety of different estimates suggests, that fertility had fallen by about a third from the 1880 level, the crude birth rate in 1910 was about 35. The implied crude death rate was then about 25 (10 = 35 − 25). If this estimate is close to the truth, the implication is that black mortality declined by about 25 percent between the 1870s and the decade after 1910.[16]

Blacks, even more than whites, experienced higher mortality in cities than in the countryside. In the death registration area of 1910 the black death rate in places of 10,000 or more was 27.1; in smaller places (including purely rural areas) it was 19.5. Census officials in 1918 considered it "highly probable" that black mortality was much lower in the rural South than in the registration area. They reasoned that "in the North, the urban Negro population, at least to the extent that it is a migrant population native of the South, is subjected to conditions similar in some respects to those encountered by the foreign immigrant, and the difficulties of adjustment to these conditions may be reflected in the higher mortalities from such causes as tuberculosis and pneumonia."[17] In the registration area of 1910 the tuberculosis death rate for blacks was more than three times the rate for whites, and the pneumonia death rate for blacks more than twice the rate for whites.[18] Table 2.4 presents some fairly reliable evidence of racial mortality differentials in large cities, where death registration was practiced. These data also reveal the mortality reductions occurring in most American cities early in the twentieth century. Fragmentary evidence suggests that such reductions also occurred during the late nineteenth century: between the 1870s and the period 1900–1905, black mortality rates declined substantially in Baltimore, New Orleans, the District of Columbia, Louisville, Memphis, Atlanta, Charleston, and Richmond.[19]

A variety of evidence points toward a significant reduction in black mortality during the period 1865–1914. The obvious question is: what accounts for this reduction? In considering this question, one must examine four possible sources of improvement in mortality conditions: changes in the natural virulence of pathogens; medical advances; new public health measures; and improvements in levels of living, particularly in housing conditions and diets. Consider each of these possibilities in turn.

First, the virulence of scarlet fever and diphtheria pathogens probably declined after 1880. However, as only a tiny proportion of black deaths resulted from these diseases, it is unlikely that the changes in their virulence could have been of substantial importance in reducing overall black mortality. Second, medical advances were of little or no consequence in reducing mortality during the period 1865–1914; even

Table 2.4. *Deaths per 1,000 population, selected cities, by race, 1900–1910*

City	1910		1900	
	Black	White	Black	White
Northern cities				
Boston	23.3	17.1	26.9	20.3
Chicago	24.3	15.0	23.6	15.2
Cincinnati	28.9	16.7	29.7	17.6
Columbus	20.4	15.0	22.8	15.3
Indianapolis	25.0	15.4	24.0	16.3
Kansas City	27.1	14.7	24.9	15.3
New York	25.9	15.8	32.1	20.4
Philadelphia	26.9	16.8	30.2	20.4
Pittsburgh	23.4	17.7	25.8	19.2
St. Louis	26.0	15.1	30.9	17.1
Southern cities				
Atlanta	25.4	15.5	27.3	18.6
Baltimore	30.6	17.2	33.5	19.2
Charleston	39.3	18.9	44.4	22.9
Louisville	26.9	14.4	27.3	16.9
Memphis	28.3	16.8	24.4	20.7
Nashville	26.0	15.0	32.1	18.8
New Orleans	32.8	17.2	41.0	21.2
Richmond	30.2	18.1	37.7	23.7
Savannah	34.1	19.4	38.1	23.4
Washington	29.1	15.8	31.0	18.3

Source: U.S. Bureau of the Census, *Negro Population, 1790–1915* (Washington, 1918), p. 320.

if significant advances had occurred, the bulk of the black population, being both poor and rural, would have had quite limited access to them. Third, public health improvements made virtually no impact on the countryside before 1915; and in the cities, where a public health movement was in progress after 1880, most blacks lived in slums or outlying areas poorly served by the new practices in sewerage and water supply.[20]

Finally, then, improvements in levels of living emerge by a process of elimination as probably the prime influence in reducing mortality. This conclusion should hardly come as a surprise, because better clothing, housing, and diet have probably been everywhere the main determinants in the long-term reduction of mortality. Recent studies of changes in American health conditions find that a rising level of living was probably the main force during the years before 1920, at least for the rural population, and suggest that dietary and housing improvements deserve most of the credit.[21] It is simply inconceivable that black mortality before 1915 could have fallen very far if levels of living had not been improving. Therefore the mortality experience of the black population during the first half century of freedom provides an important, if indirect, kind of evidence for an assessment of changes in black real income levels. (Chapter 5 below provides direct evidence of substantial improvements in the level of living.)

Though the exact levels and rates of decline remain in question, the fact of secular decline in both fertility and mortality is of major significance for the interpretation of black economic history. Declining fertility led to a fall in the number of children (dependents) per adult (worker), which eased the burden of family support. Declining mortality was itself a Good Thing, and in all likelihood it was associated with reduced morbidity, greater physical vitality, and consequently with increased labor productivity as well. Many other consequences might be conjectured, but all such speculations cry out for empirical tests that have not yet been performed. Clearly the demographic history of black Americans is in need of much additional research.

Regional distribution of the population

The regional distribution of the black population in 1865 was for the most part the product of force, not choice. Nine-tenths of all blacks having been slaves before the Civil War, they had been distributed at the pleasure of their masters. Only in the South had American slavery continued beyond the early nineteenth century and, accordingly, the black population was concentrated there. Of course the South had its own westward movement before 1860, and in this the blacks participated fully, perhaps even disproportionately. Plantation owners establishing themselves on the fertile new western lands carried tens of thousands of slaves to the frontier regions. These planters did not distribute themselves uniformly but rather sought out the prime locations for growing cotton and cane, generally the alluvial valleys and accessible uplands. On the eve of the Civil War the black population was distributed in close correspondence with the areas of plantation agriculture: in eastern Virginia and northeastern North Carolina, throughout South Carolina, across central Georgia and Alabama, along the lower Mississippi River, and in the Red River Valley of Louisiana and the river valleys of southeastern Texas (see Figure 2.1).

As soon as emancipation became effective the black population began to shift. Most of this movement was local, and many blacks who left

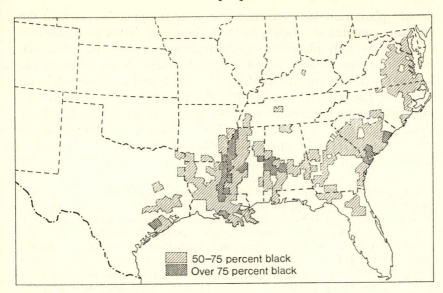

Figure 2.1. Southern counties with population 50–75 percent black and over 75 percent black, 1860. *Source:* U.S. Bureau of the Census, *Negro Population, 1790–1915* (Washington, 1918), p. 115

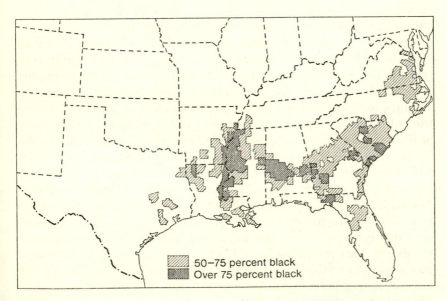

Figure 2.2. Southern counties with population 50–75 percent black and over 75 percent black, 1910. *Source:* U.S. Bureau of the Census, *Negro Population, 1790–1915* (Washington, 1918), p. 115.

the old plantation soon returned. Probably the great majority of the migrants confined themselves to their county of origin or contiguous counties, the only places about which they possessed much information.[22] But some blacks moved longer distances. A few went to the North. Far more went westward, seeking out superior opportunities on the fresh lands of the lower Mississippi Valley. Labor agents and western planters lured many with the offer of higher wages in Mississippi, Louisiana, Arkansas, and Texas, sometimes contracting to finance the travel of hundreds of workers in a single party. Reporting from Georgia in 1866, C. W. Howard observed:

[E]very railroad train during this winter has been loaded with negroes going to the west under promise of increased wages, and the unfortunate people have in many cases been made the subject of infamous speculation. It is estimated that twenty-five thousand negroes have left South Carolina this winter for Florida and the west, and the number which have left Georgia is much greater, as for some time the average number passing through Atlanta has been 1,000 daily. This depletion of labor still actively continues, and it is a matter of increasing importance to the planters. They offer ten to twelve dollars per month, besides food, house, firewood, and land for a garden, but the negroes are promised more in the west, and accordingly emigrate.[23]

These movements set a pattern for interstate migration that persisted until the drastic reduction of foreign immigration and the consequent enlargement of employment opportunities for blacks in the North after 1914 broke the old pattern and established a new one.[24]

Migration, as suggested earlier, may usefully be viewed as a form of investment. The expected returns consist of the additional earnings obtainable in the new location. The costs of migration are both tangible and psychic: transportation costs include both direct outlays and any earnings foregone between jobs; psychic costs inhere in the separation from old friends, relatives, and familiar places, and in the uncertainties of life in the new place. Whether the investment in migration is desirable depends on the magnitude of expected gains, the period over which they will accrue, and the magnitude of the costs borne by the migrant. Under the *ceteris paribus* condition, several hypotheses follow from this theory of migration. First, for obvious reasons, migrants go to regions where higher earnings prevail; second, because transport costs that reduce the gain from migration increase with the distance of the move, short moves are more likely than long ones; third, because they expect to realize the gains over a longer period, and perhaps also because they experience smaller psychic costs, young adults are more likely to move than older people.

Table 2.5 presents estimates of net migration that allow a broad test of the hypothesis that migrants sought regions where higher earnings

Table 2.5. *Net migration in thousands, by race and region, 1870–1910 (rate per 1,000 average population in parentheses)*

Decade	Northeast		South		North Central		West	
	Native white	Black	Native white	Black	Native white	Black	Native white	Black
1870–1880	−374	26	91	−68	26	42	257	n.a.
	(−33)	(55)	(11)	(−14)	(2)	(124)	(274)	
1880–1890	−240	61	−271	−88	−43	28	554	n.a.
	(−18)	(107)	(−26)	(−15)	(−3)	(65)	(325)	
1890–1900	101	136	−30	−185	−445	49	374	n.a.
	(6)	(200)	(−2)	(−26)	(−23)	(104)	(141)	
1900–1910	−196	109	−69	−194	−1,110	63	1,375	22
	(−11)	(137)	(−4)	(−24)	(−48)	(122)	(329)	(542)

Source: Hope T. Eldridge and Dorothy Swaine Thomas, *Population Redistribution and Economic Growth, United States, 1870–1950: III. Demographic Analyses and Interrelations* (Philadelphia, 1964), pp. 90, 99.

prevailed. Indeed, the main feature of the interregional movements during the period 1870–1910 was that many young blacks, most of them aged 20–40, did leave the South, where earnings were relatively low. They moved to both the Northeast and the North Central regions, where nonagricultural jobs offering higher earnings were more abundant, particularly personal service employments in the great urban centers such as New York, Philadelphia, and Chicago. Migration to the Far West, which involved for most a longer, more costly journey, seldom occurred before the early twentieth century and even then involved relatively few. The rate of black migration from the South exceeded the white rate in three of the four decades before 1910, the difference during the 1890s and 1900s being especially marked. And, unlike the whites, the blacks migrated from the South more rapidly during the period 1890–1910 than during the preceding two decades. Evidently the data in Table 2.5, as well as the age distribution of the migrants, are broadly consistent with the hypotheses implied by the theory of wealth-maximizing migration.[25]

Not all Southern states experienced a net loss of blacks through migration. States with net out-migration of blacks in at least three of the four decades after 1870 included Virginia, the Carolinas, Georgia, Kentucky, Tennessee, Alabama, and Mississippi. On the other hand, Arkansas, Oklahoma, and Texas witnessed a positive net migration of blacks during three of those four decades. Louisiana had net gains during the first half of the period, net losses during the second half.[26] This pattern of interstate migration within the South apparently arose from the pattern of opportunities available to black farmers and farm laborers during the first half century after emancipation.

Stanley Lebergott has tested in a crude way the hypothesis that interstate migration of blacks within the South depended on differentials in agricultural opportunities. His tests relate the wage rate of farm laborers in a given census year to the net interstate migration rate of black males aged 25–44 during the subsequent decade. Finding the two variables positively correlated, he concludes that "in all years the influence of forces associated with wage-rate differentials is clearly linked to migration differentials."[27] Lebergott does not report the correlation coefficients, but from his scatter diagrams it appears that the correlations, while positive, are quite low and for some decades are probably not statistically significant at customary test levels. That the association studied by Lebergott is weak does not in itself refute the hypothesis. Obviously other influences were also at work and, unless those variables are controlled, the true relation between farm wage rates and interstate migration remains obscure. Many of the blacks who migrated to Arkansas, Texas, and Oklahoma sought opportunities as farm owners or tenants, not as farm wage earners. Others were responding to opportunities in nonagricultural employments, available mainly in the rapidly expanding southwestern cities. Moreover, the net migration totals for Southern states reflected not only the relative opportunities within the South but also the relative attraction of opportunities outside the South. The pull of the North no doubt affected some Southern states (e.g., Virginia) more than others (e.g., Alabama) because of differences in the associated costs of information and transportation. Despite all these complications, a simple association between the farm wage rate and the net migration rate does exist, which suggests that the hypothesis deserves further consideration and a more exacting test.[28]

Clearly the black population was moving from state to state, from region to region, in search of superior economic opportunities. But, in spite of these movements, the most outstanding feature of the regional distribution of the black population during the period 1865–1914 was its stability. In 1910 the blacks lived, by and large, in the same areas they had inhabited in 1860. (Compare Figure 2.1 and Figure 2.2.) At both dates about nine-tenths of the population inhabited the South. This distribution persisted despite the positive net migration to the North because Northern blacks were predominantly urban, with higher mortality and lower fertility than those in the South; a positive net migration was required merely for the North to maintain its constant share of the total black population. A comparison of Figure 2.2 with Figure 2.3 shows that the areas where the black population was most

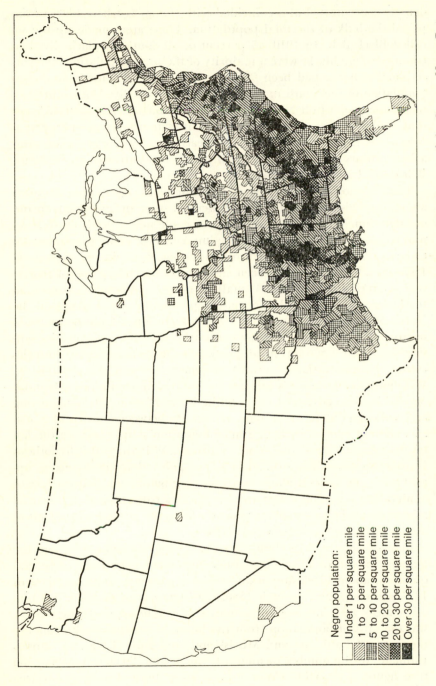

Negro population:

▢ Under 1 per square mile
▨ 1 to 5 per square mile
▦ 5 to 10 per square mile
▩ 10 to 20 per square mile
▨ 20 to 30 per square mile
■ Over 30 per square mile

Figure 2.3. Density of black population, by county, United States, 1910. *Source:* U.S. Bureau of the Census, *Negro Population, 1790–1915* (Washington, 1918), p. 110.

densely concentrated also coincided with the areas where blacks comprised the bulk of the total population. These areas made up the so-
called Black Belt. In 1910, 45 percent of all Southern blacks lived in
counties where blacks were a majority of the total population; the corresponding figure had been 57 percent in 1880. "Of the total Negro
population of the South in 1910 only 4.6 per cent lived in counties in
which the proportion Negro in the population was less than 12.5 per
cent, while 12.1 per cent lived in counties in which the proportion
Negro was 75 per cent or more."[29] Clearly the black population after
a half century of freedom was still highly concentrated in the Black
Belt created in the days of slavery.

The direction of the net migration of the black population, as shown
above, is consistent with hypotheses derived from an investment theory
of migration. Whether the number of people migrating is also consistent is more difficult to test, and the impression of many scholars seems
to be that "not enough" black migration occurred during the period
1865–1914.[30] It has already been shown that the magnitude of the actual migration flows was too small to make a substantial impact on
the broad regional distribution of the population, particularly on the
North–South distribution. That greater migration did not occur could
be attributed to a lack of many genuinely superior opportunities outside the South, ignorance of opportunities that did exist, or obstacles
of cost or coercion that prevented movement or made it more difficult.
Without making clear his underlying behavioral assumptions, Gunnar
Myrdal has also advanced the hypothesis that "before 1915 an existing
and widening difference in living conditions between South and North
. . . did not express itself in a mass migration simply because the latter did not get a start and become a pattern."[31] Perhaps this hypothesis
is really no more than a corollary of the point about ignorance of opportunities mentioned above because, presumably, the major effect of
a migration's "getting a start and becoming a pattern" is that potential
migrants are then in a better position to secure cheap, reliable information about opportunities elsewhere.

In advancing his hypothesis, Myrdal apparently chose to ignore the
famous "exodus of 1879," an episode that sheds some light on several
questions about black migration.[32] The exodus got under way late in
1877 and continued through 1880, reaching a crest in 1879. Though
other areas were involved in a small way, the heart of the movement
was the shift of population from the lower Mississippi Valley (mainly
the states of Louisiana and Mississippi), and from Texas, to Kansas.
Estimates of the number of migrants range from 20,000 to 60,000; the
true figure is probably closer to the lower limit. Contemporary accounts emphasized pressures pushing people from the South more than

attractions pulling them to the North: the migrants complained of personal insecurity, political repression, and economic exploitation; the activities of several black agitators and propaganda describing Kansas as a veritable Garden of Eden also played a role. Though some Southern planters attempted to impede the migration of black laborers and tenants by persuasion, interference with steamboat landings, or legal harassment, most whites apparently realized that such measures were futile. At a convention held at Vicksburg, Mississippi, in May 1879, the planters resolved "that it is the constitutional right of the colored people to migrate where they please, and to whatever State they may select for their residence." The resolution went on to urge the blacks not to act precipitously and to recommend that they fulfill any outstanding obligations to work or to pay land rent before departing.[33] In fact the planters had little to fear, for the exodus came to an abrupt halt in 1880.

Those "exodusters" who returned from Kansas gave such dismal reports of the barren country, the bleak climate and the harder work necessary to open new lands for cultivation that others were deterred from following their example. For ten years the migrants continued to filter back to their old homes or to seek new opportunities in other states. Possibly a third of them remained in Kansas and many of these eventually became prosperous citizens.[34]

The exodus of 1879 suggests several conclusions. First, a single mass migration was not enough to precipitate a continuing stream of similar dimensions. Myrdal's emphasis on "getting a start and becoming a pattern" is evidently lacking in some respect. Second, resistance to the migration by Southern whites was largely ineffectual; when the blacks chose to leave in large numbers the planters could not stop them. As Charles Nordhoff had observed three years before the exodus,

this readiness to better their fortunes by emigration seemed one of the best signs I saw in the South of the real independence of the negro; and I found it most fully developed in the very State [Georgia] where, according to the commonly received reports of Southern Republican politicians, the negro is still in a condition little better than slavery. If this were true, of course, he would not be moving away, for he would be tied to the soil.[35]

Third, opportunities in the North were not always so grand as to constitute great improvements for the average Southern black. Kansas – and the same might be said for other Northern states – demanded hard work in a hostile climate if an unskilled worker was to gain a subsistence. Looking south in the midst of a Topeka winter, many a black migrant may well have thought the Yazoo Delta not so bad after all.

Taking a more general view, it is not clear that a massive interregional migration would have brought large net gains in wealth or welfare for the black population. In the North the blacks faced strong competition from immigrants in unskilled jobs.[36] Information about distant opportunities was costly, especially for illiterate, rural blacks. Travel itself was expensive. In the North the blacks still had to contend with racial discrimination in many forms, a less pervasive discrimination than they faced in the South but nonetheless real. In some industries, such as the construction trades, getting employment was probably more difficult in the North than in the South. In brief, for most blacks as they were, in the world as it was, an investment in migration to the North was probably not a paying proposition, particularly if many blacks decided simultaneously to migrate to the same place, thereby threatening and inciting the hostility of the native laborers. Black leaders like Frederick Douglass and Booker T. Washington, who urged their people to make the best of opportunities within the South, may have been making economic sense. Of course, many Southern blacks did find genuine opportunity in other regions and gained considerably from migration.[37] My conclusion is merely that their achievements probably could not have been equaled had a very much larger number chosen to move north. Many blacks, especially those in skilled crafts or in business and professions catering to a segregated clientele, had perfectly sensible reasons for remaining in the South.[38]

Urban–rural distribution of the population

Superimposed on the interstate and interregional movement of the black population was a steady increase in the proportion of the population living in urban places. As the rate of natural increase was slower in urban than in rural places and international migration was inconsequential, this urbanization necessarily occurred as a result of net migration from the countryside. The exact sources of the migration cannot be identified, but it is probable that interstate migration was responsible for most of the increase of the urban black population in the North and the West while intrastate migration accounted for the bulk of the increase of black population in Southern cities. Whatever its sources, the movement into cities is a fact of central importance in the economic history of black Americans.

Any definition of "urban place" is arbitrary. The Census Bureau has classified as urban the population living in incorporated places of 2,500 or more inhabitants, and this definition is adequate for describing trends over the period 1870–1910. Table 2.6 shows that, according to this definition, just over 13 percent of all blacks lived in urban places in 1870; 40 years later the proportion had more than doubled, reaching

Table 2.6. *Percentage urban, by race and region, 1870–1910*

Race and region	1870	1880	1890	1900	1910
Native white	22.4	25.8	32.7	37.8	43.5
Northeast	37.9	44.6	53.3	60.8	66.5
South	7.7	8.3	12.0	14.2	19.5
North Central	16.8	20.9	29.5	35.5	41.7
West	21.0	25.0	35.6	39.4	47.9
Foreign-born white	53.6	55.5	60.5	65.5	71.2
Northeast	68.9	75.1	77.6	81.7	84.1
South	55.0	47.1	48.9	44.7	46.1
North Central	37.0	37.6	47.1	51.9	60.3
West	45.6	49.8	46.1	48.2	54.0
Black	13.4	14.3	19.7	22.6	27.3
Northeast	43.7	50.5	59.8	66.1	71.1
South	8.8	9.0	13.5	15.5	19.7
North Central	37.1	42.6	55.8	64.4	72.6
West	45.7	51.5	54.1	67.4	78.4

Source: Hope T. Eldridge and Dorothy Swaine Thomas, *Population Redistribution and Economic Growth, United States, 1870–1950: III. Demographic Analyses and Interrelations* (Philadelphia, 1964), p. 204.

27 percent in 1910. During this period the black urban population expanded at about the same rate as the total urban population in the United States. The black urban population increased by 44 percent in the 1870s, 57 percent in the 1880s, 35 percent in the 1890s, and 34 percent in the 1900s. The peak growth rate of the 1880s was generated mainly within the South, where the black population in cities increased by 71 percent.[39] Great regional differences prevailed: by 1910 the black population in the North and the West had become predominantly urban; but in the South, despite four decades of steady urbanization, only one black in every five lived in an urban place (see Table 2.6). Within any given region the blacks were more urbanized than the native whites, although the difference in the South was insignificant. Only the great concentration of black population in the South accounted for its predominantly rural character in the aggregate. The 43 cities for which information is displayed in Table 2.7 contained about half of the black urban population in 1910.

Urbanization was a major influence affecting the welfare of the black population during the period 1865–1914. Cities offered an array of consumption and investment opportunities not available in the country-

Table 2.7. *Cities with black population over 10,000, 1910*

City	Black population	% black in total population
Washington, D.C.	94,446	28.5
New York, N.Y.	91,790	1.9
New Orleans, La.	89,262	26.3
Baltimore, Md.	84,749	15.2
Philadelphia, Pa.	84,459	5.5
Memphis, Tenn.	52,441	40.0
Birmingham, Ala.	52,305	39.4
Atlanta, Ga.	51,902	33.5
Richmond, Va.	46,733	36.6
Chicago, Ill.	44,103	2.0
St. Louis, Mo.	43,960	6.4
Louisville, Ky.	40,522	18.1
Nashville, Tenn.	36,523	33.1
Savannah, Ga.	33,246	51.1
Charleston, S.C.	31,056	52.8
Jacksonville, Fla.	29,293	50.8
Pittsburgh, Pa.	25,623	4.8
Norfolk, Va.	25,039	37.1
Houston, Tex.	23,929	30.4
Kansas City, Mo.	23,566	9.5
Mobile, Ala.	22,763	44.2
Indianapolis, Ind.	21,816	9.3
Cincinnati, Ohio	19,639	5.4
Montgomery, Ala.	19,322	50.7
Augusta, Ga.	18,344	44.7
Macon, Ga.	18,150	44.6
Dallas, Tex.	18,024	19.6
Chattanooga, Tenn.	17,942	40.2
Little Rock, Ark.	14,539	31.6
Shreveport, La.	13,896	49.6
Boston, Mass.	13,564	2.0
Fort Worth, Tex.	13,280	18.1
Columbus, Ohio	12,739	7.0
Wilmington, N.C.	12,107	47.0
Vicksburg, Miss.	12,053	57.9
Charlotte, N.C.	11,752	34.6
Portsmouth, Va.	11,617	35.0

Table 2.7. (*continued*)

City	Black population	% black in total population
Columbia, S.C.	11,546	43.9
Petersburg, Va.	11,014	45.7
Lexington, Ky.	11,011	31.4
San Antonio, Tex.	10,716	11.1
Jackson, Miss.	10,554	49.6
Pensacola, Fla.	10,214	44.4

Source: U.S. Bureau of the Census, *Negro Population, 1790–1915* (Washington, 1918), p. 93.

side: the schools were better and more accessible; housing was better, albeit still poor by some standards; greater variety was available in food and other consumption goods; medical assistance was easier to obtain; churches and other social institutions were more abundant and flourishing. In the city, black people were less exposed to white intimidation, gaining some security from mere numbers. A large, concentrated, black community allowed the emergence of a more complex and developed black community with its own merchants, craftsmen, and professional people. Those blacks who rose to genuine prominence – the Talented Tenth for whom W. E. B. Du Bois argued so forcefully – almost all resided in cities. The countryside was not always and everywhere repressive, and opportunities of a certain limited kind were accessible there even to black people; but the cities, though still restrictive in the social latitude permitted to blacks, were generally freer, more hopeful and prosperous places to live, and unquestionably more exciting. Certainly the average urban worker earned more than his cousin on the plantation, and the benefits of mere money were hardly to be despised.[40] In brief, the cities offered greater material opportunities, and black people responded with a massive migration. That the investment paid off can scarcely be doubted, for the reverse movement – from cities to the countryside – was no more than a trickle in the opposing flood. As Du Bois expressed it, "if . . . the chances are against the Negro in the village, one thing is certain: he seldom returns to the farm."[41]

Summary: Population growth and migration

At the close of the Civil War the very survival of the black population was in question. Though predictions of imminent race extinction proved false and the population continued to grow, the rate of growth declined steadily after the 1870s. This retardation occurred because fertility fell more rapidly than mortality. That fertility declined steeply after 1880 no one seriously doubts. The trend of mortality is more uncertain: though the death rate declined considerably after 1900, it probably fell more slowly during the late nineteenth century. Urbanization, which occurred throughout the entire half century after 1865, promoted a slower rate of growth of the black population in two ways, because the urban population experienced both lower fertility and higher mortality than the rural population. In migrating to cities and to the North and the Southwest, black people behaved as a theory of wealth-maximizing investment would predict. Whether the magnitude of the interregional migrations fell short of the optimum is uncertain, for it is not clear that blacks could have realized a high return in the event of a massive migration from the South before 1915. In any event, the period 1865–1914 did witness major changes in the demographic characteristics of the black population: reduced fertility and mortality; regional redistribution, the net effect of which was to shift the center of population in a southwesterly direction; and an urbanization movement that more than doubled the proportion living in cities. It seems that all these changes tended to improve the welfare of the black population, but unmixed blessings they were not.

3

The people at work, 1865–1880

We have only to reflect for a moment upon the situation in which these people found themselves when liberated. Consider their ignorance, their poverty, their destitution, and their absolute dependence upon the very class by which they had been held in bondage for centuries, a class whose every sentiment was averse to their freedom, and we shall be prepared to marvel that they have, under the circumstances, done so well.

Frederick Douglass, 1880

The Northern politicians and soldiers who effected the emancipation of the American slave population disagreed about the appropriate design of a postemancipation economy and the part that blacks would play in it. Some, like the Radical Republicans George Washington Julian and Thaddeus Stevens, wanted to confiscate the land of wealthy rebels for free distribution among the freedmen. Others proposed that land abandoned by Southerners during the war be sold to the freedmen on easy terms. Some, like Senator Charles Sumner, wished to retain the Freedmen's Bureau indefinitely as a regulatory agency mediating between the freedmen and their erstwhile masters to insure fair play. Most, however, gave little thought to the matter, supposing that no special action by the federal government was necessary and that the situation would turn out all right if simply left under the unimpeded influence of market forces.

The course actually pursued was one of limited and temporary intervention. By 1869 the Freedmen's Bureau had ceased to act as a regulator of race relations or labor markets. The last remaining elements of the federal army of occupation left the South in 1877. Though the federal government sold a small amount of abandoned land to freedmen and a special Southern Homestead Act opened the public domain of the South to them on temporarily privileged terms, only a minute fraction of the blacks obtained land during the immediate postwar years. "Forty acres and a mule" became synonymous with the black man's disappointment in the federal government.[1] With their dreams of quickly becoming landowners shattered, most blacks had no choice but to turn to the emerging free labor market for their salvation. And from the very beginning, market forces – mingled with recurring episodes of violence, intimidation, and fraud – predominated in shaping the economic future of the freedmen.

The transition from slavery to a free labor market

When the Civil War ended, Northern reporters hurried to the South, eager to tell the world about the conditions prevailing in the defeated section and to discover how the Southerners were reacting to the social upheaval of forced emancipation. One question especially concerned them: "Will the Negro work?" Now, looking back with over a century of hindsight, it is difficult to understand how this question could have been taken so seriously. But if the question seems odd, the answer given by the Southern whites was curious indeed. A North Carolina man told the correspondent of *The Nation* that a "nigger hated work, and had no ambition; he would do just enough to keep him from actual starvation." The man's wife, however, "believed that pretty much all the niggers she knew would a little rather starve to death than work for themselves or others." Such views were not confined to the "poor whites." As General Christopher C. Andrews reported to the Joint Committee on Reconstruction early in 1866, "the prevailing opinion among the whites was that free labor would be a failure."[2]

When General Carl Schurz made a tour of inspection through the South late in 1865 he took special pains to learn about the Southerners' attitudes toward the system of free labor. He found their opinions in remarkable agreement: at least 19 of 20 told him, "you cannot make the negro work without physical compulsion." He heard this hundreds of times, in so many different places, in so nearly the same words that he finally accepted it as the prevailing view. There were exceptions to this belief, but too few, he judged, to affect the rule. Most white Southerners believed that the blacks would not respond to normal economic incentives. "They insisted," said General Andrews, echoing Schurz, "that the whip was the only means of making the blacks work."[3]

Southern whites had misled themselves with uncritical inductive reasoning. True, the blacks (slaves), whom they had long observed, had typically been unwilling to work unless physically compelled. So thoroughly had the whites confused black behavior with slave behavior, it was difficult for them to realize that under slavery – property rights being what they were – avoiding the lash was the slave's only incentive aside from petty gifts and occasional time off that the master might arbitrarily bestow. The freedman, endowed with property rights over his own labor services, responded quickly to the prospect of a pecuniary return.[4]

It turned out, then, that the freedmen would work, but this fact failed to silence the cries of many whites for powers of physical compulsion over black labor. For although the freedmen would work, they now had some bargaining power in determining the conditions under which they would work, and these, not surprisingly, differed from the conditions under which they had labored as slaves. The old masters not only objected to the higher cost of labor but considered it degrading to deal with their former slaves as equal parties to an exchange in the labor market. "Men did not feel kindly that their old slaves should take time to consider the question of hiring with them, and should presume to haggle about wages. The least manifestation of a disposition to assert obtrusively his independence, brought the late slave into danger."[5]

Indeed, even the most docile freedman might encounter danger at any moment, for the postwar atmosphere seethed with racial hatred, and 1865 witnessed an orgy of persecution of the freedmen. The reports of Northern officers and agents of the Freedmen's Bureau list violent incidents in sickening detail. General E. M. Gregory reported from Texas that "cases almost defy any attempt to record them, and are reckoned by hundreds, ranging from downright murder, savage beatings, merciless whippings, hunting men with trained bloodhounds, through all the lessor degrees of cruelty and crime." From Mobile, Alabama, a federal captain wrote to his superior officer describing beatings, hangings, shootings, torturings, and drownings of blacks in a revolting variety.[6] Every Southern state had its share of the atrocities. Only the immediate presence of Northern troops seemed to diminish their incidence.

Most observers identified the "poor whites" as the principal perpetrators of these outrages. As Benjamin C. Truman, a Northern journalist, saw the situation in 1866, the former slave owners were the black man's "best friends in the South," while the poor whites were his enemies, abusing him horribly. "In a state of slavery they hated him; and, now that he is free, there is no striking abatement of this sentiment. . . . On the streets, by the roadside, in his wretched hut, in the field of labor – everywhere," said Truman, "the inoffensive negro is exposed to their petty and contemptible persecutions."[7] Without disputing Truman's main point, one might simply add that the black man's "best friends in the South" often chose to exhibit their friendship in a most offensive manner. Although friendly, and even cordial, relations existed between some freedmen and their former masters, many an erstwhile slave owner reached instinctively for the whip handle when dealing with a black.

Immediately after the emancipation, then, labor market conditions were nothing short of chaotic. People were moving about in great numbers, some apparently aimlessly. Impoverished and highly uncertain about the future, employers found contracts difficult to make and to enforce, for the whole legal order was in a state of flux. The whites feared a black insurrection, while the blacks feared reenslavement, and mutual distrust made the establishment of contractual relations even more difficult. Troops and vigilantes intervened spasmodically to impose "order," as postwar social disorganization, unemployment, and lingering political bitterness created a favorable environment for theft and feuding. Such conditions persisted through 1865 in many areas. By 1866, however, the situation had begun to stabilize, the amount of migratory traffic was declining, and most blacks were at work.

The planters' fears about the labor supply were not entirely groundless, however, for the aggregate supply of black labor did fall from its prewar level. The reasons seem fairly transparent. A major supporting pillar of the slave regime had been the ability of the master to extract labor services from the slave without considering the sacrifice of leisure by the slave as a real cost of production. Hence slave men worked more hours per year than free men, and slave women and children were regularly employed as well. Once labor market conditions stabilized in the late 1860s, it was apparent that women and children had partly withdrawn their services from field work and that men were not generally willing to work as many hours per year as they had as slaves. Contemporaries often ascribed this behavior to "aping the whites," but simply viewing it in the light of the new property rights and new opportunities available to the blacks offers a more satisfying explanation. Black men obviously valued the housekeeping and childrearing services of black women; and holding women off the labor market as showpieces in idleness – an oft-repeated claim – seems implausible in general, though conceivable in a few cases. Black parents after 1865 could sometimes choose to educate their children instead of sending them to the fields or to other employment. In brief, as a free man the black could respond to a variety of new opportunities, and one result was a reduction in the aggregate amount of black labor supplied.

Still, to say that the blacks worked less than before is hardly to assert that much loafing took place. Travelers in the South in the 1870s reported that black men were generally at work and that black women and children, while less frequently employed than under slavery, commonly worked alongside the men, especially during the cotton-chopping and picking seasons.[8] The census of 1890, the first to make racial distinctions in the returns pertaining to occupations, revealed that of the black population 10 years of age and over, 79 percent of the males and 36 percent of the females were gainfully employed. The figures were probably underestimates, many family workers on farms being left out.

For whites the proportions at work were smaller, the percentages being 77 for males and 14 for females. Considering both sexes together, 58 percent of the blacks and 47 percent of the whites were gainfully occupied.[9] Participation in the labor force, then, was considerably higher for blacks than for whites. Oddly enough, this evidence led no one to ask: "Will the white work?"

Agricultural labor and land tenure, 1865–1880

By almost any standard, the black labor force was closely associated with agriculture during the first 15 years after emancipation. Although there are no comprehensive data to reveal exactly what proportion of the workers was occupied in agriculture, it was obviously a large majority. Clearly, no one can understand black economic history without giving detailed attention to the Southern rural economy.

Slavery disappeared slowly in the Southern countryside. Some masters tried to conceal the knowledge of emancipation from their slaves, and in certain interior districts this subterfuge proved effective for months. Others attempted, usually unsuccessfully, to terrorize their former slaves into remaining with them in an unchanged status. Many planters, perhaps the majority, called together their slaves, informed them of their freedom, and offered to make contracts for continued labor. In 1865 many plantations simply went on as usual, the freedmen laboring as they always had and receiving as compensation the usual cabin, clothes, and rations. The persistence of slavery varied inversely with the proximity of Northern garrisons. A year after the Confederate surrender at Appomattox Court House, federal troops still had not occupied some areas in sufficient numbers to extinguish the *de facto* relation of master and slave.[10] But, as time passed, information spread and, as the blacks became more confident of the reality and permanence of their emancipation, the bonds of slavery crumbled even in the back country. Certainly by 1867 the peculiar institution had expired everywhere in the South.

Dependent freed persons raised a special problem for their former masters and for the federal authorities. Under slavery, owners had supported the old and the infirm in order to maintain the morale of those at work, but under the new regime no such motive remained; those unable to work represented a cost without a corresponding benefit for the employer. Some planters simply drove away the old people, but many continued to maintain them despite the cost. Freed children without parents present raised a similar problem. Agents of the Freedmen's Bureau bound out some until they were of age and compelled the former owners to care for others. Nowhere was the reckless nature of the emancipation more evident than in the cases of the very old, the very young, and the infirm, many of whom perished soon after emancipation, victims of hunger, exposure, and disease. "For a few years immediately subsequent to the war," a contemporary observer noted, "the number of deaths among colored infants was appalling."[11] Even for those able to work, the new conditions posed a serious challenge.

In many parts of the Southern countryside free labor markets had scarcely existed before the Civil War, and in 1865 no one was quite sure how to bring together the land, labor, and other resources necessary for a renewal of agricultural production. The whites, of course, knew something about Northern customs of hiring farm laborers, but they generally dismissed this knowledge as inapplicable to their situation. They greatly feared that labor contracts with the blacks would be unenforceable. "The employer," said one observer, "accustomed only to the system of compulsory labor, is slow to believe that he can secure faithful services by the stimulus of wages." From Arkansas, a civilian agent of the Freedmen's Bureau reported: "I am pressing the point vigorously upon our people that *bodily coercion* fell as an incident of slavery. Many of our best farmers confess that I am right; others growl and wish to be allowed to *enforce* their contracts, the simple English of which is to 'whip the nigger.' "[12]

In many areas of the South the Freedmen's Bureau played a key role in facilitating the transition from slavery to a free labor market. Congress created this agency, officially known as the Bureau of Refugees, Freedmen, and Abandoned Lands, in March 1865. Although some civilians served as agents, most officials of the bureau, including its commissioner, General Oliver O. Howard, were Northern soldiers. The bureau performed various relief functions, providing rations, clothing, and medical attention to the destitute, both black and white, and helped to establish numerous schools for the blacks. It acted as an employment agency, allocating workers to various employers and transporting freedmen to the areas of highest wages. Of perhaps greatest importance, it became the legal authority in all cases involving the freedmen. It established guidelines for the payment of "fair" wages or shares of the crop to black laborers and stood ready to approve contracts and adjudicate disputes. Charles Stearns, a Northerner who took up residence in Georgia as a planter-missionary after the war, clearly described the bureau's judicial activities:

It was the custom of the officers of the Bureau to inspect every contract between the freedmen and their employers, when offered to them for that purpose; and if they approved of its provisions, they promised both parties military protection, in enforcing the contracts. This was a great point gained by the whites, for of what avail was a contract with irresponsible men without means for its enforcements? If a black man failed to do his duty, he was immediately brought before the Bureau, and obliged to conform to his agreement, and many of the rebels gladly availed themselves of this protection. On the contrary, if an employer failed to do justice to his hands, he too, must appear before this august tribunal, and make amends for his conduct.[13]

While such legal order as existed in the labor market grew largely out of the bureau's efforts, many areas were too isolated to be much influenced by the handful of officials assigned to serve a large district. In such places only trial and error could serve to develop the knowledge and confidence required for the smooth functioning of a free labor market. Even in areas better supplied with agents, most planters were hostile toward the bureau and resisted its authority. General Schurz admitted late in 1865 that "the success achieved by the Freedmen's Bureau is as yet very incomplete," but he insisted that it had nevertheless provided an indispensable service. He estimated that not half of the labor performed in 1865 would have been done except for the bureau's efforts. "The confusion and disorder of the transition period would have been infinitely greater," he declared, "had not an agency interfered which possessed the confidence of the emancipated slaves; which would disabuse them of any extravagant notions and expectations and be trusted; which would administer them good advice and be voluntarily obeyed."[14] Even if one discounts Schurz's assessment to compensate for his bias in favor of the bureau, the conclusion is still inescapable that the agency had a profound influence in bridging the gap created by the mutual distrust and hostility between planters and freedmen immediately after the war. By serving as mediators and employment agents, the officials of the Freedmen's Bureau helped to cool the racial passions that inflamed the South in 1865, and made a significant contribution to the development of the free labor market. Except for conducting an educational department and paying bounties to black soldiers, the bureau ceased to operate in 1869.[15]

Immediately after the war, the payment of wages in some form was the most common way to compensate laborers. The wages were usually paid partly in goods and partly in money, but some laborers received no cash at all. Near Danville, Virginia, a Northern journalist encountered an old black man whose "contract" for 1865, a mere note signed by his former master, entitled him to ten barrels of corn "in full of his wages, his wife's and children's."[16] More typical of wage contracts was the following Georgia agreement:[17]

Columbus, Ga., Jan. 2, 1866

Contract and agreement entered into between R. A. Martin, of the first part, and Kendle Souther, freedman, for himself and family, of the second part. The second part agrees to labor faithfully for the first part, and to obey all orders given by the same, and to be responsible for all property entrusted to his care; the first part promises to furnish him with a house to live in so long as he may be in his employment, and to pay him $135 and board for them that labors, and sell him provisions at the market price for them that don't work, and nothing more. In witness whereof we have set our hands and signatures.

R. A. Martin
his
Kendle X Souther.
mark

Wages naturally varied with the condition of the laborer. "Full hands," adult men in good condition, commanded the highest wages, generally $10–15 per month; women and children got considerably less. Real wages also varied from place to place, being generally higher in Louisiana, Texas, and Arkansas than in the states along the Atlantic coast. The data in Table 3.1 are averages of figures collected by the commissioner of agriculture from correspondents in the various states; the amounts shown represent the total value of money wages plus rations, the latter generally consisting of three or four pounds of salt pork and a peck of corn meal per week. Wage contracts sometimes called for the provision of medical attendance or some clothing; some provided the worker an acre or two for a garden spot; almost all gave him a cabin, fuel, and rations besides cash. Commonly, half the money

Table 3.1. *Money wages ($) plus value of rations, agricultural labor, by state, 1867–68*

State	1867			1868		
	Men	Women	Youth	Men	Women	Youth
Virginia	102	43	46	102	41	45
North Carolina	104	45	47	89	41	39
South Carolina	100	55	43	93	52	42
Georgia	125	65	46	83	55	47
Florida	139	85	52	97	50	44
Alabama	117	71	52	87	50	40
Mississippi	149	93	61	90	66	40
Louisiana	150	104	65	104	75	60
Texas	139	84	67	130	72	63
Arkansas	158	94	78	115	75	67
Tennessee	136	67	65	109	51	45

Source: U.S. Department of Agriculture, *Report of the Commissioner of Agriculture for the Year 1867* (Washington, 1868), p. 416.

wage was paid weekly or monthly, the other half retained by the employer until the end of the contract period, which gave the employee an incentive not to break his contract and reduced the cash requirements of the employer. In addition, employers sometimes levied fines for absence from work, shoddy work, damage to equipment or stock, and other faults in the laborer's performance. Contracts in the early years typically required the laborer to be civil, obedient, respectful, honest, faithful, and so forth. Judging from contractual terms and from the remarks of contemporaries, one might almost believe that the planters were as concerned about the "impudence" of the freedmen as they were about the wage rate.[18]

On many plantations, wage payments proved unsatisfactory to both employers and employees. Planters complained that laborers shirked on the job, which necessitated a heavy expense for supervising them; laborers sometimes deserted the fields at critical times, especially during the cotton-picking season, in response to attractive offers from other employers. Accustomed to the bound labor force of the slave regime, the planters considered a corps of black wage laborers uncertain in the extreme. The workers also disliked the wage system. Working in gangs under the watchful eye of an overseer smacked too much of the old regime, especially when the overseer resorted to his old methods, brandishing a pistol or whipping the laborers to stimulate their efforts. Moreover, many complained that the employers failed to abide by the terms of their contracts: wages were not paid in full, poor-quality rations were supplied, and extra work was demanded without extra pay. These problems led to a shift on many plantations from wage systems to share-rent systems.

Many writers seem to believe that share tenancy was a method of race control imposed on helpless blacks by all-powerful whites,[19] but the evidence is almost entirely inconsistent with such an interpretation. In fact, most blacks had a continuum of preferences in which, other things being the same, landownership was most preferred, followed by fixed-rent tenancy, share-rent tenancy, and – the least preferred – working for wages. In the beginning the practical choice was usually between shares and wages. If any difference existed here, it was probably that the freedmen preferred sharing to wage payments more than the planters did. On one Alabama plantation "the negroes demanded shares, threatening to leave in case of refusal."[20] That the share system soon came to involve many white tenants on the same terms as the blacks also argues against the contention that it was a device of race control.

Crop-sharing arrangements had existed during the war in certain areas occupied by Northern forces, and share systems appeared throughout the South in 1865 and 1866. The terms of share contracts varied enormously with respect to how farm inputs and outputs were divided between the landlord and the tenant. A Northern journalist reported the terms of a very simple Virginia contract as follows:

The undersigned bind themselves to stay on the — — plantation from Nov. 15th, year of 1865, to Nov. 15th, year of 1866. We agree to work on said plantation for Mr. W—. He is to pay the rent of the plantation, and he is to pay all the expense of the crops. Mr. W— agrees to give us payment for labor by sharing equally with the Negroes – one half the crop to be his, one half to be ours, one half the wheat, one half the oats, one half the corn, one half of every crop on the place, excepting that all the fodder and straw is to belong to Mr. W—. Mr. W— is to give us rations and clothing, and the expense is to be paid back out of our half of the crop. We are to act polite to him, and to be obedient and industrious, and make no disturbance in the place.[21]

Involving an unusually large farm and a rare delegation of responsibilities, the following Georgia share contract evidently applied to a freedman of considerable skill and trusted character:

State of Georgia, Muscogee Co.

An agreement entered into the 7th day of December between D. W. Urquhart, proprietor, on one part, and a freedman, Thornton Allen, on the other part, witnesseth that the said Urquhart covenants and agrees to furnish the said Thornton Allen a house and lands, to wit: The Joe Diamond place, with 140 acres, more or less, of land for cultivation; and, furthermore, to furnish the said Thornton Allen $500 worth of provisions and two mules to assist in cultivating said land. And the said Thornton agrees on his part to well and faithfully cultivate said land, and put not less than 60 acres in cotton, and all the balance in corn and other grain and suitable crops of sweet-potatoes and melons, to put the orchard and vineyard in proper trim and cultivation, and that he, the said Thornton, will faithfully market the products of said orchard, vineyard, melons, and potatoes, and freely and honestly pay over to said Urquhart the one-half of the products of lands so cultivated and the products so marketed, and pay the one-half of the corn and cotton on lands so cultivated into the store of the said Urquhart.[22]

Evidently share rents varied greatly, the proportion paid the landlord ranging from 1/4 to 19/20, although it is misleading to call the larger shares "rents" because they compensated landlords for much more than the use of land. In general, the more inputs furnished by a party to the contract the greater was his share of the output. Laborers who provided only their labor services might get as much as half, but often they received a smaller share. Land alone seldom commanded less than a one-quarter share. Mules and their feed might be worth a share of one-sixth to one-third. Different share ratios could apply to different crops raised on the same farm. A common arrangement where the landlord supplied only land was that his rent consist of one-third

of the corn and one-quarter of the cotton. Minor crops such as potatoes, sorghum, and melons were sometimes divided in the same fractions as the major crops, sometimes left entirely to the tenant. Another
common arrangement called for a share rent on some crops, a fixed
rent on others, for example, one-half of the cotton plus 50 bushels of
corn. The complexity and variety of these arrangements make them
difficult to analyze, but clearly they were quite flexible contracts, easily
altered to suit the varying demands of landlords and tenants. Above
all, they were neither standardized nor one-sided. Black tenants had
from the very beginning a strong voice in determining the terms of
share-rent contracts.

Many landlords resented the bargaining power of the black share
tenants and attempted to reduce it by forming combinations – what
economists call "cartels" – to restrict the terms of contracts. Testifying
before the Joint Committee on Reconstruction, General George E.
Spencer told of a combination of planters formed in Tuscaloosa
County, Alabama, in 1866. The planters there refused to give more
than one-eighth of the net proceeds of the crop to the tenants. When
a certain Mr. Beale contracted to give his tenants one-sixth of the crop,
the planters "called a meeting, sent for Mr. Beale, and told him he
must change that arrangement; and a committee went from the meeting down to the plantation, and told the negroes there the arrangement
must be changed, and forced them to change." Similar associations appeared in various parts of the South as planters perceived the advantages of united action in the labor market.[23]

But perceiving advantages and realizing them were not the same
thing, and many Southerners were skeptical that the planters' cartels
could succeed in exerting real monopsony power. When a contributor
to *DeBow's Review* in 1869 identified lack of cooperation as the planters' prime shortcoming, the editor took issue with him in the introduction to the article. "It would be difficult and discouraging," said the
editor, "to form combinations to control wages. The laborer is entitled
to a just compensation, and will indeed, in the end, always obtain a
fair share of what his labor sells for in the perfected market." Six years
later another observer declared in the same spirit: "No attempts at
intimidation, no forms of contract, no combinations among planters,
no penalties of the law, can effect this improvement [in the planters'
position in the labor market]."[24]

Three distinct forms of evidence indicate that the planters' cartels
were in fact generally unsuccessful in accomplishing their desired ends:
first, the repeated proposals for cooperation, which would have been
unnecessary had effective combinations been in existence; second, testimony that cartels crumbled in the face of intense competition for

labor; and third, increases in the prevailing share ratios paid to tenants, a change that effective combinations would have prevented. In addition, as General Clinton B. Fisk testified early in 1866, the officers of the Freedmen's Bureau took an active part in destroying restrictive combinations of planters immediately after the war.[25]

That many planters desired cartels to exert monopsony power in the labor market is easily documented. Newspapers and popular periodicals carried numerous appeals for organization. A contributor to the *Southern Cultivator* in 1865 proposed that the planters stand together in enforcing contracts; with the landlords acting as one, the freedman *"must* consent or starve." Four years later a planter bemoaned in the pages of *DeBow's Review* that "there was no concert of action on the part of the planters to oppose these ever increasing exactions [of the freedmen]." And as late as 1889 the same refrain was heard in the *Cultivator:* "If they desire success let the farmers, as a body; cooperate together, and work by rule, order and system; attend to their own labor, and let other's labor alone."[26] Evidently something was preventing successful organization, for otherwise these repeated proposals make no sense.

In fact, intense competition for the scarce labor services of the blacks precluded successful organization by the planters. An official of the Freedmen's Bureau reported from Lowndes County, Alabama: "Such was the demand for negro laborers . . . that any combination to abridge their freedom in seeking and changing homes, or to control the price of labor, failed utterly." "[T]he planters made a strong combination to hire no negro away from home," said General Wager Swayne. "The freedmen stood it out until the planters gave way, and they finally hired at random, at a little higher wages than were generally paid elsewhere." General Gregory referred to "a competition for labor which, in many localities [in Texas], has become a scramble." Writing in 1877, a planter recalled that for 10 years after the war "every one seemed to fear that everybody else would get ahead of him and that he would have no labor at all. Hence a universal rush at the negro – each outbidding the other, the negro in the meantime feeling like a maiden with a dozen suitors at her feet – entire master of the situation."[27] In 1871 an articulate planter described exactly why and how the competitive scramble took place:

At fair prices and with good management there is money in raising cotton. So he [the planter] speaks to one freedman after another, mounts his horse and rides hither and thither, sends an agent back and forth day after day, announces his willingness to make liberal contracts, does make large offers, bribes his own hands to hire others for him, goes to the towns and villages and addresses the many colored loiterers on the streets, stops at railway stations and sounds the freedmen he always finds strolling near, and thus by one means and another gradually obtains as many hands as he wants, or failing in that, as many as he can. The freedman will almost always hear what he has to say, will ask a great many questions, raise some foolish objections, and perhaps end the conversation by declaring he is not ready to hire yet, that he will take a day or two to think about it, or quietly announce that he has already hired. If he promises to accept your proposition and live with you, you may well doubt the fulfilment of his promise; for, while on his way to one place, he will accept a seemingly fairer offer and go elsewhere.[28]

Many contemporary observers recognized that intense competition for labor did more to enforce real freedom for the blacks than the military forces themselves. As a Tennessee man put it: "I *believe* there is no disposition on the part of our citizens to impose illiberal terms on those they employ; and I *know* they have not the ability to do so, as the demand for labor is so much in excess of the supply as to give all the advantage to the employe."[29]

Competition for labor quickly affected the terms of share agreements. Whereas many laborers had received only one-tenth or one-eighth of the crop (plus food, clothing, and shelter) in 1865, such small fractions were unknown in later years. One planter noted that in his area most freedmen remained on their old plantations in 1865 and received shares ranging from one-twelfth to one-eighth. The next year they generally changed employers and worked for wages. In 1867 they again demanded shares, but this time one-quarter for themselves. "They demanded it, and, of course they got it." From Texas in 1865 came the report that "the old line planters, who only a few weeks before had driven off their negroes, endeavored to secure their services by offering greater inducements. They offered part of the crop – first, one-fourth, then one-third, and now one-half – rather than let their plantations remain idle." By the 1870s, tenants who provided only labor normally received one-half of the crops plus a cabin, fuel, and garden plot.[30] Obviously competition for labor operated as the driving force in raising the share of the crop paid to black tenants.

While the share-rent system solved certain problems inherent in the wage system, it had difficulties of its own. Planters were delighted to have the tenant share with them the risk of fluctuating yields, but they complained that share tenants would not perform any work unless it contributed directly toward increasing the crop in which they had an interest. Hence landlords were often compelled to hire wage workers to maintain houses and ditches, to build fences, and to make other permanent improvements in their property. Share tenants would generally undertake such tasks only if they received extra pay, though occasionally such obligations were spelled out in their contracts. Landlords also complained that share tenants took every opportunity to steal some of the crop before the division of the shares. Tenants, on the other hand, resented the landlords' close oversight of the farm work and objected that landlords gave them an incorrect accounting of the crop's value when it was marketed and the proceeds divided. No doubt all these complaints had some validity; the actual frequency of contractual abuses no one will ever know.

Dissatisfaction with share-rent systems led increasingly to the adoption of fixed-rent systems. These required the payment of either a prescribed sum of money ("cash rent") or a definite amount of products ("standing rent"), the latter being more common. The amount of the fixed rent varied with the fertility and location of the land. Robert Somers, a British writer, found lands around Corinth, Mississippi, renting for $3–4 per acre in 1870. According to Charles Nordhoff's observations in the mid-1870s, Arkansas bottomlands rented for $6–10 per acre, Mississippi Delta lands for $6–10 or 80 pounds of cotton lint per acre, North Carolina lands for $3–7 or about 64 pounds lint per acre, Georgia lands for about 20 pounds lint per acre. About the same time Edward King observed rents of 72 pounds lint per acre along the Mississippi River in Louisiana. A few years later David Barrow noted that lands in Middle Georgia rented for 750 pounds lint per "one-horse farm" (usually 25–30 acres).[31]

Landlords liked the fixed-rent system because it freed them from the risk of fluctuating yields and, in the case of cash rental, from the risk of fluctuating product prices as well. It also required much less supervision, for unlike the share-rent tenant the fixed-rent tenant had an unconstrained incentive to produce an optimal output.[32] Still, this kind of rent was suitable only for tenants skillful enough to make a good crop regularly without careful supervision, that is, for tenants who would be able to pay the fixed rent when it came due at the end of the crop year. As one planter put it, "it would not do to trust all freedmen as much as this. Only those who possess a good character, a degree of diligence, and a fair knowledge of farming can be so trusted."[33] Tenants liked the system because it allowed them a maximum of independence in managing the farm. The freedmen generally regarded it as a more desirable form of tenancy than share renting, especially in places like the Georgia Black Belt, where yields fluctuated within a relatively narrow range.

The very simple fixed-rent contract of an old Georgia freedman, Ben Thomas, read as follows:[34]

By or before the 15th November, 1880, I promise to pay to David C. Barrow, 500 lbs. of white lint cotton, 40 bushels of cotton-seed, 25 bushels of corn

and the shucks therefrom, and 500 lbs. of good fodder, as rent for land on
Syll's Fork, during year 1880.
1st Jan., 1880   *his*
Witness: O. C. Watson.   Ben X Thomas.
                                                               mark

Barrow's plantation was typical of many in its shift from share-rent
tenancy to fixed-rent tenancy during the first 15 years after the war.
David C. Barrow, Jr., described in some detail just how that change
occurred. After the war the labor force was divided into two gangs,
the laborers receiving a share of the crop. Although this system worked
well for a few years, the laborers grew increasingly restive, each man
desiring to "be his own boss." Then the original gangs split up into
smaller and smaller squads, still working for shares, but this change
failed to give satisfaction. Mules received abusive treatment, and crops
were improperly divided. These problems eventually led to the adoption of a fixed-rent system, each tenant family paying 750 pounds of
lint cotton for its "one-horse farm." To facilitate the new arrangement
the landlord consented to sell mules to the tenants on credit. After the
change, the landlord hardly supervised the more capable tenants at all;
to the less able, a majority, he continued to offer occasional advice.[35]
That capable black farmers could attain a virtually independent position under a fixed-rent contract was a highly valued advantage of this
arrangement. That less skillful tenants could obtain the advice of a
skilled landlord was also a substantial benefit.

While the various systems of tenancy were developing in the first
15 years after the war, some black farmers were accumulating land of
their own. The independent owner stood at the top of black rural society. In Georgia, the only state for which comprehensive data are
available for many years before 1900, black farm owners held over
586,000 acres, with an assessed value of about $1.5 million, in 1880.
The average holding was modest (about 98 acres in a 31-county sample)
but nonetheless represented a substantial accomplishment in accumulation for persons who had only 15 years earlier escaped from the thrift-
less conditions of slavery.[36] In every Southern state successful tenants
used the proceeds of a particularly good year to purchase farms; when
credit was required, landlords typically provided it by allowing the
purchasers to pay for the land in several annual installments with interest. Lacking experience in independent management, many of the
purchasers failed to retain their property but, over the long run, the
total number of owners and the total acreage owned by blacks continued to increase. In 1876 the Department of Agriculture attempted
to ascertain from its correspondents the extent of black ownership in

the South. The proportion of freedmen occupying their own land was reported, by admittedly incomplete returns of information, to be 4 percent in Tennessee and Alabama, between 4 and 5 percent in North Carolina and Georgia, 5 percent in South Carolina and Texas, between 5 and 6 percent in Mississippi, Louisiana, and Arkansas, and 8 percent in Florida.[37]

Though some whites objected to black landownership and attempted to prevent it, such attempts generally failed. Land was simply too abundant to be monopolized by the whites, many of whom did not share their neighbor's objections to land acquisition by blacks and stood to gain by a sale. As early as 1867 the Columbus *Mississippi Sentinel* noted that "they [the blacks] can buy land in this and the adjoining counties at any price they wish, and they will do it." Sir George Campbell observed, 11 years later, that "in some places there is a feeling against letting the land pass into the hands of blacks," but he added that "there is so much land for sale that those who save money need have no difficulty in buying it." Indeed, not uncommonly, blacks acquired land by virtue of the assistance of friendly whites.[38] That the acquisition of land was so limited during the first 15 years after emancipation probably resulted more from simple poverty than from racial discrimination in the land market. Of course, the attenuation of black property rights produced by the racial discrimination of the legal authorities made investment in land less attractive than it would otherwise have been. This consideration may help to explain why blacks sometimes used their incomes for what the whites regarded as "frivolous" consumption rather than investing more in the acquisition of land and other productive assets.

In 1880 the Census Office sponsored an extensive study of cotton cultivation, and the report of this study, in two thick volumes, provides a major benchmark for evaluating changes in the condition of blacks in agriculture since emancipation. The report makes clear that a variety of contractual systems continued to operate, but some general features seem to emerge from the complexity of the situation. Evidently the most common arrangement for obtaining laborers was to rent them land for a share of the crop. Land alone generally commanded one-quarter of the cotton and one-third of the corn. Land plus mules and implements received a half share. Tenants received either half the crop or one-third of the crop plus rations. Fixed-rent tenancy was less common than share renting in most places. Fixed rents varied so greatly with the fertility and location of the land that no generalizations are possible. Laborers continued to receive wages on some plantations. $10 per month (plus the usual nonpecuniary items) was an average figure for a first-class hand, often more in the Southwestern states and often less in the Southeastern states. Day laborers received about 50 cents per day with food, 75 cents without food, or a piece-rate, commonly 50 cents per 100 pounds of seed cotton picked. Again, variations occurred according to place and season, rates being generally higher in the Southwestern states or during the cotton-picking season. Correspondents contributing information to the 1880 inquiry were also asked to state the proportion of black laborers who owned land or houses. In a few counties a majority was reported as owners, in other counties a substantial fraction, but in most the answer was simply "very few."[39] The overall impression conveyed by the 1880 report, in conjunction with reports for the immediate postwar years, is that blacks in general had made considerable progress in agriculture during the first 15 years of freedom. In 1880 they seldom labored in gangs, they lived in dispersed housing rather than the old "quarter," many had a measure of independence as tenants, and some had acquired enough land, stock, and tools to become owner operators. Their level of living was well above subsistence in most cases.[40]

But if genuine progress occurred, so did disappointment and frustration, for by and large the blacks were ignorant and powerless, and many whites took illegitimate advantage of those characteristics. In plain English, the blacks were often cheated. Perhaps the most frequent occasion for dishonesty was "settlement time," usually in December, when the landlord added up debits and credits and paid his tenant the balance due for the year. Illiterate tenants, forced to accept the landlord's statement of their accounts, were naturally suspicious, and no doubt some felt cheated when they were not. But many were genuinely robbed. Stearns told of his own experience in Georgia:

Every year negroes come to me, complaining bitterly of their employers withholding from them their dues; and particularly when they have been to work for a share of the crop. It is possible, that in some of these cases, they may not state the exact truth; but I have repeatedly asked them for all the items of their labor; the number of acres cultivated, amount of corn and cotton raised, the price it brought, and the amount they had received; and in a multitude of cases I was forced to admit, that they had been shamefully robbed, unless they are the greatest liars in existence.

Stearns added, perceptively, that "if the negro had land of his own, he would at least avoid this cheating process, and of course would be likely to receive all he earned."[41]

Again, however, competition among landlords helped to relieve a burden that would otherwise have exerted a crushing force on ignorant people largely excluded from the protection of the law. Even illiterates had some feeling for what was due to them. When the planter's exactions were very great, the tenant was almost certain to discover his ill-treatment and take the first opportunity for changing landlords. At the same time, landlords who dealt fairly with their tenants gained a local reputation that made their plantations preferred places of employment. As a Georgia planter told Nordhoff in 1875, "whoever pays his black laborers regularly and honestly can get as many as he wants at all times, and they will work faithfully." Addressing a Senate committee in 1883, an Alabama planter observed that "the planter is disposed to protect his negro laborer, or his negro tenant, because it is his interest to do so." He admitted that some did cheat the blacks, that "there has been a good deal of that," but he insisted that the majority of the planters "realize that that is not only unjust but also that it is bad policy." And he followed his statement with the familiar example of a neighbor who had dealt unjustly with his laborers and consequently could not secure laborers on his plantation.[42] That competition did moderate the extent to which the blacks were cheated is beyond question; that some cheating persisted despite competitive pressures is equally beyond doubt. The ignorance of many blacks and their exclusion from the equal protection of the law created opportunities for cheating too numerous and easily exploited to be demolished completely by competitive forces.

Competition was apparently more effective in preventing racial differences in wages or the terms of rental contracts. This racial equality in the marketplace rather astonished Sir George Campbell, who noted seeing "black and white labourers working together at the same work, and on the same wages, in a way which, to our Indian ideas of the dignity of the white race, is somewhat distressing."[43] Similarly, blacks who rented farms paid the landlord "such rent only as any white man would have to pay under the same circumstances." On one occasion in 1868 a group of white tenants signed at the bottom of the same contract that a group of blacks had signed, noting that "we are perfectly Satisfied with it and heare by bind our selves to abide and be Governed and Controwed by it." Nordhoff noted in the mid-1870s that on Arkansas plantations "white and colored renters seem to hold like relations to the owners of the land."[44] The general absence of racial discrimination from the farm labor and land rental markets probably reflects the operation of competitive forces that made the practice of such discrimination too costly for the planters to bear. On the other hand one might recognize that the poor whites labored under many of the same disadvantages as the blacks, being ignorant and powerless as a rule, and the racial equality of conditions in the rural labor markets does not necessarily imply an absence of some monopsony power in the hands of the planters. Clearly, many planters of self-styled "aristocratic" status harbored more prejudices against the poor whites than against the blacks, and discriminated accordingly in their hiring practices. Again, competitive forces and the forces of ignorance and discrimination were so inextricably entangled that a clear portrait of the rural labor markets is difficult to paint.

The new agricultural credit system

As long as the blacks in agriculture worked for wages, credit was no problem, but when they became tenants or owner operators credit was essential. Wage workers received money and rations at regular intervals during the course of the crop year. Tenants and owners, on the other hand, needed to spend both for personal consumption and for farm operations throughout the year, but not until they had produced and sold a crop would they receive any income. Had the black farmers possessed sufficient funds at the start of the year to carry them through the growing season, they would have required no credit, but almost all lacked such resources. In short, entering the credit market was part of the price paid for escaping from the status of wage laborer and becoming more independent of supervision by the white landlord.

While tenancy emerged as a dominant institution on the plantations, a new agricultural credit system grew up alongside it.[45] The heart of the new credit system was the country store. After the war small stores proliferated throughout the Southern countryside in response to the rise in the number of small purchasers growing out of emancipation and the collapse of the factorage system that had supplied credit on a larger scale to the antebellum plantations. Though these stores ostensibly served as agencies of trade not finance, in fact they engaged heavily in both. By allowing their customers to purchase goods at regular intervals during the year and waiting until harvest time for the settlement of accounts, the merchant creditors made it possible for black farmers lacking accumulated resources to operate as tenants or owner cultivators. Indeed, it is difficult to conceive of how any alternative financial agency – surely not banks or factors – could have provided credit in such small average amounts to so many poor people on such a wide scale, for only the storekeepers could cheaply monitor and regulate the loans so as to minimize the losses inherent in such high-risk lending.

Like any creditor, the country storekeeper required some form of collateral to secure him against the loss of his advances. Tenants usually possessed little or no property suitable for collateral; owner operators had land, but generally only cheap land not readily saleable. To provide an alternative form of security, the legislatures of the Southern states passed crop-lien laws soon after the war. A crop lien was "a bond for the payment of a specified amount – usually about $100 – given to the storekeeper by the farmer, and pledging the growing crop as collateral security." The lien note might be offered directly to a storekeeper, or a tenant might give the lien to his landlord, who guaranteed payment of the store account or made the advances himself. In the event of a debtor's prospective default the merchant had a simple legal remedy. "On affidavit of the lien holder that he believes his debtor means to avoid payment, the clerk of the court orders the sheriff to seize the crop, and sell the whole, or so much of it as will pay the debt with costs."[46] Though the prospective crop was subject to risks of various sorts, it did provide some security to the merchant creditors, and crop-lien credit became the mainstay of the small Southern farmers, both black and white. To insure that the collateral retained its value, storekeepers or their agents kept a close watch on the progress of the crops of their debtors. A farmer who failed to work his crops properly would receive a warning from the merchant; if he failed to take remedial action he might find his credit reduced at the store until such time as he "got his cotton out of the grass."

In accepting a lien note the merchant agreed to extend a line of credit up to a maximum for the season as specified in the contract. The amounts varied according to the demands of the farmer and the willingness of the merchant, and a tug-of-war often took place, the farmer trying to obtain more while the merchant endeavored to hold down the amount advanced. Credit limits commonly ranged from $50 to $200, larger amounts going to those farmers with larger or more fertile farms, more children of cotton-picking age, and better reputations as skilled farmers. During the growing season the farmer made periodic purchases from the store, for which he was charged "time prices" – prices to which an amount was added to reflect the delayed payment and risk borne by the seller. The difference between time prices and cash prices, along with the time elapsing between purchase of goods and settlement of account, determined the implicit interest rate actually paid on the credit extended by the merchant.

Everyone agreed that time prices, and therefore the implicit rates of interest, were "high." Just how high they were varied from one good to another, from one store to another, and even from one purchaser to another at the same store. Thomas D. Clark, the leading authority on the Southern merchant, discovered that "sometimes the mark-up price was more than twenty-five per cent, and frequently it was lower. . . . Good credit risks were charged less, and poor ones more."[47] In addition, customers who failed to "pay out" at the end of the year were usually charged explicit interest of 8 percent or more when their unpaid balance was carried over to the next year.

While everyone considered merchant credit expensive, there was –
and still is – no agreement about the cause of the exorbitant rates.
The major explanations point to scarcity of financial capital, high
risks, and monopoly power. Probably all played some part, but not all
mattered equally. No doubt the general scarcity of financial capital in
the South was a significant factor. All Southern interest rates, including
interest rates at the banks where the merchants themselves obtained
credit, were relatively high. In South Carolina, for example, Williamson found evidence that the interest rates paid by merchants and planters who borrowed money in Charleston and New York ranged from
12 to 36 percent and occasionally were even higher. Risk was also a
genuine influence in keeping time prices high. The crops covered by
the merchant's lien might fail, or bring a low price, or the tenant
might quietly migrate to an unknown destination, leaving his account
unpaid. When Somers questioned a Jewish storekeeper about his large
markups the merchant replied that "it ish large profit, but it ish profit
in de books, not profit in de pocket."[48] The surviving account books of
country merchants contain numerous entries for uncollected debts, si-
lent witnesses to the reality of the risks borne by the creditors. Whether
monopoly power played a large role still provokes dispute. Contemporaries emphasized that a farmer could not do any credit business except with the merchant to whom he had granted a lien. True enough,
but those who "paid out" could freely change merchants from one year
to the next; and despite a great deal of loose talk to the contrary, many
farmers did settle their accounts in full every year or almost every year.
The great number of stores scattered thickly throughout the rural
South also promoted competition. In South Carolina in 1882, for example, there were 4,645 stores of all kinds, or about one store for every
43 families (assuming a total population of a million, and five persons
per family). Philip Bruce's description of the merchant system in Virginia gave no hint of monopoly power. The black man, he said, ran
little risk of being improperly treated by the merchants. "Indeed there
is much competition among them to obtain his patronage, special advantages being offered as an inducement to secure his good-will." With
so many stores within a short radius, the rural black always had "a
choice of trading at any one of two or three," and he selected the one
that gave him the best terms. Bruce was, to be sure, an observer in-
clined toward minimizing the oppression of the freedmen, and one
may not wish to accept his statements at face value. Nevertheless, it
appears that monopoly power has been overemphasized by most economic historians. General capital scarcity and high risks probably
loomed larger as causes of the relatively high rates of interest implicit
in the time prices charged by Southern merchant creditors.[49]

The crop-lien credit system, then, was both a blessing and a curse to the black farmer. Without it he could not have assumed his position as an independent cultivator, but under it he had to struggle hard just to pay his store bill. Still, the credit system probably did not fundamentally determine the black man's progress in Southern agriculture. Du Bois wrote:

> The effect of this new crop-lien system on the freedman depended on his character and surrounding circumstances. A thrifty Negro in the hands of well-disposed landowners and honest merchants early became an independent landowner. A shiftless, ignorant Negro in the hands of unscrupulous landowners and Shylocks became something worse than a slave. The mass of the Negroes between these two extremes fared as chance and the weather let them.[50]

Contemporaries and historians alike have generally condemned the crop-lien credit system as an unmitigated evil, and central to their criticism has been the notion that the system made "peons" of the Southern farmers, especially the blacks. Strictly speaking, "peonage" refers to the working-out of a debt through compulsory labor. In the Southern states the lien generally applied only to the current crop and could not legally be carried over to future crops without the consent of the farmer. In some states over certain periods the laws apparently did sanction peonage or something akin to it by providing that certain breaches of debt contracts, normally subject only to civil suit, were criminal offenses; landlord creditors could then use the threat of criminal prosecution to hold indebted tenants at continued labor.[51] The farmers being perpetually in debt – as the received interpretation would have it – they had no choice of creditors and hence remained subject indefinitely to the monopoly power of the merchant or landlord. This view needs, at the very least, some clarification.

It is true that merchants and landlords often desired to retain their customers and tenants, but they surely did not desire to retain indefinitely those genuinely in debt to them. Promoting a perpetual indebtedness would have meant giving away real resources. Peonage made economic sense for the creditors only if the debt were fictitious, for then the creditor was simply holding a customer from whom he was stealing. No doubt peonage of this sort did sometimes occur – how often no one knows – but it resulted more from the ignorance and legal impotence of the black than from the crop-lien system. Given the circumstances, the whites would have found some way to rob the blacks; the crop-lien system, like the tenant system, provided the actual context for the fraud that would have occurred even in a different institutional setting. As long as hostile whites controlled the legal machinery the blacks – poor, ignorant, and powerless – were bound to be exploited. The crop-lien system was merely incidental.

But there were limits. As Bruce noted, "to allow the laborer to contract a large debt, is to tempt him to decamp without giving any notice of his intention to depart." A well-informed planter declared that "he is a bad manager who permits his freedmen to end the year in his debt." Yet he admitted that "this is frequently the case. Of course the debtor promises emphatically to stay and pay it back in work, but some morning his house will be found vacated, and you will discover that he has contracted elsewhere."[52] Once again the black man's mobility, the most precious jewel of emancipation, was his ultimate reliance in resisting oppression. Many did flee from their creditors. Unfortunately, while this provided relief for some, it only perpetuated the difficulties of those who remained, for uncollected legitimate debts meant high risks for the lenders and therefore high interest rates for all borrowers.

Nonagricultural employment

Any account of the blacks at work in the first 15 years after emancipation would be incomplete if it failed to notice those in nonagricultural occupations. Although there are no comprehensive data to indicate the exact number of nonagricultural workers, there is plenty of evidence that the number was considerable. In 1890, when about 20 percent of the black population lived in places of 2,500 or more, about 44 percent were classified as occupied outside agriculture. Using this relation as a rough basis, one can conjecture that in 1880, when about 14 percent lived in such urban places (but the census did not classify occupational returns by race), about three of every ten workers pursued nonagricultural jobs.[53] The relatively small number of people notwithstanding, it is more difficult to describe them than the agricultural population because of their greater diversity.

The freedmen pursued a wide variety of nonagricultural tasks. Under slavery many blacks had received training in blacksmithing, carpentry, masonry, painting, tailoring, barbering, and other skilled jobs. After the war these occupations continued to be filled for the most part by the same craftsmen who had pursued them as slaves.[54] A much larger number of blacks found employment in unskilled jobs of various sorts: black women worked as household servants, cooks, and laundresses; black men performed as common laborers, servants, waiters, longshoremen, porters, teamsters, miners, janitors, and deliverymen. A few occupied themselves as teachers, preachers, and undertakers, providing their services for a segregated black clientele. In the cities blacks kept small shops, restaurants, and saloons. Occasionally a black man appeared as a substantial entrepreneur in retail trade, construction, or real estate. During Reconstruction a handful of black lawyers practiced; black physicians, for obvious reasons, were almost unknown. Few factories existed in the South before 1880, so the common exclusion of blacks from employment as manufacturing operatives mattered little during those years.

It appears that black workers faced somewhat greater discrimination in nonagricultural than in agricultural labor markets. Still, the degree of discrimination was probably not great; in many jobs the workers received the same pay regardless of race. Sir George Campbell discerned no wage discrimination during his tour of Georgia in 1878. Five years later a black carpenter told the Senate Committee on Education and Labor that "there is no trouble but what the negro gets the same pay for the same work; none in the world. We work all together, right in the same shop [in Columbus, Ga.]." This witness testified that such racial equality of wages prevailed generally; and another witness, a black painter and contractor from the same city, corroborated this testimony.[55] Discrimination more commonly took the form of exclusion from an occupation, as in the textile mills, than the form of substandard wages. Many Southern whites had well-developed ideas about the various occupations, dividing them among "white man's work," "nigger jobs," and those open to all comers. But other whites had slightly different notions and, in any event, ideas and practices sometimes clashed when economic incentives dictated that "new ideas" should prevail. Where individual actions were the decisive force, economic competition and racial discrimination often conflicted, with discrimination the loser.

Certainly the composition of black nonagricultural employment was heavily weighted by workers in low-paid and menial occupations. But, in view of the low levels of skill and training of the black work force, this situation hardly demonstrates that employers regularly favored white workers over blacks when both were equally qualified. In 1880 the occupational structure of the black labor force remained largely a legacy of slavery, but it also reflected the general poverty of the black population and the racial discrimination exercised in the creation and administration of the Southern public school systems: few blacks could afford much education, and those few found their upward path obstructed by white school administrators bent on diverting resources toward the white schools. So conditions changed slowly, at times almost imperceptibly. But, despite the difficulties, nonagricultural employments continued to attract black people, and the number occupied in such jobs no doubt increased during the first 15 years after emancipation.

Summary: Freedom and necessity

When the events of 1865 and 1866 dashed the freedmen's hopes for acquiring land from the federal government, they had no choice but to find a place in the emerging free labor market. The development of contractual relations occurred fairly smoothly in the cities, where customs of hiring labor were already established, but in the countryside the transition was marked by confusion, experimentation, and violence. Out of the chaos grew the new systems of agricultural tenancy and crop-lien credit. They were complementary because the shift from wage labor to tenancy required credit not available from traditional sources, while the merchant creditors depended on the new markets created by the partitioning of the plantations and the emergence of more independent black cultivators. As the blacks became tenants, borrowers, and – more rarely – landowners, the whites made sporadic attempts to place them at a competitive disadvantage through the formation of restrictive cartels. In general, such organizations failed to achieve their objectives because intense competition for labor undermined the solidarity required to exert genuine monopsony power in the labor market or monopoly power in the land market. Competition also prevented the general emergence of racial discrimination in wage payments or farm rental agreements. Competitive pressures failed to eliminate completely the cheating of blacks by landlords and merchants, although such pressures did serve to moderate these abuses. The black man's most effective response to persecution was simply to flee, an action that could succeed after 1865 on a scale quite impossible under the slave regime. Generally powerless before the white-dominated legal (and extralegal) machinery, the blacks paid a high price for their ignorance and inexperience. Overall, however, economic progress did occur during the first 15 years after the war: the development of tenancy meant both higher incomes and greater independence from white supervision than were obtained by blacks under the wage system; land ownership conferred even greater benefits; and some found greater opportunities in nonagricultural employments. To be sure, the progress was limited but, considering the circumstances surrounding their enslavement and emancipation, one might well marvel that the freedmen did so well.

4

The people at work, 1880–1914

Industry is competing with agriculture for the limited supply of Negro workers. Negroes, responding to exactly the same natural laws that control the white farmers, have been moving cityward, entering other occupations, migrating west or north—where more money is to be made. Agricultural wages have therefore gone up and rents, relatively, have gone down.

Ray Stannard Baker, 1908

If living by the sweat of the brow was an indication of man's fall from grace, then black people truly labored under the curse. In 1890, when the census first made racial distinctions in the returns pertaining to gainful employment, the blacks reported a relatively high involvement in gainful pursuits; and during the following 20 years their measured rate of participation in the labor force increased substantially (see Table 4.1). Some of the increase, particularly for females, was probably spurious, reflecting more careful enumeration in the last census. But part of the increase was probably genuine, for the age structure of the population was changing in a way that favored greater participation in the labor market. In 1890 persons aged 10–14 made up about 20 percent of the population aged 10 or more; by 1910 their share had fallen to about 16 percent. In addition, the share of persons aged 15–19 fell by about two percentage points during this period. These changes meant that persons relatively less involved in the labor market were becoming less heavily represented in the population of potential working age. By 1910 about 71 percent of the blacks over 9 years of age were gainfully employed; for the whites, by contrast, the ratio was only 51 percent.[1] Surely the question "Will the Negro work?" had been settled once and for all.

Farmers and farm laborers continued to constitute the bulk of the gainfully employed throughout the period 1880–1914. Because of the problems of properly accounting for family workers in agriculture, it is difficult to say just how the actual labor force was divided between agricultural and other pursuits at different times. The census data for male workers, which are probably more reliable than the figures for females, show that agricultural employment did not grow as fast as other types of employment during the period 1890–1910 (see Table 4.1). The agricultural share of total male employment fell from about 62

Table 4.1. *Employment status of blacks 10 years of age and over, by sex,
1890–1910* [a]

	Males			Females		
	1910	1900	1890	1910	1900	1890
Total number (000's)	3,637	3,182	2,646	3,681	3,234	2,683
Percentages						
Gainfully employed	87.4	84.1	79.4	54.7	40.7	36.2
In agricultural pursuits	50.3	49.1	49.2	28.6	18.0	15.9
In other pursuits	37.1	35.0	30.3	26.2	22.7	20.3

[a] "It seems probable that a large proportion of the apparent increase in the
gainful, and specifically in the agricultural, employment of Negro as of white
women in the decade 1900–1910, is to be attributed directly to the fact that
instructions to enumerators in 1910 were, as regards women, more specific
and comprehensive," U.S. Bureau of the Census, *Negro Population, 1790–1915*
(Washington, 1918), p. 507.
Source: Ibid., p. 504.

percent in 1890 to about 58 percent in 1910, but nearly all the decline
occurred in the 1890s, a period of unusual depression in Southern
agriculture. The decline, of course, was only relative; the absolute
numbers of black farmers and farm laborers grew rapidly during these
years. Clearly, agriculture continued to provide the most typical setting
for black labor until well into the twentieth century.

Agricultural labor, land tenure, and credit

By 1880, if not earlier, the main features of the postbellum Southern
rural economy had taken shape, and no major organizational changes
occurred during the subsequent 35 years. But because more studies
were performed and more data collected after 1880, one can assess the
workings of the economy and the role of the blacks in it more easily for
the more recent years. The evidence indicates that the real wage rates
of black farm laborers probably increased somewhat over time. Until
the late 1890s, a falling general price level produced this effect even
when nominal wages remained unchanged. Substantial changes in the
prevailing forms of land rental also occurred.

At the turn of the century the Department of Agriculture modified
its usual procedure for collecting data on farm wage rates, asking its
correspondents to submit data separately for black and white laborers.
Information was obtained for the years 1898, 1899, and 1902. Never

before had such an enormous body of wage data been collected and systematically compiled: the study in 1902 obtained information from over 23,000 correspondents; the number of respondents to the earlier investigations, not revealed in the published reports, was probably in the same neighborhood. Contributors included the regular county crop reporters and their assistants, state statistical agents and their correspondents, and a "great number" of farmers. Although the department acknowledged that returns were deficient for some counties, no source of comparable scope is available, and the reports are not subject to such obvious bias that one would be warranted in disregarding them.[2]

Table 4.2, which is based on these data, shows two different measures of the ratio of the white money wage rate to the black money wage rate: for ordinary and for harvest labor, both without board. Data for

Table 4.2. *Money wage rates in Southern agriculture, by state and race, 1898, 1899, and 1902*

State	Wages/day, in current dollars, without board, ordinary labor			Wages/day, in current dollars, without board, harvest labor		
	Whites (1)	Blacks (2)	Ratio (1)/(2)	Whites (3)	Blacks (4)	Ratio (3)/(4)
Delaware	1.00	0.96	1.04	1.37	1.33	1.03
Maryland	0.96	0.88	1.09	1.35	1.25	1.08
Virginia	0.75	0.71	1.06	1.20	1.14	1.05
North Carolina	0.63	0.59	1.07	1.00	0.93	1.08
South Carolina	0.57	0.51	1.12	0.89	0.79	1.13
Georgia	0.65	0.58	1.12	0.96	0.87	1.10
Florida	0.92	0.82	1.12	1.05	0.98	1.07
Alabama	0.69	0.61	1.13	0.98	0.84	1.17
Mississippi	0.74	0.69	1.07	0.94	0.86	1.09
Louisiana	0.90	0.79	1.14	1.15	1.02	1.13
Texas	0.96	0.83	1.16	1.23	1.08	1.14
Arkansas	0.83	0.80	1.04	1.22	1.14	1.07
Tennessee	0.72	0.69	1.04	1.15	1.10	1.05
West Virginia	0.93	0.87	1.07	1.29	1.25	1.03
Kentucky	0.79	0.78	1.01	1.30	1.32	0.98
Unweighted mean	0.80	0.74	1.08	1.14	1.06	1.08

Source: Calculated from data in James H. Blodgett, "Wages of Farm Labor in the United States," U.S. Department of Agriculture, Bureau of Statistics, *Miscellaneous Series, Bulletin No. 26* (Washington, 1903), pp. 37–38.

1898, 1899, and 1902, which the Department of Agriculture's bulletins present separately, have been averaged in the table. The two measures of the racial wage ratio give quite similar results. The ratios range from 0.98 in Kentucky (though the department warned against a possible bias because of incomplete data from this state) to 1.17 in Alabama. On the average the white money wage rate exceeded the black money wage rate by about 8 percent.

This racial differential appears small, yet it probably overstates the true differential in real wages for two reasons. First, the figures for whites probably include a relatively greater number of wage rates paid to workers with special skills or more responsibility.[3] In this case the whites would be expected to earn higher wages because they supply, on the average, more valuable labor services. Second, black workers typically received substantial compensation in kind that their white counterparts did not. The Department of Agriculture's first study refers repeatedly to this difference in mode of payment and cautions against misinterpretation of the data. The following statements clearly describe the differences at issue:

In general, the negro has lower wages than the white. This is not so much from comparison of an individual negro with an individual white as because of a condition affecting negroes as a body, which has established customs of privileges and allowances for negroes as to work and compensation that apply to whites in the States employing large numbers of negroes only in a very limited degree. . . . Rations are more generally furnished to colored laborers than to white – to such an extent, in fact, that the cost of rations in considerable areas stands for cost of food for colored laborers. . . . All this affects the rate of nominal wages. It is not prominently a question of color, but it is essentially a question of social economy in which color becomes involved, because so many of the laborers with such customs of life are colored.[4]

These statements imply that money wage figures like those in Table 4.2 overstate the real wage difference between black and white farm laborers in the South at the turn of the century. Because money wages differed on the average by only 8 percent – that is, by about 6 cents per day for ordinary labor, perhaps 2 cents more during harvest – even a very slight allowance for the greater compensation in kind of the blacks would bring the real wages of the two groups into approximate equality.[5]

Other evidence also indicates an absence of racial discrimination in the farm labor markets of the South. When the United States Industrial Commission questioned witnesses from various parts of the South in 1900, planters from Georgia, Mississippi, and Tennessee were unanimous in stating under oath that "we give them [blacks and whites] about the same thing."[6] Apparently the only study to adduce evidence of discrimination in wage payments is an article by Frenise Logan on

North Carolina. Logan asserts that "with respect to wages, the weight of evidence seems to support the view that Negro agricultural laborers were employed at wages lower than those paid to their white counterparts." However, anyone who bothers to track down Logan's source, the report for 1887 of the North Carolina Bureau of Labor Statistics, will discover that Logan has produced a remarkable distortion of the evidence; in fact, this evidence supports just the opposite conclusion.[7] In short, the real weight of evidence points toward a virtual absence of racial wage differences in the rural South at the turn of the century.[8]

This racial equality of wages prevailed for two reasons. First, the average productivity of blacks and whites was about the same in unskilled labor. Though some planters preferred blacks to whites, proclaiming black labor "the best that we have," others preferred whites when they were available. In either case their preferences had little to do with differences in productivity but depended more on the farmers' tastes and their self-perceptions of social standing. More "aristocratic" planters preferred black laborers, while yeoman farmers were more likely to hire a white farm hand.[9] Second, as the Report of the Industrial Commission observed, "any white labor of the same grade of service is leveled in the competition." Just how starkly this racial competition operated was revealed by R. J. Redding, Director of the Georgia Agricultural Experiment Station, when he appeared before the Industrial Commission in 1900. He testified that, on the farms he managed, whites frequently made application for jobs. "But when the white men come and are willing to work we have to say: We can not afford to pay you any more, because I can get a negro for 60 cents a day; if you are willing to work at that price the first vacancy we have you can have it." And from time to time white men consented to employment on those terms.[10] Obviously, with widespread competition for labor in a market containing thousands of employers, not all of whom valued the exercise of racial discrimination, systematic racial wage differentials could not long persist.

Tenancy remained the prevailing status of black farm operators. According to a recent estimate for the cotton regions of the South in 1880, about 80 percent of the black farm operators were tenants.[11] One may well doubt the representativeness of this estimate, since it implies a far lower percentage of tenancy than that reported by the Department of Agriculture's correspondents in 1876 or by the special census correspondents in 1880 – in an area noted for its extreme degree of tenancy. But, whatever the precise ratio, tenants far outnumbered owners. In 1890 the census takers made their first attempt to count farm owners and tenants classified by race (see Table 4.3). Their enumeration indicated that about 78 percent of the black farmers in the United States

Table 4.3. *Land tenure status of black farm operators, by region, 1890*

Region	Owners	Tenants
North Atlantic	1,090	698
South Atlantic	53,261	164,742
North Central	7,530	6,260
South Central	58,570	257,108
Western	287	86
United States	120,738	428,894

Source: Calculated from data in Department of the Interior, Census Division, *Report on Farms and Homes* (Washington, 1896), p. 175.

were tenants. If this proportion is approximately correct, as it appears to be, it casts further doubt on the estimate for 1880, since both contemporary comment and a statistical record for Georgia point toward a considerable decrease in the relative prevalence of black tenancy during the 1880s. The absolute number of tenants, however, increased steadily. From about 429,000 in 1890, the number of black tenants climbed to over 557,000 in 1900, and to almost 673,000 in 1910.[12]

As the number of tenants increased, fixed-rent contracts became more prevalent relative to share-rent forms, at least until 1900. In a sample of 1,581 black tenants in the cotton regions in 1880, almost two-thirds paid a share rent;[13] the estimate is consistent with contemporary testimony. When the census first distinguished tenants by both race and rental type 20 years later, the number of black tenants paying fixed rents almost equaled the number paying share rents. During the first decade of the twentieth century the trend reversed itself as share tenancy expanded considerably faster than fixed-rent forms. By 1910 about 57 percent of the black tenants paid a share rent.[14]

These changes in prevailing forms of land rental reflected a variety of developments in Southern agriculture. The expansion of fixed-rent tenancy during the late nineteenth century may have occurred in part as a response to the growth in the number of experienced black farmers to whom landlords were willing to grant such contracts. Also, the cotton economy experienced a severe price depression during the 1890s, and many landlords concluded that their managerial talents would be better employed in an urban occupation. No longer able to supervise their plantations closely, they adopted fixed-rent contracts, which required less supervision because they provided a greater incentive for the tenant. The steady accumulation of land by country storekeepers encouraged fixed rental for the same reasons.[15] A long-term decrease in the riskiness of cotton production could also have encouraged a relative decline of share systems, a major function of which is to spread risk between the tenant and the landlord. This interpretation is consistent with the resurgence of share renting that occurred along with the spread of the boll weevil beyond Texas early in the twentieth century, an event that greatly increased the risk of cotton cultivation. A recent econometric study of the cotton states in 1910 indicates that the "mix" of share-rent and fixed-rent forms of tenancy was indeed connected with the level of yield risk, greater risk being associated with relatively more share renting.[16]

That study also finds that the farmer's race probably had no systematic influence on the form of rental agreement he obtained, given that both races faced the same risk conditions – a conclusion corroborated by a related study of the Georgia cotton-belt counties in the period 1880–1900.[17] Contemporary testimony is consistent with these findings: planters asserted that blacks and whites not only obtained the same form of contracts under similar circumstances but that the terms of their contracts were identical as well. As one planter put it in 1900, "all share alike. The contracts are made on the same basis to each race."[18] Apparently, competition in the land rental market precluded the emergence of racial differences in contracts, other things being the same.

Noticing that black tenants tended to operate smaller farms than whites, some writers have suggested that this difference reflected racial discrimination.[19] The planters themselves asserted that tenants got as much as they could handle; since the demand for labor reached a peak during the harvest season, the number of available harvest workers was crucial. On cotton farms – and most black farmers did grow cotton – the number of family workers available for picking cotton set a limit on the size of the farm. When John C. Kyle, a Mississippi planter, was asked about tenant farm sizes, he said simply: "It depends on the size of the family." It also depended on the fertility of the land, more fertile land producing greater yields and therefore requiring more harvest labor per acre, and on the mix of crops grown, cotton requiring more labor than corn. Because black tenants tended to occupy more fertile land and to grow more cotton than their white counterparts, it was predictable that their farms would be smaller. Perhaps these considerations do not fully account for the relatively small size of black farms, but if a genuine racial difference existed it was not large.[20]

Blacks continued to acquire land. In Georgia, for which a continuous annual series is available showing black landownership from 1874 forward, the rural acreage held by blacks increased from about 587,000 acres in 1880 to about 1,608,000 acres in 1910. Accumulation of land depended in part on the vagaries of the cotton economy, for tenants generally relied on the proceeds of a good year to make the down payment on land of their own; moreover, the ability to complete the payments depended on crop yields and prices. Though their land holdings had increased steadily for almost 30 years after the war, the blacks of Georgia failed to accumulate any additional land between 1892 and 1900, when cotton prices and incomes suffered a severe depression. Recovery of the cotton economy after 1900 stimulated a renewed upsurge of acquisitions in the early twentieth century. In 1900 a committee of the American Economic Association estimated that in the entire United States black farmers owned property, the bulk of it being land, valued at about $230,000,000. In the Black Belt, where most rural blacks lived, relatively few achieved landownership, but the absolute number of owners was greatest in that area.[21]

With notable exceptions, black owners held small farms on poor land. In the main, simple poverty probably accounts for this tendency. In part, however, the average size of the farms owned by blacks is misleading. As Du Bois noted, many of them were "serving merely as the partial support of persons with supplementary occupations." He judged that "practically all the farms under 10 acres are of this sort, and might be counted as large gardens. Many are situated just outside the corporation limits of towns and cities, and thus escape being listed or taxed as town lots."[22]

Though the farm land owned by blacks was generally inferior, the black owners themselves were generally the best of the rural population. "[T]he fact that a negro is a land-owner is a proof," said Philip Bruce, "that he is superior in certain qualities of his character to the great mass of his race." They were, added Enoch Banks, "respected alike by the whites and the members of their own race."[23] Despite the possible exaggeration in such observations, the point remains: black landowners tended to constitute the most talented and ambitious class in black rural society.

White hostility toward black landownership gradually waned as more and more blacks acquired land. George Henry White, a North Carolina black who served in the U.S. Congress at the turn of the century, told the Industrial Commission in 1900 that the whites did not object to the accumulation of land by blacks. "I can not say," he testified, "that I know of any prejudice against the colored man's accumulating property." Several other witnesses told the same story, and some whites even expressed the idea that black landowners were approved because they made "better citizens" and did not "get into trouble with the neighbors as frequently as colored people who do not own land and are ready to move at any time." In 1905 Banks reported that in Georgia "the attitude of the typical white landowner is not one that would dictate a refusal to sell land to a negro because of his color, nor would the color of the purchaser alter in any wise the terms upon which the land might be obtained." Not infrequently, blacks acquired land in part because of aid from friendly whites, who provided advice, loans, or legal assistance. In discussing such manifestations of interracial friendship, T. J. Woofter was moved to remark that "the North believes in the Negro as a race and condemns him as an individual, while the South believes in him as an individual and condemns him as a race" – a dictum that contained a grain of truth.[24]

Black farmers generally produced the crops best suited to their skills and experience and to the soils, climates, and markets to which they had access. As Table 4.4 shows, cotton was the leading crop, with corn the only major competitor for acreage, but significant amounts of other crops were grown. Sweet potatoes occupied a large acreage, and considerable quantities of garden produce were grown. Livestock was raised on many farms: of black-operated farms in 1910, 38 percent reported cattle, 50 percent mules, 62 percent horses, 68 percent hogs, and 80 percent poultry.[25] Black farmers reporting no livestock were almost all sharecroppers to whom landlords furnished draft animals from central locations. To raise corn, hay, and food crops only for home use and cotton as the cash crop formed the usual pattern.

Table 4.4. *Acres in specified crops on farms of black farmers, all Southern states, 1899 and 1909*

Crop	Acreage (in 000's) 1899	Acreage (in 000's) 1909
Cotton	9,656	12,097
Corn	6,994	7,377
Hay and forage	317	469
Oats	262	322
Wheat	435	204
Sweet potatoes	133	166
Tobacco	142	170
Potatoes	30	51
Rice	49	29

Source: U.S. Bureau of the Census, *Negro Population, 1790–1915* (Washington, 1918), p. 601.

It has become traditional to assert that Southern farmers, especially the blacks, grew "too much" cotton and "too little" food, but the validity of the proposition is open to question. The argument rests on the alleged power of the merchant creditor under the crop-lien system to dictate, as Fred Shannon put it, "that cotton, more cotton, and almost cotton alone should be grown. . . . So the cropper who dared to till a truck patch was quickly warned that he was lowering his credit."[26] Careful students of the merchant credit system, however, have failed to find evidence that merchants typically acted in this way. Jacqueline Bull stated that "a rather careful search has failed to reveal any lien notes which stated that cotton alone must be planted." Thomas D. Clark observed that "many merchants have been known to advise customers to plant more food and feed crops in order to leave more of their cotton money clear." He also questioned "the logic of claiming that credit was reduced because customers reduced their cotton acreage," noting that "the margin of profit actually would have been greater for the merchant if a majority of his customers had been able to grow adequate foodstuff, and to clear a modest cotton crop with which to purchase a larger assortment of higher quality merchandise." And quite recently the econometric studies of Stephen DeCanio have seriously challenged the whole notion that cotton was "overproduced."[27] A more plausible hypothesis is that the tendency of blacks to produce more cotton than similar whites stemmed from their occupancy of soils particularly suited for that crop and from their lack of equal skills in the production of alternative crops.

Some supporters of the thesis that merchants possessed great monopoly power have also asserted that the credit system discriminated against blacks. The evidence for this position is inferential,[28] and available direct evidence generally contradicts it. Speaking before the American Economic Association in 1901, Alfred Holt Stone, a planter from the Yazoo-Mississippi Delta and an articulate student of race relations, asserted that the racial factor played no part in the credit system of the Delta region:

The negro is dealt with just as his established reputation and the value of the security he has to offer may justify. . . . The amount advanced is governed by the character of the individual and the security. There is, however, this difference; the white man gets his advances in cash, available at stated intervals, while the negro gets the most of his in the shape of supplies. If, however, the negro has established for himself a reputation and credit, and is entitled to it under the standard applying to the white man, he can secure advances in the same manner. On the other hand, if the white man is the owner of only two mules, he gets his just as does the negro. Of negroes of reputation and credit, there are in the delta a great many; of white men without property there are, fortunately for all concerned, extremely few. It is a matter of credit, and not of race.

In the same spirit Banks judged that the black farmers of Georgia could "obtain goods from merchants upon as good terms as do white men similarly circumstanced, and their complexion has no influence upon the rate of interest." Similarly a planter merchant from South Carolina told the Industrial Commission that, when merchants determined their markups, they made no distinction according to the color of the customer.[29] Evidently, competition among merchants and landlords generally prevented racial discrimination in the provision of merchant credit. Of course, to say that the creditors did not discriminate on a purely racial basis is not to assert that blacks obtained credit easily or cheaply. Because of their poor reputations as borrowers and their lack of good collateral, most blacks could borrow only with difficulty and then at relatively high interest rates. That poor whites faced the same situation gave small consolation to the hard-pressed black farmers.

With credit charges always high and crop prices and yields fluctuating, black farmers sometimes could not "pay out" at the end of the year at the store. Just how frequently this occurred no one really knows, and the evidence is contradictory. Many contemporaries spoke as though virtually all black farmers lived in perpetual debt. Pitt Dillingham estimated that "probably ninety per cent. of these colored farmers on the average find the balance at the store against them." George K. Holmes' hyperbolic account, which leaves the impression that Southern farmers were locked without exception in thralldom to the merchants, has been frequently cited by uncritical historians. Both Dillingham and Holmes were writing in the mid-1890s, when the collapse of the cotton market no doubt did give rise to widespread indebtedness. During better times more farmers cleared their accounts with the merchants at the end of the year. George Henry White testified in 1900 that, although debts were sometimes carried over from year to year so that the debtor was never able to clear his account, "I do not want to impress you that this is the rule."[30]

The tendency to see the black farmers as locked in perpetual debt springs in part from a confusion of concepts. One must distinguish between the farmer who borrowed every year but cleared his account from time to time and the farmer whose unpaid debt balance remained on the merchant's books indefinitely and who never cleared his account. The former was hardly a peon, while the latter may or may not have been, depending on other conditions. Evidently most black farmers borrowed every year; how many "paid out" is the great unknown. J. H.

Hale, an unusual farmer who operated farms in both Georgia and Connecticut, told the Industrial Commission that "many of them do have their debts lapse over from year to year; but I think a majority get a clean settlement once in two or three years, when they have an exceptionally good crop or prices are a little high." After reconsidering his statement, he judged that "the majority of them get out of debt each year, in October, but start in again in January with a new one." Some, he said, "have a moderate bank account and . . . do business on business principles."[31] Many statements in the historical literature about peonage and the power of the merchants under the crop-lien system are merely uncritical assertions based upon the implicit – and economically unsound – assumption that any debt is a Bad Thing. That black farmers regularly borrowed from the merchant creditors did not *ipso facto* make them peons.

Whether indebtedness would lead to peonage depended on the desire and ability of the creditor to immobilize his debtor and dictate his activities. Again there has been much loose talk. The evidence suggests that relatively few lenders had sufficient power to hold tenants against their will. The options open to indebted tenants were revealed clearly in the testimony of O. B. Stevens, Georgia's Commissioner of Agriculture, before the Industrial Commission in 1901. Notice that in the course of the dialogue the tenant's status somehow rises from slave to free man:

Q. [by a member of the commission] Now, a man in continual debt, wearing out the land there for 10 or 15 years, is practically in slavery?
A. [by Stevens] Yes; I think that is it.
Q. He is so tied up that it is impossible for him ever to escape it?
A. Yes; I think so.
Q. And one successive debt follows another there like an endless chain, and there is no hope for a man?
A. In many cases that is true.
Q. It would take probably a great season and an advance in crops to some abnormal prices probably to lift him out of that debt, would it not?
A. Yes.
Q. Normally he could not get out of debt?
A. Normally he would not at all. A great many of the tenants go on these lands possibly and farm them, say, for 5 years, and then they have poor prices and poor crops, and they become discouraged and throw up the whole thing and get out.
Q. At the end of any one year they do not have to work there the next year?
A. Oh, no.
Q. Is there any reason why a man should not take another place and make a new start?
A. Not at all. . . . There is nothing whatever to force a man to stay on the farm. They usually rent these lands from year to year. The lands are not leased for continuous years, but usually they are rented from year to year,

and if the landlord becomes dissatisfied at the end of the year he need not retain the tenant longer unless he wants to keep him. If the tenant is dissatisfied for any cause, he has a perfect right to go whenever he wants to. The landlord has no lien and no claim upon the property of the tenant whatever except for rent and advances, and those only apply to the present crop.

Q. What would be the position of a man, however, who had defaulted on one farm? What would be his probability of being able to get another farm in that locality, provided he did not liquidate his indebtedness in the first instance?

A. Oh, he would not be regarded as a first-class tenant. But there is always plenty of room there for everybody, and he always gets a place and gets along in some way. Some people always take him up. . . . I have never seen a man in Georgia yet who wanted to work that could not get a place.[32]

Not uncommonly, an indebted black who wished to change landlords did so by persuading the new landlord to pay his debt to the old landlord. The tenant then assumed his new contract bringing an interest-bearing debt. Amounts paid in such transfers ranged from \$25 to \$200.[33] Where genuine forced labor existed in the rural South it almost invariably rested on illegal or extralegal intimidation and the complicity of the legal authorities.[34] Such conditions derived from the inability of the black man to secure equal protection before the law and, to a lesser extent, from his ignorance. The credit system or indebtedness *per se* had little to do with genuine peonage.

George Henry White identified the ignorance of many black farmers as a grave deficiency. "There is a great deal of fraud perpetrated on the ignorant," he said; "they keep no books, and in the fall the account is what the landlord and the storeman choose to make it. They can not dispute it; they have kept no account." But others, he noted, did keep accounts, and "there are many who thrive." No doubt many whites habitually extracted petty sums from ignorant blacks. Such behavior, as L. C. Gray viewed it in 1912, did not often violate the letter of common honesty, being rather the "advantage which the very strong takes of the very helpless. Not infrequently it is tempered by moderation." Nevertheless, it was pervasive. As a black man in the Brazos Valley told Gray: "Boss, some cuts de nigger too close to de bone, but dey all gash him a little."[35]

That they did not "gash" him more owed something to competitive forces. Harry Hammond, an articulate South Carolina planter, testified in 1901 that "Negro laborers, without being able to explain their mathematics, have a very clear idea of what is due them, and employers usually settle fairly to avoid the reputation of being bad paymasters, which would interfere seriously with their securing labor." O. B. Stevens confirmed that a planter known to cheat his laborers "does not get any more labor at all." So important was their reputation for honesty that some planters took special pains to allay doubts

in the minds of black workers. John C. Calhoun III, an Arkansas
planter and a grandson of the famous antebellum Senator, never contracted with an illiterate, and therefore suspicious, tenant too hastily:
"I never allow a negro to sign a written contract with me before he
has taken it home with him and had some friend to read it over and
consult with him about it, because I want some obligation attached
to my contracts."[36] Clearly, in the face of competitive pressures in the
labor and land rental markets landlords could not repeatedly deal
unfairly with the blacks and expect to escape without some undesirable
repercussions.

In an attempt to use the powers of the law to reduce the competition
for labor, Southern states enacted legislation against the enticement of
laborers or tenants. Such laws applied only to those currently under
contract, but even there they had little effect. As early as 1871, a
Southern planter observed that

occasionally an advertisement appears in a newspaper, declaring that such
and such a freedman has broken his labor contract, and that whoever hires
him shall be prosecuted according to law; but it rarely or never occurs that
such a prosecution takes place, though the freedman is hired by some other
planter. Indeed, it is a difficult matter to discover an absconded freedman, for
he can readily find a home go where he will, so great is the demand for
laborers.

When questioned about the antienticement law in 1900, a Georgia
planter responded that he had "run up against it once or twice" and
he judged that it did not "amount to very much one way or the other."
Similarly, laws placing prohibitive taxes on agents recruiting laborers
to leave the state seem to have had little effect beyond driving the
agents underground.[37]

A more effective device was to hold a tenant in place by threatening
to prosecute him for a technical violation of some criminal law. George
Henry White testified that "since the adoption of the homestead law
in the State [North Carolina] nearly all debts that could be collected
in the absence of the homestead are now reduced to criminal offenses."
As a result the landlords were "almost forced for their own protection
to invoke this criminal law to collect what otherwise they could collect
under the civil procedure." White emphasized that such technical violations of the criminal law were not invoked by the "better element"
of the landlords but only by "some shyster fellow who wants to stop
me when I am disposed to go elsewhere with a view of bettering my
condition."[38] Tenants still possessed – and often exercised – the option
of surreptitious flight if conditions became intolerable.

More common than the use of law to suppress competition was the
exertion of illegal force and violence, an outstanding example being

the behavior known as "whitecapping." This appeared in various parts of the South, but the best documented episodes occurred in Mississippi in the 1890s and the 1900s. There white farmers formed secret organizations to combat the influence of the merchants in the labor and land rental markets. They opposed the unsupervised rental of land to blacks and hoped to frighten the black tenants into accepting employment on the plantations of resident landlords. To accomplish their ends they issued warnings, burned homes, beat blacks, and fired shots into houses. This strategy failed utterly. Frightened blacks did abandon the lands they had rented from the merchants, but instead of transferring to neighboring plantations they quite sensibly left the area entirely. From southwestern Mississippi, where whitecapping flourished during the years 1892–1893 and 1902–1906, black farmers migrated by the hundreds to the Delta. Recognizing the potential for attracting laborers, labor agents from the Delta encouraged this migration by providing information about employment opportunities in their more peaceful area. The violence was finally suppressed, on both occasions, by legal action that led to the dissolution of the whitecap organizations.[39]

The interaction of landlords and tenants continued to provide the occasion for much coercion and violence. In addition to the perennial disputes surrounding settlements, the landlord's control over the tenant's entire family raised thorny problems, for the tenant sometimes challenged the landlord's prerogative. One such incident occurred in Lowndes County, Alabama, in the late 1890s. As Dillingham told the story:

[A] woman, the wife of a colored man, had been ordered out into the field; she claimed she was sick; the husband then said to the man who ordered her out that she should not go; that she was sick. The white man went for his shotgun. When he came back the black man was ready with his gun, and shot the white man first. Then finally came the lynching. The black man was hung up and riddled with shot.[40]

This incident very nearly plunged the county into a renewal of the open race warfare that had occurred there previously, but on this occasion cooler heads prevailed.

Excluded from the protection of the law, rural blacks had to rely on the protection generated by competitive pressures in the market. Calhoun, the Arkansas planter, asserted in 1883 that "the constant demand for their labor affords them the amplest protection." Stone appealed to the same argument in describing the condition of the blacks in the Delta two decades later:

It is not claimed that there are no instances of injustice to the negro. Not at all. But I do claim that nowhere else is his general treatment fairer, – nowhere is his remedy more certain. This is but corollary to the proposition that nowhere in the same extent of territory will be found a greater or more constant demand for his labor. Nowhere does he find a better market for his service, nowhere is he freer to change his local habitation.

A Tennessee planter told the Industrial Commission that he took special pains to insure his tenants good treatment, "as labor is not so plentiful."[41] Evidently these Delta planters were telling a true story; at least the blacks seemed to agree, for the Delta persistently drew blacks from other areas of the South.

Ultimately migration provided the surest remedy for the oppressed black. As Bruce clearly recognized, "if the employer or his overseer is harsh and indiscriminating in his discipline, taxing the energies of the freedman to a point that shows a lack of proper regard for him, the latter is disposed to resent it by leaving." Moreover, "there is no way whatever of retaining them if the plantation with which they are temporarily connected is situated near a convenient means of transportation."[42] Those who complained of the black's "shiftlessness" might well have looked closer; they would have seen the surest justice to which he could appeal. The constant flux of the population bore witness that the appeal was being made.

The legacy of a landless emancipation

Table 4.5 displays data that describe the distribution of farmers and land among the major racial and tenure classes in Southern agriculture in 1910. More than 52 percent of the white farmers owned all the

Table 4.5. *Number of farm operators and acreage, by race and tenure class, all Southern states, 1910*

Tenure class	Colored		White	
	Farmers (000's)	Acreage (000's)	Farmers (000's)	Acreage (000's)
Full owners	175	12,847	1,154	181,343
Part owners	43	2,844	172	33,580
Fixed-rent tenants	286	12,876	229	26,276
Share-rent tenants	385	13,691	637	46,328
Managers	1	350	15	24,316
Totals	890	42,608	2,207	311,843

Source: U.S. Bureau of the Census, *Negro Population, 1790–1915* (Washington, 1918), pp. 609, 612.

land they cultivated, and this land made up over 58 percent of all white-operated acreage. In contrast, less than 20 percent of all black farmers were full owners, and their land constituted only about 30 percent of all black-operated acreage. (Strictly speaking, the data in Table 4.5 represent all "colored" farmers, including Indians, Orientals, and blacks; but for present purposes "black" and "colored" can be treated as virtually synonymous in the South.) Part ownership was also more prevalent among whites. It is hardly surprising that farm ownership was more common among whites than among blacks. Perhaps more remarkable is that, only 45 years after the landless emancipation, 175,000 Southern blacks were full farm owners, and another 43,000 owned some part (about 57 percent on the average) of the land they cultivated; the estimated value of farm property operated by black full owners was $275 million and an allowance for the property held by part owners would push the total well over $300 million.[43] Almost 40 percent of the white farmers rented all the land they cultivated, this land making up about 23 percent of all white-operated acreage. Of the black farmers, 75 percent rented all the land they cultivated, this land being about 63 percent of all black-operated acreage. In brief, despite substantial accumulation of farm property by the freedmen and their descendants, black farmers in 1910 were still less frequently owners and more frequently tenants than were white farmers.

The meaning of these data depends on the perspective in which one views them. With secure private property rights the most obvious benefit of landownership was simply that it allowed the owner to appropriate the returns generated by the property, that is, ownership of a productive asset implied a higher income for the owner, other things being the same. On the conservative assumptions that the farm land owned by blacks in 1910 was worth only $300 million and that it yielded only a 5 percent return, rural landownership raised black incomes by $15 million, which averaged about $69 per owner (assuming only 218,000 owners). This is probably well below the true figure. Whether the amount is "large" or "small" depends, again, on the standard by which it is judged.

Perhaps a relevant standard, and in any event an interesting one, can be drawn from the proposals for land distribution to the freedmen immediately after the emancipation. Suppose that the freedmen had received 40 acres per family. One can make a rough calculation of the value of such a grant. There were in 1865 about 4.5 million freedmen of all ages. Assuming that one-fifth of them were heads of households qualified to receive a land grant, the blacks would have obtained about 36 million acres (40 acres times 900,000 recipients). At the land values prevailing in 1865 this land would have been worth only a few dollars per acre, but its value would have risen as the Southern rural economy recovered. Even if the value at the end of the war was only $2.50 per acre, the grant would have represented a transfer of $100 to each family. Had the blacks retained ownership of the land grants until 1910, the value would then have been at least $720 million (36 million acres times $20 per acre).[44] An annual yield of 5 percent on this sum equals $36 million, or about $3.60 per capita of the entire black population – an amount less than the weekly earnings of an unskilled farm wage laborer in the South at that time.

Another way to assess the rural land held by black owners in 1910, which was probably well in excess of 14 million acres, is to compare it with the 36 million acres that the land grant would have provided in 1865 to a population only half as large. The grant of 40 acres per family would have given the freedmen of 1865 about 8 acres per capita. As events actually occurred, the blacks acquired by their own efforts, over a period of 45 years, an average of about 1.5 acres of farm land per capita.

A land grant would have had its greatest impact immediately after the war, for it would have provided black laborers with the major cooperating resource at a time when cotton prices were relatively high. Even then, however, the freedmen would have required credit, skills in independent management, and other resources such as draft animals and implements to make a success of their farming activities. Over time, as the population expanded, the influence of the initial land grant would have dissipated. Nevertheless, a large proportion of rural laborers would have benefited. An individual share tenant commonly paid one-quarter of the cotton and one-third of the grain for the use of land; had he owned the land, those amounts would have accrued to him. Perhaps, too, a black population beginning with a sizable endowment of land in 1865 would have been in a better position to accumulate still more. Clearly, additional accumulation of property was essential if the blacks were ever to raise their incomes to the level of the whites. Obtaining 40 acres and a mule was by itself far from enough to bring the freedmen's income level anywhere near the level of the whites.

Landownership would have conveyed other advantages, however. Not the least of them was a reduction in transactions with hostile whites, especially landlords. Countless disputes and episodes of violence and intimidation might have been avoided had the blacks owned rather than rented land. Settlement problems and difficulties connected with the management of family workers would have diminished. A tempting opportunity for the whites to cheat the blacks would have been eliminated. And, perhaps most importantly, a black population of landowners might well have developed greater skills, self-reliance, and initiative. The dependency and paternalism that characterized the Southern system of tenancy would not have done so much damage to the independence of rural blacks.

"Forty acres and a mule" was no panacea for the economic ills of the black population. Even with such a grant, many difficulties would have remained, especially the ignorance and inexperience that made the blacks so vulnerable to their hostile white neighbors. And without an equal standing before the law, many blacks would no doubt have been robbed of their property in one way or another. But, after all this is said, it remains true that the absence of a land grant was a major deficiency of Reconstruction policy from the perspective of the blacks. A land grant would not have produced miracles, but it would have given the freedmen a sharp boost in their struggle for genuine economic progress.

Nonagricultural employment

The census of 1890, the first to make racial distinctions in the returns pertaining to occupations, showed black employment overwhelmingly concentrated in two sectors: 56 percent of the gainfully employed worked in agriculture, 31 percent in domestic and personal service (see Table 4.6). Of agriculture enough has already been said. The most remarkable feature of the nonagricultural employment situation was the predominant position of the domestic and personal services, which accounted for over 70 percent of the jobs. This sector included servants, waiters, laundresses, and a host of others, of whom only the barbers could be said to possess much skill. In the trade, transportation, manufacturing, and mechanical sectors, which together provided about 26 percent of nonagricultural employment, most of the workers were common laborers, although carpenters, masons, and blacksmiths together numbered more than 40,000. A tiny professional group made up about 2.5 percent of the nonagricultural labor force. Of the professionals, 80 percent were either teachers or clergymen, and neither of these groups had attained more than rudimentary educations on the average. In general the black nonagricultural labor force in 1890 was overwhelmingly unskilled, providing the muscle power in the meanest, dirtiest, and least-paid occupations.

During the two decades after 1890 the composition of the nonagricultural labor force changed considerably (see Table 4.6). Employment in domestic and personal service grew slowly, and its share of nonagricultural employment had fallen to 59 percent by 1910; employment in the trade and transportation sector grew rapidly, raising its share to

Table 4.6. *Numbers (in 000's) of gainfully employed blacks, by industrial sector, 1890–1910*

Sector	1890	1900	1910
Agricultural pursuits	1,728	2,143	2,881
Professional service	34	47	66
Domestic and personal service	957	1,318	1,358
Trade and transportation	146	209	334
Manufacturing and mechanical pursuits	208	275	553
All occupations	3,073	3,992	5,193

Source: U.S. Bureau of the Census, *Negro Population, 1790–1915* (Washington, 1918), p. 526.

over 14 percent; manufacturing and mechanical pursuits expanded still faster, accounting for 24 percent in 1910. While expanding faster than the average, professional employment still accounted for only 3 percent of nonagricultural employment in 1910, with teaching and preaching remaining the prevailing professional jobs.

According to a standard classification of the census occupational data employed by Becker in his study of discrimination, the number of blacks in skilled jobs expanded relatively rapidly during the period 1890–1910, increasing from about 7 percent to over 9 percent of the male labor force (excluding farmers and farm tenants). This classification must be viewed with some reservations, because it includes among the skilled a large number who were in fact often without skills (e.g., many teachers and preachers); but the direction of the trend portrayed is probably accurate. The Seventeenth Annual Atlanta Conference in 1912 concluded that "Negro American skilled labor is undoubtedly gaining ground both North and South."[45] This conclusion deserves emphasis, since somehow the myth that black employment in skilled occupations declined during the postbellum period has become firmly entrenched in the historical literature.[46] The facts are quite simple. First, before 1890 no comprehensive data on the occupational distribution of the black labor force are available, and all conclusions about changes in its skill composition are necessarily conjectural. No one has ever adduced evidence that the *overall* black labor force suffered a relative decline in skilled employment between 1865 and 1890. Second, available census data for 1890–1910, classified by a standard procedure into skilled and unskilled components, show that the former grew faster than the latter in nonagricultural employment. As nonagricul-

Table 4.7. *Weekly earnings of blacks in nonagricultural occupations,*[a] *Atlanta, Nashville, and Cambridge, 1896*

City and occupation	Number with average weekly earnings of								Mean earnings ($)
	Less than $2.00	$2.00 –3.99	$4.00 –5.99	$6.00 –7.99	$8.00 –9.99	$10.00 –11.99	$12.00 –13.99	$14.00 and more	
Atlanta									
Drivers		4	20	6		2		2	5.95
Laborers	5	11	18	14	3	1			4.79
Porters			4	3	3	1			6.70
Washerwomen	15	15	1	1					2.24
Cooks	1	11	1	1	2				3.54
Nashville									
Drivers			2	10	1	2		1	7.21
Laborers	3	7	16	24	2				5.19
Porters		1	2	7	2	4	2	1	8.21
Washerwomen	4	14							2.11
Cambridge, Mass.									
Laborers			1	3	13	9	17		10.21

[a] The criteria for inclusion in this table are that the individual reported both the number of weeks he was employed and his weekly earnings and that he reported no work in another occupation during the year. Occupations shown are all those for which at least 10 persons in a given city reported complete information. "Drivers" include drivers, hackmen, draymen, coachmen, and teamsters. "Laborers" include a few not listed under that title but who were obviously engaged in common unskilled labor (e.g., railroad car cleaner).
Source: Compiled from data in U.S. Department of Labor, "Condition of the Negro in Various Cities," *Bulletin No. 10* (May 1897), pp. 304–320.

tural employment was growing relative to total employment, it follows *a fortiori* that black employment in skilled nonagricultural jobs was increasing relative to the black labor force. Anyone is, of course, entitled to question the basic data or to quarrel with the classification procedure. But, until someone offers a convincing critique of this sort, the conclusion remains that overall black employment in skilled jobs was relatively on the increase, at least after 1890. The myth of deteriorating skills can be laid to rest.

Of the black male labor force (excluding farmers and farm tenants) in 1910, about 9 percent worked in skilled occupations, over 6 percent in semiskilled, and the rest in unskilled jobs.[47] Notable among the skilled were 32,000 carpenters, 24,000 masons, 11,000 blacksmiths, and 8,000 tailors. Blacks had made a beginning in employment as factory operatives, 33,000 being occupied in the iron and steel industry, 24,000 in tobacco factories, and 6,000 in cotton mills.[48] But, despite the significant diversification of employment that had occurred, the majority of those in nonagricultural jobs remained in domestic and personal service. Black workers were still the mudsill of the occupational structure.

Table 4.7 displays sample data on the earnings of blacks in some typical unskilled nonagricultural jobs. The data have been compiled from what is perhaps the most comprehensive, systematic, and carefully conducted investigation of its kind made before World War I. Although the data are subject to reporting errors of unknown magnitude, they appear fairly unbiased and consistent with other, more fragmentary information. This evidence reveals several interesting features of black nonagricultural employment.

First, the earnings of unskilled workers varied widely, both within and across occupational classifications. No doubt much of the variation within occupations reflects differences in hours worked and in the intensity of the labor performed. Washerwomen, for example, might launder the clothes of one family or many families in a week; and as payment was more or less by the "piece," low earnings indicate less work performed rather than lower pay for identical work. Similar remarks apply to family cooks and certain laborers. The variations show that many black workers belonged to the labor force in a rather casual or marginal way, being less than "fully employed" as a rule. No doubt such workers accounted in large part for the unusually high participation in the labor force recorded for the black population. Sometimes partial employment was all that the worker desired, as when housewives took in a little washing or went out for a short while each day to cook or clean house in order to supplement the family income. In other cases, like those involving old or physically handicapped persons, limited employment required the full capacity of the worker. And for some, perhaps, casual employment was all they could find at the time, and they accepted it as a stopgap while continuing to search for a superior alternative. Especially was this the situation of many young people in domestic service.

Differences in earnings among occupations also reflected in part the extent of employment, because some jobs (e.g., driving) generally provided steadier work than others (e.g., construction labor). But variations in earnings also arose from differences in skill and responsibility. In reality, not all jobs classified as unskilled called for the identical application of mute muscle power. That porters and drivers earned more than common laborers is perhaps attributable to the greater exercise of responsibility and initiative sometimes associated with their jobs. In any event the differences in earnings were considerable: Atlanta's porters earned 40 percent more than its laborers, and in Nashville the premium reached almost 60 percent (see Table 4.7).

Artisans with a definite skill could expect to earn twice as much as common laborers, and sometimes even more. While the laborers in Memphis received little more than a dollar a day at the turn of the century, the carpenters, painters, tailors, blacksmiths, and engineers reported wages ranging from $2.00 to $3.00 a day; plumbers, brick masons, plasterers, and stone cutters reported even higher earnings.[49] Similar skill differentials were reported in Atlanta and elsewhere in the South.[50] Clearly, the possession of a skill commanded a substantial premium in the labor market. Given this fact, why did the black labor force acquire skills so slowly?

Evidently the exercise of a skilled art, at least in the South, was easier for a black than the acquisition of the requisite skill. Black craftsmen, particularly in the building trades, could work side by side with their white counterparts in the South, provided they had the appropriate training. But where could they obtain this training? Du Bois in 1902 described the predicament of the black artisan in the late nineteenth century:

The industrial conditions in the country were rapidly changing. Slowly but surely the new industrial South began to arise and with it came new demands on the mechanic. Now the Negro mechanic could not in the very nature of the case meet these demands; he knew how to do a few things by rule of thumb – he could build one of the rambling old-fashioned southern mansions, he could build a slave shanty; he could construct a rough sugar hogshead and resole a shoe; in exceptional cases he could do even careful and ingenious work in certain lines; but as a rule he knew little of the niceties of modern carpentry or iron-working, he knew practically nothing of mills and machinery, very little about railroads – in fact he was expecially ignorant in those very lines of mechanical and industrial development in which the South has taken the longest strides in the last thirty years. And if he was ignorant, who was to teach him? Certainly not his white fellow workmen, for they were his bitterest opponents because of strong race-prejudice and because of the fact that the Negro works for low wages. Apprenticeship to the older Negro mechanics was but partially successful for they could not teach what they had never learned. In fact it was only through the lever of low wages that the Negro secured any share in the new industries. By that means he was enabled to replace white laborers in many branches, but he thereby increased the enmity of trades-unions and labor-leaders. Such in brief was the complicated effect of emancipation on the Negro artisan and one could not well imagine a situation more difficult to remedy.[51]

Somehow many blacks managed to overcome these difficulties, as the growing number of black craftsmen attests. No doubt learning from experience on the job played a large part.

One device for dealing with the difficulties of securing training was the black industrial school, of which Hampton Institute and Tuskegee Institute were the best known. Because of the enormous prestige and power of Booker T. Washington, Tuskegee's principal, and because of the widely discussed dispute between the supporters of industrial education and the proponents of more liberal higher education, no student of black history is unaware of the movement to promote training in the skilled crafts. Despite the notoriety of these efforts, however, the industrial schools failed to make a substantial impact on the problem of industrial training. Du Bois estimated that during the last two decades of the nineteenth century all the schools giving industrial training to blacks produced only about 1,000 actual artisans.[52] In fact the majority of those graduated from schools such as Tuskegee and Hampton went on to become teachers in the segregated schools of the South. Insofar as the training of skilled craftsmen is concerned, the industrial schools must be considered insignificant.[53]

With formal training generally inaccessible, the alternative of apprenticeship must be tried, but here black workmen often encountered the hostility of the trade unions. During the late nineteenth and early twentieth centuries unions became increasingly entrenched in the skilled crafts. Not all excluded blacks from membership; where blacks were sufficiently numerous to threaten the union's monopoly power in the labor market, they usually found a welcome in the union. The best examples of this situation occurred among the longshoremen and the miners, but then skills scarcely played a part in these cases. A list compiled in 1902 placed some of the more important craft unions in the order of increasing hostility toward the black:

Miners – Welcome Negroes in nearly all cases.
Longshoremen – Welcome Negroes in nearly all cases.
Cigar-makers – Admit practically all applicants.

Barbers – Admit many, but restrain Negroes when possible.
Seamen – Admit many, but prefer whites.
Firemen – Admit many, but prefer whites.
Tobacco Workers – Admit many, but prefer whites.
Carriage and Wagon Workers – Admit some, but do not seek Negroes.
Brick-makers – Admit some, but do not seek Negroes.
Coopers – Admit some, but do not seek Negroes.
Broom-makers – Admit some, but do not seek Negroes.
Plasterers – Admit freely in South and a few in North.
Carpenters – Admit many in South, almost none in North.
Masons – Admit a few in South, almost none in North.
Painters – Admit a few in South, almost none in North.[54]

The unions sometimes organized blacks in segregated locals. At times the black and white locals cooperated with and supported one another; at other times the separate local was merely a device used by the white unionists to reduce the threat of black strikebreaking. Wherever trade unions flourished, black men lived in fear of exclusion from opportunities for employment. Small wonder that black leaders almost unanimously condemned the unions and sometimes actually applauded the involvement of blacks in strikebreaking. Washington was a lifelong foe of trade unions, although his animosity softened somewhat toward the end of his life; and Du Bois called them the greatest enemy of the black working man.[55]

While the blacks gained a reputation – not entirely undeserved – for strikebreaking, the unions sometimes used their power to force blacks out of employment, on occasion by violent means. During the last 20 years of the nineteenth century the Labor Department recorded information on 50 strikes conducted for the avowed purpose of resisting the employment of blacks; and investigators believed that considerably more such strikes actually occurred, many of them in the North being concealed within the classification of strikes against nonunion workers. Significantly, of the 50 strikes recorded, 38 failed to achieve their objective.[56] In one instance, when blacks were hired to fill skilled positions at the Black Diamond Steel Works near Pittsburgh, Irish puddlers struck against their introduction. This strategy backfired: the employer fired the Irish and kept the blacks.[57] On other occasions, however, the white workers succeeded in keeping black workers out. Perhaps most commonly, especially in the North, the conflict never manifested itself, for the employer, fearful of his white employee's reactions, simply refused to hire black workers in the first place.

Where the whites belonged to a union and the blacks did not, the former usually obtained higher wages than the latter. In this case wage discrimination occurred but was racial only in an indirect sense. Some-

times, however, employers practiced racial discrimination in the payment of wages even where no unions were involved. To identify the
purely discriminatory component of such wage differences is usually
difficult. The average black worker was less skilled and more frequently
absent from the job than his average white counterpart and for those
reasons would have received a smaller wage quite apart from the question of race.[58] Therefore, the large body of evidence showing racial
differences in wages is difficult to interpret.[59] This is not to say that
purely racial discrimination in wage payments never occurred. A classic case was described by a black locomotive fireman for the Southern
Railway:

If I take a train from here [Atlanta] to Greenville, S.C., I get for that trip
$2.60, the white engineer gets $6.00. But if that same train had the same
engineer and a *white* fireman, the engineer would get his $6.00 just the same but
the fireman would get $3.25. He gets 65 cts. more for doing the same work
I do. At the end of the run we have to make out our time on a card,
which, with the other necessary wording has two spaces marked "white" and
"colored" respectively. I cross out the "colored" and get $2.60; he crosses out
the "white" and gets $3.25. That's all the difference there is between our
work.[60]

Seldom, however, did such pure cases arise.

One reason for doubting that every racial wage difference represented racial discrimination is that in a large number of cases blacks
and whites obtained the same pay for the same work. Particularly did
this occur in unskilled jobs, but investigators also reported many instances of equal pay in the skilled crafts. In Memphis, black plasterers
and brickmasons belonged to the same union and received the same
pay as their white fellows. Blacksmiths in various Texas towns were
described as receiving "wages according to their skill. White men having the same degree of skill would receive no more." Houston had at
least two white contractors who paid carpenters "according to skill,
white and black alike." One investigator reported that Atlanta's black
artisans received "the prevailing scale of wages," but others adduced
evidence of racial differences in that city. From Jacksonville came the
report that "usually . . . there is no discrimination in wages [for arti-
sans], but this is not always true." Brickmasons and stone cutters in
eastern Georgia received "the same wages of whites in the same trade."
In New Orleans, "there is no apparent discrimination in wages in this
city and the trade unions are open to Negroes in most cases." In the
mines of West Virginia, blacks got the "same as white men for like
work." And reports from various Mississippi towns, from Greensboro
and Hillsboro, North Carolina, and from Murfreesboro, Tennessee,
indicated an absence of racial discrimination in the wages paid to artisans.[61]

That racial equality and racial differences of wage payment existed side by side throughout the economy can be explained in various ways. One interpretation maintains that the instances of equal pay occurred where the quality of the labor performed was the same, while instances of racial differences in pay occurred where the black labor was in fact of relatively poor quality. This view is compatible with the evidence that the average black laborer was less productive than the average white but that considerable variation existed, some blacks being fully as productive as some whites. As Du Bois expressed it, "some of these [black craftsmen] are progressive, efficient workmen. More are careless, slovenly and ill-trained."[62]

An alternative explanation – and one difficult to test against the preceding hypothesis in practice – maintains that some blacks obtained what their labor was worth, getting the same pay as the whites for the same work, while other blacks received less for the same work because their employers judged every black man, even the most capable, in the light of the low average performance of blacks. This view stresses the high cost of learning about the productive attributes of a particular individual and the use of racial identity as a "signal" conveying to the employer some information – at times incorrect information – about these attributes. Such an explanation is consistent with the constant complaints of accomplished blacks that white employers refused to consider them on their individual merits because of previous unfortunate experience with or beliefs about the low productivity of black workers as a group. With his usual insight, Du Bois recognized this problem, too:

[T]he individual black workman is rated not by his own efficiency, but by the efficiency of a whole group of black fellow workmen which may often be low. . . . Again, though a man ordinarily does not dismiss all his white mill-hands because some turn out badly, yet it repeatedly happens that men dismiss all their colored servants and condemn their race because one or two in their employ have proven untrustworthy.[63]

One might expect that this kind of discrimination, arising not from racial antipathy but rather from the costliness of information and the mistakes inherent in the use of imperfect information, would have a greater impact on initial employment and wages than on the wages paid to blacks with some experience in a given firm. After a time on the job, superior workers demonstrate their true productivity, and the employer's initial misgivings dissipate. This learning process may fail to reduce the initial wage differential, however; if the employer recognizes that the worker faces the same problem in alternative employments, he may continue to pay the same wage because he is the only employer who knows the worker's actual attributes. The worker may continue to receive only his "opportunity wage" (what he could get in the next best alternative) even after he has demonstrated to one employer that his labor is worth more. The persistence of such discrimination depends crucially on how costly it is for potential employers to obtain information about the worker's actual productivity. In many actual situations, as in rural areas or small towns where workers were well known, these costs were probably very low and the associated problem of little or no consequence. In large cities – and particularly in the North, where blacks constituted a minute part of the labor force and therefore could be excluded from employment or paid poorly with no noticeable effect on the overall labor market – such problems probably arose more often and were more serious for the black worker. It is perhaps not entirely coincidental that Du Bois recognized and discussed this type of discrimination in his study of Philadelphia.

Still another hypothesis is that racial wage differences grew out of pure racial discrimination and that nondiscriminating employers had too small an impact on the labor market for competitive forces to eliminate the racial differences everywhere. This view is compatible with the existence of pure racial wage discrimination, like that practiced by the Southern Railway in the payment of its firemen, in situations that involve labor of identical quality and in which the terms of the contracts are well known to many participants in the labor market. No doubt some local labor markets contained a greater proportion of discriminating employers than others, and therefore the prevalence and degree of racial wage differentials varied from place to place.

Probably all three interpretations have a measure of validity. Black labor was relatively unproductive on the average; individual blacks were sometimes judged by the accomplishments of the mass; and pure racial discrimination did sometimes occur. It is unlikely that anyone will ever possess enough information to sort out these alternative, but not necessarily incompatible, explanations well enough to assign numerical weights to them. In view of these problems of interpretation, perhaps the most remarkable fact about black participation in the nonagricultural labor market was that blacks and whites often commanded the same wages for what was judged the same work. Though pure discrimination surely occurred, its scope and magnitude varied widely from place to place and over time. In a number of well-documented instances, especially in the South, local labor markets displayed no trace of racial discrimination. In those cases white employers, evidently valuing wealth more than the pleasures of racial discrimination, simply refused to pay their white workmen a premium for their color.

Black business and the "group economy"

While Jim Crow achieved somewhat less than complete success in the labor market, he increasingly extended his sway over other facets of American society after 1890, particularly in the South, where nine-tenths of the blacks lived. By various devices, every Southern state engineered a virtually complete disfranchisement of the blacks. In 1896 the United States Supreme Court upheld the legality of public segregation provided that facilities were "separate but equal" (Plessy *v.* Ferguson), thus opening the doors for a sweeping, legally sanctioned separation of the races on railways and streetcars, in parks and theatres, and even in residential neighborhoods. As everyone knows, the "separate-but-equal" facilities provided for blacks were in fact almost invariably inferior, usually grossly inferior. Racial discrimination in the provision of public funds for education, long an established practice, grew by leaps and bounds after 1900. Lynching reached almost incredible proportions: during the years 1882–1915 about 3,000 blacks died at the hands of mobs;[64] and increasingly the lynchers found a place for torture, burning, and dismemberment in their savagery. Urban race riots became more frequent, major violence occurring in Wilmington, North Carolina (1898), New York City (1900), Atlanta (1906), Springfield, Illinois (1908), and elsewhere.

Small wonder that many blacks had little hope of even eventual acceptance by white society and increasingly sought to build a community of their own, complete with its own economic institutions, within the walls created by segregation and discrimination. Ideally this "group economy," as Du Bois called it, would enable the blacks to survive and prosper by substituting transactions with one another for transactions with the hostile white world. In this scheme, blacks must not only labor in skilled and unskilled jobs, but they must do so for black employers, producing goods and services for black consumers. The black community must have its own newspapers, banks, and insurance companies, its own churches, hospitals, and welfare agencies. Every dollar must remain within the confines of the ghetto.

Perceiving that such an appeal to racial solidarity might be turned into private profits, increasing numbers of blacks established business enterprises. Du Bois estimated that about 5,000 blacks operated businesses in 1890. The National Negro Business League, an organization founded by Booker T. Washington, estimated that the number reached 20,000 in 1900 and 40,000 in 1914, but these figures are probably overstatements. Most of these enterprises were small – so small that they could be operated with little or no hired help – and most involved retailing or personal services. Grocery stores, restaurants, saloons, pool rooms, barber shops, undertakers, real estate agencies, and boarding houses were common. Of the 1,906 black businesses surveyed in 1899, only 12 represented investments of $50,000 or more; and 79 percent of them involved capital sums of less than $2,500. The largest enterprises included insurance companies, banks, newspapers, and real estate agencies, but even they were small by the standards of the white world.[65]

Urbanization probably played a more significant role than propaganda espousing racial solidarity in promoting black business. Du Bois asserted that "it is density of Negro population in the main that gives the Negro businessman his best chance."[66] Statistical tests of this hypothesis indicate that it is consistent with the facts. For example, among the Southern states in 1910 the average relation between urbanization and black retail merchants was such that a state with 100,000 gainfully occupied black males and 30 percent of its black population urbanized had 1,967 black merchants; had the black population been only 10 percent urbanized, the state would have had only 360 black merchants.[67] The same statistical tests also indicate that black merchants were more likely to thrive in the South than in the North, given the same degree of urbanization.

Black businesses experienced a high rate of failure which, for several reasons, is hardly surprising. Small businesses have always experienced a high rate of failure, regardless of the ethnic identity of their operators. Inexperienced management, difficulties in securing investment capital and credit, and competition from larger, better-equipped enterprises characteristically plague such undertakings. Besides coping with these problems, black businessmen sometimes had to contend with racial discrimination by bankers, suppliers, and customers. By comparison with white businessmen, they could expect less police protection of their property and greater insecurity of their property rights in cases brought before the courts. As a successful black businessman in Atlanta emphasized, "if we can have justice in the courts, and fair protection, we can learn to compete with the white stores and get along all right."[68] Finally, the black consumers, upon whom most black businessmen depended for the great bulk of their sales, gave only grudging support to black enterprises, especially when competing white businesses offered superior variety or quality, lower prices, or more liberal credit. One observer declared that black consumers would "walk three blocks or more to trade with a white man, when there is a Negro store next to their door. They say the Negro does not have as good material as the white man. In all cases that is not true."[69] Black businessmen and proponents of the group economy appealed to black consumers to patronize black businesses even though a small sacrifice might be entailed, but consumers generally turned a deaf ear to these appeals for racial solidarity. Though the number of black business establishments increased considerably in the early twentieth century, black consumers continued to make the bulk of their purchases from white merchants. Only in personal services such as barbering and undertaking, where the racial etiquette of the South ruled out white suppliers, did blacks secure a firm hold on the market. As Table 4.8 shows, black representation in the merchant class remained relatively low, even in the large cities, where the odds of success were higher than in the countryside.

The group economy, then, never attained the dimensions projected by its proponents. That the realization fell short of the ideal can hardly be counted a failure, however, for in fact the ideal was unattainable from the start. Black people were simply too poor, too dis-

Table 4.8. *Male retail merchants* [a] *per 1,000 gainfully occupied males, blacks, native-born whites, and foreign-born whites, 13 large cities, 1890–1910*

City	1890			1900			1910		
	Black	Native-born whites	Foreign-born whites	Black	Native-born whites	Foreign-born whites	Black	Native-born whites	Foreign-born whites
Atlanta	14	94	192	13	71	215	15	64	229
Baltimore	26	78	89	15	52	78	20	54	103
Boston	28	77	65	11	52	49	13	38	64
Chicago	11	63	62	11	37	48	12	35	57
Cincinnati	16	53	85	11	35	67	13	41	79
Louisville	10	64	100	4	49	89	12	51	134
Memphis	12	99	190	4	72	157	13	69	193
Nashville	15	98	237	10	75	216	17	71	247
New Orleans	9	66	155	4	53	123	10	57	186
New York	18	76	95	8	49	75	8	40	93
Philadelphia	18	73	72	14	55	61	21	49	82
Richmond	24	104	213	22	69	163	21	59	204
St. Louis	9	52	75	11	37	61	11	46	76
Aggregates									
13 cities	16	71	83	10	48	66	14	44	83
6 Northern [b]	16	70	80	11	46	64	13	41	80
7 Southern [b]	16	78	120	9	56	101	15	58	140

[a] In 1890 the classification is "merchants, dealers, and peddlers"; in 1900 it is "merchants and dealers (exc. wholesale)"; in 1910 it is "retail dealers." The data for 1900 and 1910 appear to be fairly comparable, but the data for 1890 are, by comparison, inflated by the inclusion of peddlers and, to a lesser extent, of wholesalers.
[b] Cities considered Northern are Boston, Chicago, Cincinnati, New York, Philadelphia, and St. Louis; the remaining cities are considered Southern. In 1890 New York includes only New York and Brooklyn; thereafter, all of greater New York city.
Sources: Ratios calculated from data in U.S. Census Office, *Report on Population of the United States at the Eleventh Census: 1890, Pt. II* (Washington, 1897); U.S. Bureau of the Census, *Special Reports: Occupations at the Twelfth Census* (Washington, 1904); and *idem, Population, 1910: Occupation Statistics* (Washington, 1914).

persed, and too inexperienced to create an economic world of their own within the American economy. The effort was a natural reaction to the constricting forces of segregation, discrimination, violence, and disfranchisement that characterized the quarter century after 1890. But in this "taking advantage of the disadvantages" the blacks could not go far when the disadvantages were virtually all they had to work with. In view of the difficulties they had confronted, they could in 1915 look with modest pride on their accomplishments in business. Yet the great majority of blacks still worked for white employers and spent their money in white stores. Despite talk of "a nation within a nation," and despite the well-defined physical and institutional ghettos that took shape in many of the larger cities, blacks continued to play an integral part in the overall American economy as workers and consumers.

Summary: The evolution of the black labor force

Black participation in the labor force, already relatively high in 1890, rose even higher in the following quarter century, though many of the black laborers occupied rather marginal, "underemployed" positions. While its dominance waned slightly, agriculture remained the setting for most black labor. Characteristic features of the Southern rural economy, well established by 1880, persisted up to the First World War: most black farm operators rented land under share-rent or fixed-rent arrangements, while a smaller but more rapidly growing number acquired titles to farm land. Competitive pressures generally precluded racial discrimination in agricultural wage rates, land rental contracts, and merchant credit terms. The ignorance and legal impotence of rural blacks, however, continued to expose them to fraud and intimidation at the hands of landlords and merchants. No doubt some tenants – no one really knows how many – fell into virtual peonage as a result of legal, or more often illegal, immobilization for indebtedness; but high mobility was a prevailing characteristic of rural blacks as a group, and landlords or merchants normally could not prevent their movement. Fifty years after emancipation, despite considerable acquisition of land by blacks, three-fourths of all black farmers were tenants. "Forty acres and a mule," that great might-have-been of Reconstruction, could have alleviated this condition somewhat, but historians have no doubt exaggerated the economic impact of such a grant; its quantitative importance after two generations would have been modest indeed, even under the most optimistic assumptions.

A growing proportion of the black labor force entered nonagricultural occupations. Domestic and personal service provided employment for the great majority of these workers, although employment in trade, transportation, mining, and manufacturing grew more rapidly. The number of blacks in skilled jobs expanded faster than the black labor force, at least after 1890, but trade union policies made apprenticeship difficult or impossible in many trades and blocked a more rapid acquisition of skills. While wage and employment discrimination sometimes occurred, its scope and magnitude varied widely from place to place; in many local labor markets black workers pursued a wide variety of trades and received equal pay for equal work. Growing legal segregation, disfranchisement, and racial violence led some blacks to urge the creation of a "group economy" where blacks could lead their lives in prosperous isolation from the hostile white world. A proliferation of small businesses operated by blacks did occur, but these frail undertakings fell far short of constituting a workable group economy. Too poor, too dispersed, and too inexperienced to build an economic world of their own, black people continued to play an integral, if subordinate, part in the overall economy as workers and consumers.

5

The fruits of their labors

Accounts of discrimination and race prejudice probably play a
larger part in the formation of the popular belief concerning the
colored people than do statistics of improvement.

T. J. Woofter, Jr., 1920

Any assessment of black economic history in the half century after
emancipation requires evidence on changes in the people's real income
over time. Did freedom actually, as many appear to believe, offer little
opportunity for blacks to improve their material condition? Or did
they in fact participate in the rapid economic growth that characterized
the American economy in the post-Civil War era? If so, did the rate of
growth of black income per capita exceed, equal, or fall short of the
average rate for the overall economy? Reliable estimates of incomes,
classified by race, would permit one to answer these questions and shed
much light on the economic history of black Americans. Unfortunately
no one has attempted to construct such estimates; indeed the underlying evidence for the calculations is so scanty that the project is
fraught with difficulties, some of them perhaps insurmountable. Still,
the issue cannot be ignored, for unless one explicitly considers the level
and growth of black incomes one is apt to slide into uncritical assumptions. Crude estimates are not necessarily more accurate than unexam-
ined assumptions, but they have the virtue of exposing their limitations
for all to see. For the years around the turn of the century, relevant
data are relatively abundant, permitting an estimate of black income
circa 1900. For comparative purposes an estimate for the late 1860s
can be constructed, though this estimate has a much flimsier basis than
the later one.

Estimates of black incomes

For the years around the turn of the century, perhaps as much information is available for the North as for the South. This is unfortunate,
as only one-tenth of the black population lived in the North, and these
people were decidedly unrepresentative of the entire black population.
Still, in the present context, one cannot afford to throw away any information. Probably the most painstaking attempt to estimate the in-

comes of Northern blacks appears in W. E. B. Du Bois' *Philadelphia Negro.* The Philadelphia data – probably fairly representative of the North generally, for most Northern blacks lived in large cities – apply to 1896. (About this time commodity prices reached their lowest point of the period 1865–1914, a fact that one must recall in assessing changes in nominal income.) Du Bois recognized that the data contained considerable error, but he judged the errors to be more or less offsetting and the averages fairly unbiased. In a sample of 2,276 families in the city's Seventh Ward, he found at the bottom 192 families with annual incomes of $150 or less, at the top 123 families with $1,000 or more; the bulk of the families, about two-thirds of them, had incomes in the $200–500 range. The median family income was between $350 and $400, the mean about $470.[1] As the average black family in the Seventh Ward contained only 3.2 members,[2] the family income data imply a mean income per capita in the neighborhood of $150.

Du Bois also undertook, with the aid of some of his students, to obtain income data for blacks in several Georgia towns about 1898. In the small village of Lithonia the 16 families studied had a median family income of about $300 and 6.3 persons per family; the implied median income per capita was less than $50. In Covington 50 families described as "rather above the average for the town" had a median family income somewhere in the range $300–500 and 3.8 persons per family; the implied median income per capita was in the range $79–132. In Athens 45 families of "the better class of colored folks" had a median family income somewhere in the range $500–750 and 3.6 persons per family; the implied median income per capita was in the range $139–208.[3] Du Bois regarded the Georgia families studied as unrepresentative of the mass of the race and their incomes as significantly higher than those of average rural blacks.

More systematic data are available for 124 "representative families" of Atlanta in 1900. For this group the median family income was between $300 and $400, the mean $350. The size of the families was not reported. On the assumption that the average family contained 3.5 persons, the implied mean income per capita was about $100. Additional data were supplied for 25 "typical Negro families" in Atlanta in 1900. For this group the median family income was $320, the mean $374, and the average family size 3.3 persons; the implied mean income per capita was about $113.[4]

A study by Du Bois of 262 families in Farmville, Virginia, in 1897, showed a median family income in the range $250–350 and an average family size of about 4.6 persons; the implied median income per capita was therefore in the range $54–76. A similar study by Richard R. Wright, Jr., of 501 families in Xenia, Ohio, in 1903 showed that the median family income was approximately $350 and the average family size about 3.6; the implied median income per capita was therefore almost $100.[5]

An alternative, and somewhat conjectural, method of ascertaining income levels for urban blacks is to build up an estimate from the component variables in terms of which the desired measure can be defined. Thus average annual family income, Y_f, can be defined as follows, where E is average days employed per year, W is average daily earnings, and L is average number of wage earners per family: $Y_f = (E)(W)(L)$. One can substitute plausible values into the right side of the equation to obtain an estimate of average family income. Assuming 240 days of employment per year,[6] daily earnings of $1.00, and 1.5 wage earners per family, $Y_f = (240)(\$1.00)(1.5) = \$360$. If the representative urban family contained 3.6 members, their average income per capita would have been, according to this calculation, $100. This estimate agrees well with the data from the sample surveys by Du Bois and others discussed above.

To summarize, the existing evidence suggests that urban blacks had an average income per capita in the neighborhood of $100 at the end of the nineteenth century. The data on which this conclusion rests may be criticized in several ways. Direct evidence on black incomes is simply very scanty and the representativeness of the existing data uncertain. Similarly, the quality of data on employment, earnings, labor force participation, and family size – the component parts of an indirect estimate – is open to question. In view of the possible errors surrounding the data and their manipulation, a cautious interpretation requires not a point estimate but a confidence interval of some sort. Since the construction of a formally defined confidence interval is impossible, perhaps the most prudent policy is simply to postulate a wide potential error. Assuming that an error of plus or minus 25 percent is sufficiently large to bracket the truth, one can say that the average annual income of black urban dwellers around 1900 probably lay between $75 and $125 per capita.

Even if one regards this estimate as adequate the problem of estimating rural incomes remains. At the turn of the century more than three-fourths of the black population was rural. Special difficulties attend any estimate of income for this group: labor force participation is difficult to define because of the intermittent employment of women and children; a large part of earnings accrued in the form of goods and services rather than money; fluctuations in yields and prices gave rise to great variability of income, which complicates the identification of a typical year. Perhaps the only thing known with certainty is that rural incomes on the average fell below urban incomes. On this point contemporaries spoke with one voice. But determining how much lower is a challenging task.

There is virtually no direct evidence on the magnitude of the incomes earned by rural blacks. Farm tenants almost invariably, and farm owners quite frequently, spoke of how much they "cleared"; even so knowledgeable an investigator as Du Bois once made a table to show for a group of farmers the various amounts cleared.[7] This usage, however, is singularly uninformative. When a tenant declared that he had cleared a certain amount, he meant that he had that much left after settling his accounts with the landlord and the credit merchant at the end of the year. Obviously, then, the amount cleared depended not only on the tenant's gross earnings but also on the amounts "advanced" by the landlord and the storekeeper during the year. Two men might clear the same amount while obtaining vastly different advances and therefore equally different real incomes. Information on clearings simply reveals nothing about farmers' real incomes. One must resort to an alternative kind of information.

Again, one can build up a crude estimate from some definitional components. Seeking only the neighborhood of the truth, I shall simplify drastically. And once more, when my best point estimate has been made, I shall acknowledge the possibility of large potential error around it. Nevertheless, some interesting conclusions will emerge even from such crude estimates.

To proceed, suppose that the rural population pursued only two occupations in 1900: farm laborer and farmer. This is not actually true, of course; but it approximates the truth, and the assumption will serve its purpose as long as the income estimate it helps to generate is not highly unrepresentative of the average income in other rural occupations. The procedure will be to construct estimates of income for farm laborers and for farmers, then to obtain a properly weighted average of them, and finally to adjust this figure so that it represents the average income per capita of the entire rural population.

To obtain an estimate of the average annual income of farm laborers one can employ a definition similar to that used above for urban workers: $Y = (E)(W)$. (The only difference is that this equation defines the income of the individual worker, not the family.) In consideration of the many days during which agricultural work was impossible because of slack labor requirements in the winter or inclement weather during the growing season, assume an average of only 200 days of paid employment per year. From data presented in Chapter 4 (Table 4.2), assuming that workers received the harvest wage for 50 days and the ordinary wage for the other 150 days employed, the average money wage per day is computed as $0.82.[8] Annual earnings were then

$Y = (200)(\$0.82) = \$164$. These money earnings, however, represented only part of the farm laborer's total real income. In addition he typically received the use of a house and garden plot, free fuel, and rations. A Georgia farmer estimated in 1900 that the value of such perquisites was about $5 per month. A number of earlier estimates of the value of rations alone ranged from $30 to $75 per year, the mode being about $50.[9] With even a niggardly allowance for the value of income in kind one can place the average income of a full-time farm laborer at $200. The true figure was probably greater.

To obtain an estimate of the average annual income of black farm operators I shall make the calculation supposing that the representative farmer was a sharecropper on an average-sized plot (31 acres improved) devoting himself entirely to the cultivation of cotton, of which he obtained the average yield (about $\frac{1}{3}$ bale per acre), which sold for 10 cents a pound.[10] These assumptions probably have the net effect of understating the truth. The representative farmer would have produced about 10 bales of cotton worth about $50 per bale. (Cotton seed also had considerable value, deliberately ignored here.) After paying the landlord half of the proceeds for the use of land, tools, and animals, he would have $250 for himself.[11] During the year, tenants commonly obtained additional income by working for daily wages on their own or nearby plantations; in the winter some supplemented their incomes by working in the cane harvest, in the forests, or on levee or railroad construction projects.[12] In the interest of producing a conservative figure I shall estimate such earnings, plus the value of housing, garden plots, and fuel, to total only $50 per year. The total annual income of the representative black farmer in 1900 was then, according to this crude calculation, about $300.[13]

The average annual income of rural black workers in 1900, by my earlier assumption, is a weighted average of the incomes of farm laborers and farmers. The census of 1900 counted about 1,339,000 black farm laborers and 758,000 black farmers.[14] However, not all those counted as farm laborers received a money income or worked full time in the fields. Some 687,000 of them were listed as laborers on the "home farm" and were probably for the most part unpaid family workers whose labor contributed toward producing the incomes attributed above to black farmers. Of the remaining 652,000 laborers, listed as "working out,"[15] probably many worked less than full time, occupying themselves only during the cotton-chopping and picking seasons. My guess – a deliberately conservative guess – is that the total number of black full-time-equivalent farm laborers in 1900 was in the neighborhood of 500,000.[16] Using this number as a weight, one can now calculate the average annual income of full-time-equivalent, employed blacks in the farm sector in 1900 at about $260.[17] In fact, many rural blacks were neither farm laborers nor farmers; they worked as domestics, laborers, miners, craftsmen, and at a variety of other occupations. I shall assume that their average income was the same as that earned in agriculture and that their total number in 1900 was only 450,000. This, together with previously determined data, implies that the full-time-equivalent participation of the rural population in the labor force was 25 percent, which probably falls short of the truth. This participation rate, in conjunction with the estimated average rural income level of $260 per worker, implies a rural income of $65 per capita.[18] This is probably an understatement. Again, to be safe I shall postulate a wide range of error, plus or minus 25 percent. I conclude that the average annual income per capita of rural blacks in 1900 probably lay between $49 and $81.

The average annual income per capita of the entire black population about 1900 can now be computed. This is simply a weighted average of the urban and rural figures computed above, where the weights are the proportions of the population urban (0.23) and rural (0.77), as shown in Chapter 2 (Table 2.6). My best point estimate is about $73 per capita;[19] an interval of plus or minus 25 percent puts the probable range of the estimate between $55 and $91. The tenuous foundation of these estimates can hardly be overemphasized, but they do provide a quantitative basis for considering changes in the material condition of the black population during the last third of the nineteenth century.[20]

To place the income estimate for 1900 in a comparative context one requires an estimate for the immediate postbellum period. Relatively few systematic data are available for that period. The most comprehensive collection of relevant information is the agricultural wage data displayed in Table 3.1 above. For present purposes it is fortunate that agricultural employment was relatively more important in the late 1860s than in 1900 and also that, within agriculture, wage labor was probably relatively more important at the earlier date. For these reasons agricultural wage data convey more representative information about average black income in 1867–68 than they would at a later date. The Department of Agriculture obtained these data from its "regular corps of reporters and agricultural editors, and [from] planters distinguished in their vocation." The Department expressed its appreciation "for the care and fidelity with which its inquiries were met" but gave no indication of the number of responses received.[21] No doubt the data contain errors of various sorts, but the (independently verifiable) patterns of interstate and age-sex differences within the data suggest that they are probably fairly reliable. In any event no alternative collection of similar scope exists, and no one would be warranted in dismissing the data out of hand.

To go from data on agricultural wage rates to an estimate of black income per capita requires a number of assumptions. I shall attempt to make these assumptions so that an upper limit estimate of income will result; this in turn will give rise to a lower limit estimate of the rate of growth after 1867–68, which is my ultimate objective. In brief, the calculations are biased against a high rate of growth of black income between 1867–68 and 1900. If the estimated figures nevertheless imply a high rate of growth, one can be fairly sure that it actually obtained.

The procedures and assumptions employed in constructing an estimate of black income per capita in 1867–68 are as follows. First, average the agricultural wage data shown separately for 1867 and 1868 in Table 3.1; then weight these averages according to the 1860 population shares (which are probably more reliable than the 1870 shares) of the states in the aggregate they constitute. The resulting figure is $111, which is the weighted average value of money income plus the value of rations. Farm laborers also typically received housing, garden plots, and fuel. If one assumes that the annual value of these perquisites was quite considerable, one can place total real income in the neighborhood of $150. Next suppose that the income of black farmers was, as calculated for 1900, 50 percent above that of farm laborers; in the present case this is $225. Then assume that the rural labor force was equally divided between farm laborers and farmers; the weighted average, which provides an estimate of average rural income per worker, is $188.[22] Assuming that the full-time-equivalent participation in the rural labor force was 0.25, as assumed for 1900, the resulting estimate of rural income per capita is $47.[23] Next suppose that the urban income level in 1867–68 was, as in 1900, about 50 percent above the rural level. This assumption, along with the 1870 urban–rural shares of the population shown in Table 2.6, permits calculation of the overall black income per capita, $50.[24] This is almost certainly an overstatement. Finally, comparison of this figure with the estimate for 1900 requires deflation to take into account changes in the price level. No existing price index is really appropriate for this purpose. The widely employed Warren-Pearson price index indicates that the price level fell by almost 50 percent between 1867–68 and 1900.[25] Still following the strategy of biasing the income estimate for the initial years upward, I shall assume that the $50 estimate in 1867–68 dollars was equivalent to $30 in 1900 purchasing power. Limits of plus or minus 25 percent bound the estimate at about $22 and $38.

Finally, one can draw some conclusions about changes over time, although they must be as tenuous as the estimates that underlie them. The first conclusion, of which one can be quite certain, is that the level of income per capita of blacks in 1900 stood considerably above the level of 1867–68. At the very least, the average income had increased from about $38 to about $55, that is, by almost half again; more probably it increased from about $30 to about $73, that is, approximately one and a half times; and it might have grown from about $22 to about $91, that is, it might have quadrupled. The intermediate estimates imply a rate of growth of about 2.7 percent per year, which is considerably greater than the growth rate of income per capita in the overall American economy during that period, about 2 percent.[26] This is not to say that black incomes increased by a steady 2.7 percent every year after 1867–68. No doubt some periods, like the mid-1890s, saw little or no growth. Nevertheless, the likelihood that over a third of a century black incomes advanced more rapidly than white incomes is a matter of great significance. True, my estimate of the growth rate may be too high; but then again, it may be too low. I believe that the latter is more likely, as the estimates are deliberately biased against a high rate of growth. The quantitative evidence indicates strongly that black people shared in the growing material prosperity of the American economy in the late nineteenth century. No matter which estimate is accepted, however, it remains true that the black income level in 1900 lay far below the white level in absolute terms. But evidence that the blacks of 1900 remained poor in some absolute sense or poor relative to the whites in no way contradicts the estimates showing relatively rapid growth of black incomes during the last third of the nineteenth century.[27]

Budgets

Another way to assess the increase in black real income over time is by examining evidence on the actual content of the consumption basket. How much of their income did people spend for food, housing, and clothing, and what was the quality of these "necessities"? To what other uses did they put their incomes? Was much allocated to "frivolous" consumption or simply "thrown away" as many critics alleged? Reliable, representative evidence on the disposition of black incomes would provide answers to these questions. Needless to say, such evidence does not exist. Fragmentary, sketchy, and crudely estimated data are the only ones available. Nevertheless, the existing evidence is sufficient to establish several important conclusions beyond reasonable question.

Table 5.1. *Distributions of income and expenditure for 121 representative black families, Atlanta, c. 1900*

Annual Income ($)		Number of Families	Percentage [a] of all expenditures for:				
Range	Mean		Rent	Food	Clothing	Taxes	Other expenses and savings
100–199	139	18	12	37	20	0	31
200–299	249	34	12	50	21	2	15
300–399	333	30	9	42	21	3	26
400–499	433	19	9	36	16	3	36
500–749	564	20	7	31	16	3	44

Source: Adapted from data in W. E. B. Du Bois, "The Negro Landholder of Georgia," U.S. Department of Labor, *Bulletin No. 35* (July 1901), p. 664.
[a] Percentages may not sum to 100 because of rounding.

Table 5.1 displays one of the best organized collections of data on expenditure patterns. Several interesting features of these data can be noted. Evidently "necessities" accounted for considerably less than the total expenditure of even those families with the lowest incomes. Probably some of those listed as having family incomes below $200 were servants or cooks with opportunities for procuring food from their employers' kitchens; hence their low proportion of expenditure for food relative to those in the next income class. Families with incomes of $200–299 could provide for their food, clothing, and shelter and still have 15 percent of their incomes available for other uses. And this margin varied directly with family income. Those in the $500–749 class used fully 44 percent of their income for other expenditures and savings. (No doubt some of this went for medical care and might reasonably be counted a "necessity.") Taxes required relatively modest sums. In general, the higher the income, the smaller was the proportion spent for rent, food, and clothing and therefore the greater was the proportional allowance for other things.[28]

Budget data for rural families are fragmentary at best. Writing in 1913, the sociologist Robert E. Park estimated the annual expenditure of an average black tenant at about $288, distributed as follows: clothing, $77; groceries, $125; physician and medicines, $9; church and school, $5; and other things, $72. He noted that considerable variation occurred from year to year because of fluctuations in crop yields and prices. Moreover, "a thrifty farmer . . . can reduce the amount of his purchases [of food] at the store to almost nothing. He can raise his own cane and make his own syrup; he can . . . supply himself with pork and corn meal from his own farm. This is what he usually does as soon as he sets out to buy a farm of his own." In a study of the black family published in 1908, Du Bois presented several budgets for farm families. These indicated considerable allocations to churches and secret orders, amusements, medical care, and incidentals, besides the usual outlays for food, clothing, and shelter. After examining numerous store accounts, George T. Surface estimated in 1909 that black coal miners spent over 90 percent of their incomes, with an average of 40 percent for food, 25 percent for clothing, and the remainder for other things.[29]

Scattered data are available for the North. In his study of Philadelphia, Du Bois presented several budgets. One of those he judged most representative of the mass of the race in that city was for a family of three which allocated its income of $455 as follows: rent, $96; food, $190; fuel, $35; clothing, other expenditures, and savings, $134. In Xenia, Ohio, a black laborer's annual budget included $36 for rent, $208 for food, $33 for fuel, $28 for clothing, $21 for medical care, $20 for funeral expenses, $13 for life insurance, $10 for tobacco, and $30 for miscellaneous expenses – the total $399.[30] Whatever else such information may show, it does establish that these black families allocated substantial parts of their incomes to consumption items other than "necessities." In addition, some saving was probably the rule rather than the exception.[31]

Suggestive, if rather backhanded, evidence that the black level of living had advanced considerably above subsistence is the continual complaint of whites, especially planters, that the blacks "wasted" a large part of their incomes. Alfred Holt Stone was typical of many paternalistic employers when he railed against his black tenants' purchases of illustrated Bibles, patent nostrums, hair straighteners, skin bleaches, pistols, sewing machines, organs, pianos, and clocks.[32] Perhaps Stone's tenants were unusually prosperous, or perhaps his description of their purchasing habits was biased. But Du Bois agreed that the black consumer "threw away" far more than he should:

Probably few poor nations waste more money by thoughtless and unreasonable expenditure than the American Negro, and especially those living in large cities like Philadelphia. First, they waste much money in poor food and in unhealthful methods of cooking. The meat bill of the average Negro family would surprise a French or German peasant or even an Englishman. The crowds that line Lombard street on Sundays are dressed far beyond their means; much money is wasted in extravagantly furnished parlors, dining-rooms, guest chambers and other visible parts of the homes. Thousands of dollars are annually wasted in excessive rents, in doubtful "societies" of all kinds and descriptions, in amusements of various kinds, and in miscellaneous ornaments and gewgaws. All this is a natural heritage of a slave system, but it is not the less a matter of serious import to a people in such economic stress as Negroes now are. The Negro has much to learn of the Jew and Italian, as to living within his means and saving every penny from excessive and waste-expenditures.[33]

Complaints like this constituted obvious attempts to impose the writer's "superior" values on the mass of black consumers. But the positive message is clear: black people possessed a considerable margin of income beyond that required for "necessities."

To sum up, budget data are limited and insufficiently detailed, but they do establish some important facts. Food, clothing, and shelter no doubt claimed the greater part of black expenditures, but a considerable margin remained for allocation to amusement, medical care, insurance, churches and societies, travel, and consumer durables. The budget data are surely consistent with the income estimates of the previous section. To be sure, the average level of living remained relatively low, but withal far above the level of the late 1860s.

Diets

Food consumption occupies a central place in any population's level of living. Obviously people must eat to survive, and for many this aspect of the struggle for survival serves at the same time as a source of immediate and profound satisfaction. But the importance of diet transcends these obvious considerations, for the amounts and kinds of food consumed can set in train a host of repercussions for a population's life expectancy, morbidity, working productivity, and even for its capacity to learn and to transmit intelligence from one generation to the next.[34] Blacks devoted a large part of their real incomes to the acquisition of foodstuffs. To assess their level of living one must know something about what they got in exchange.

Historians are virtually unanimous in their accounts of the diets of rural blacks. They agree that the "three M's" – meat, meal, and molasses – comprised the bulk of the food consumed. Thomas D. Clark, after examining thousands of accounts in the records of Southern country stores, declared that "from Virginia to Texas food purchases were pretty much alike. Every personal account of any consequence included frequent purchases of the staples, meat, meal, molasses, flour, sugar, salt, and coffee."[35] The "meat" hardly deserved its name, consisting almost entirely of fat. Investigators in the Black Belt of Alabama in the 1890s reported that

the only kind of meat which seemed to be in at all common use among the country people was fat pork. Whenever they spoke of meat they always meant fat pork. Some of them knew it by no other name, nor did they seem to know much of any other meat except that of opossum and rabbits, which they occasionally hunted, and of chickens which they raised to a limited extent.

The report observed that "all meats are fried or otherwise cooked until they are crisp" and added, somewhat gratuitously, that "very many [of these people] suffer from indigestion in some form."[36] The corn meal was mixed with water, and sometimes a little salt, and baked on the flat surface of a hoe or griddle in the fireplace (hence "hoe-cake"). The molasses was mixed with the grease left from the cooking of the salt pork and sopped up with cornbread; sometimes molasses mixed with hot water formed a beverage. Some families consumed a little fresh milk, but it was common for those with a cow to forego drinking the milk and instead to make butter, which they bartered for staple items at the country store. Most of the Alabama families studied consumed eggs occasionally. A similar study in eastern Virginia revealed essentially the same overall dietary pattern except that the rural blacks there consumed substantial amounts of fish along with their steady "hog and hominy."[37]

To supplement the staple items of their diet many, though by no means all, rural families kept a garden. Blacks typically grew a smaller assortment of vegetables than did their white neighbors. One investigator in Alabama found that "not more than half a dozen varieties of vegetable foods are grown by those [blacks] producing vegetables for their own consumption, and in a number of cases the variety is much smaller." Most frequently cultivated were turnips, collards, string beans, corn, Irish potatoes, cowpeas, and sweet potatoes.[38] The use of such vegetables helped to offset the vitamin deficiencies inherent in a diet of the three M's, but the prevailing practice of thoroughly cooking most vegetables in water probably reduced the quantities of vitamins available in the fresh garden produce.

Scientists measured the calories and proteins in the sample diets. They concluded that

the negro dietaries show on the average a liberal allowance of fuel ingredients. . . . But the quantities of protein in the negro dietaries are extremely small, in general from one-half to two-thirds the amounts which the standards call for and which are actually found in the food of well-to-do and well-nourished people of different classes in the United States and in Europe.

The averages for the Alabama families studied were 3,270 calories and 62 grams of protein per day per man-equivalent, but the variance around these averages was quite large, some families falling far below the average.[39] Not only was the protein content of the diets low, but most of it came from vegetable sources that did not provide "complete" protein, that is, all the essential amino acids. There is little doubt that many vitamins – which were still undiscovered at the time of these studies – were also deficient in the typical diet of the rural blacks. The Virginia families studied had more nutritious diets by virtue of their substantial consumption of fish,[40] but they, too, were probably deficient in certain vitamins. Later investigators perceived indirect evidence of such a deficiency in the relationship between poor years in the cotton economy and the subsequently increased incidence of pellagra, a niacin-deficiency disease, among tenants.[41]

The dietary studies sponsored by the Department of Agriculture examined mainly the poorest class of the black rural population. Although the diets studied probably represented those of a large part of the rural population, many blacks in the countryside enjoyed considerably better nourishment. The more prosperous tenants and the owner operators were more likely to keep a garden with a greater variety of vegetables. Similarly, they were more likely to have a milk cow, some hogs, and a substantial number of chickens. With a more abundant supply of milk, fresh meat, eggs, and vegetables, they consumed a more healthful diet. Moreover, having larger farms, they generally earned more from the sale of cash crops and therefore could bring home a greater variety of food from the store on Saturday. All this is not to say that they neglected the characteristic Southern staples, but merely to emphasize that in diet, as in almost everything else, the more prosperous black farmers differed from the poorest sharecroppers and laborers. Not everyone in the countryside subsisted on an uninterrupted regimen of hog and hominy.[42]

City dwellers could take advantage of a more varied supply of foodstuffs, and the existing evidence shows that they did in fact enjoy better diets. Students at Atlanta University collected information on the food purchases of 20 laborers and artisans in Atlanta in 1908. Representative of the unskilled workers with family incomes of $6–10 per week was a common laborer whose food purchases included wheat flour, corn meal, sweet potatoes, dried peas and beans, green vegetables, fresh beef, salt pork, fish, lard, butter, coffee, cocoa, sugar, and dried fruits. A carpenter with a weekly income of $18 represented the more highly paid artisan group; he purchased the same items as the laborer (except for the fish and the cocoa) *plus* macaroni, rice, Irish potatoes, bacon, sausage, cheese, fresh milk, condensed milk, eggs, tea, and molasses.[43] In general, the higher the family income the more varied and nutritious was a family's diet. Urban blacks, with considerably higher real incomes than their rural cousins, could demand better diets, and the greater availability of a variety of foods in the city made it possible for their demands to be satisfied.

In brief, black diets varied as widely as the people themselves. Much depended on income, especially in the cities. But the accessibility of various foodstuffs changed with the character of one's location, urban or rural, North or South. No doubt many, particularly in the countryside, subsisted on an undisturbed regimen of meat, meal, and molasses. But not every country family submitted to this nutritional insult, and by maintaining a substantial garden, a cow, and some chickens, many families enjoyed a better diet. Urban dwellers capitalized on the dual advantages of higher incomes and greater accessibility to a more varied assortment of foodstuffs. While some city people persisted in their attachment to hog and hominy, most apparently took advantage of their superior opportunities to consume a more balanced and nutritious diet.

Housing

Second only to diet as an important component of a population's level of living is housing. Obviously people must be shielded from the rain and snow, shaded from the sun's summer rays, and protected from the cold of winter. Housing may perform these functions better or worse according to its quality. And, while providing its inmates with immediate satisfaction, a house also helps to determine their life expectancy, morbidity, working productivity, and all the more indirect repercussions of their health conditions.[44] Although information about the quality of black housing is scanty, fragmentary, and largely impressionistic, enough is known to establish certain generalizations about urban–rural differences and trends over time. Urban blacks, as shown above, expended a substantial part of their incomes for house rental or purchase. Rural blacks typically paid no explicit house rent; they either owned their houses or received housing as part of their compensation as farm laborers or tenants. But in both urban and rural locations, housing services in fact accounted for a substantial fraction of the people's real incomes, and an assessment of the black level of living requires a knowledge of the amount and quality of housing services enjoyed.

The housing stock available to blacks after emancipation was, for the most part, constituted of structures inherited from the slave regime. These varied from place to place but possessed some common characteristics. Only a few were made of brick or stone; most, especially in the more newly settled regions, were made of logs, while a smaller number were constructed of sawn planks. Most were small, usually less than 20 feet square, and possessed only a single room and a dirt floor. A fireplace provided the sole source of heat and, at night, of light. Windows with glass panes were almost unknown; even windows with wooden shutters were uncommon. Construction was crude in both materials and workmanship and, as a result, the walls were often cracked, freely admitting the wind, and the ceilings leaked during rains. Privileged house servants and urban slaves had sometimes received better accommodations than the plantation field hands. Overall, however, Du Bois was no doubt correct when he asserted that "the house of the slave . . . [provided] little or nothing save bare rough shelter."[45]

Houses in the countryside were gradually improved in the half century after emancipation. Log cabins gave way to frame dwellings. After traveling from South Carolina to Washington, D.C., in 1901, Harry Hammond observed: "I did not see but one log house from the car window all the way through; the log cabin is disappearing." He also noted that "the dirt floor has disappeared entirely." Du Bois corroborated this testimony, adding that "glass windows have been introduced here and there."[46] Houses were also enlarged. Appearing before the Industrial Commission at the turn of the century, J. H. Hale, who operated farms in both Georgia and Connecticut, testified:

The original plantation houses of the South, I regret to say, were mostly 1-room affairs, 20 or 25 feet square, and those were mostly of logs. The modern house is a frame house, boarded and sheathed, with 3 rooms – a general family room, which is used only to put the family beds in, and then a separate bedroom, and a kitchen. The general modern tenant house now is a 3-room house.[47]

More spacious housing reduced the probability that infectious diseases like tuberculosis and diphtheria would spread to all susceptible members of the household. Better-insulated houses meant greater comfort in the winter, a household environment in which the body could better resist the inroads of infectious disease.

Black landowners had themselves to thank for improvements in their housing, but the mass of rural blacks, employed as farm laborers or tenants, enjoyed such gains as a result of the competitive behavior of employers in the rural labor markets. As Alfred Holt Stone, a Delta planter, remarked: "In the competition for laborers a steadily improving class of plantation houses is not the least of the inducements offered." O. B. Stevens, Georgia's commissioner of agriculture, told the Industrial Commission in 1901 that "landlords have been forced to build better tenant houses and provide them with modern systems that are adopted all around, in order to retain and keep the best labor. That is really the way that a great many of our best people succeed in keeping their labor, and the better class of labor, by making everything around them as comfortable as possible." Du Bois agreed that "to some extent laborers were induced to remain on farms by offers of higher wages and better houses."[48] Thus, not through any benevolence of spirit but merely as a self-serving device in the competition of labor, Southern landlords contributed toward raising the level of living of rural blacks by constructing better houses for them.

That the average housing conditions of rural blacks improved during the half century after emancipation is undeniable but, measured by any other standard than the miserable past, the gain was often difficult to perceive; much black housing in the countryside remained nothing short of squalid. Du Bois in 1908 gave a vivid description of the poorer rural homes:

[A]s cooking, washing and sleeping go on in the same room an accumulation of stale sickly odors are [sic] manifest to every visitor. . . . A room so largely in use is with difficulty kept clean. The dish-water forms a pool beside the door; animals stray into the house; there are either no privies or bad ones; facilities for bathing even the face and hands are poor, and there is almost no provision for washing other parts of the body; the beds are filled with vermin. To be neat and tidy in such homes is almost impossible. Now and then one does find a tiny cabin shining and clean, but this is not the rule. . . . The average country home leaks in the roof and is poorly protected against changes in the weather. A hard storm means the shutting out of all air and light; cold weather leads to overheating, draughts, or poor ventilation; hot weather breeds diseases. The conditions are aggravated in cases where the huge old-fashioned fireplace has been replaced by a poor smoky stove. . . . So far as actual sleeping space goes, the crowding of human beings together in the Black Belt is greater than in the tenement district of large cities like New York.[49]

As Du Bois himself recognized, however, "there are other sections where the homes are larger and the conditions greatly improved." Robert E. Park described one such region, near Christianburg, Virginia, in 1913:

The homes of the Negro farmers in this region would be regarded as comfortable for a small farmer in any part of the country. They are frequently two-story frame buildings, surrounded by a garden and numerous outbuildings. The interior of these homes is neat and well kept. They contain a few books, some pictures and the usual assortment of women's handiwork. A general air of comfort and contentment pervades the homes and the community.

Park also described a similar neighborhood near Tuskegee, Alabama, where "a large proportion of colored farmers in Macon County live at present in neat four- and five-room cottages." He observed further that "wherever one meets a little colony of Negro land owners and wherever one meets a Negro who has risen to the position of farm manager, one invariably finds improvement in the character and condition of the Negro home."[50] In housing, as in diet and almost everything else, the more prosperous rural blacks compared very favorably with the mass of poor sharecroppers and laborers.

The housing conditions of urban blacks varied even more widely. Historians are fortunate to possess some quantitative evidence that reveals something of these conditions. Of 262 families in Farmville, Virginia, in 1890, 17 occupied one room, 134 two rooms, 45 three rooms, and 66 four or more rooms, the average being almost three rooms per family. In Covington, Georgia, another small town, the average family around the turn of the century occupied two or three rooms, a common arrangement consisting of two rooms divided by a hall, with a kitchen attached at the back of the hall and often with a front porch. In Xenia, Ohio, of 501 families studied in 1903, 16 occupied one room, 57 two rooms, 130 three rooms, 117 four rooms, 79 five rooms, and 102 six or more rooms, the average being more than four rooms per family. In villages and small towns like these the more prosperous blacks improved their houses by adding rooms, larger windows, and more furniture, by differentiating parlor, bedroom, and kitchen, and by making the home tidier and decorating it more tastefully.[51]

Table 5.2, which displays information gathered in the Labor Department's extensive study of urban blacks in 1896, provides evidence on the amount of living space enjoyed by blacks in some of the larger urban places. The data reveal that almost half of the Atlanta families studied occupied three or more rooms;[52] in Nashville and the other Southern cities studied almost three-fourths had that many rooms; and in Cambridge the proportion rose even higher. In the total sample

Table 5.2. *Rooms per family, urban blacks, 1896*

City	Families living in:							Total families
	1 room	2 rooms	3 rooms	4 rooms	5 rooms	rooms	7 or more rooms	
Atlanta, Ga.	58	116	84	25	17	16	8	324
Nashville, Tenn.	9	55	124	34	14	5	5	246
Cambridge, Mass.	5	7	28	21	18	7	10	96
Other cities a	45	98	72	117	63	33	38	466
Total	117	276	308	197	112	61	61	1,132

a The other cities sampled included Savannah, Macon, Athens, and Cartersville (Ga.), Washington, D.C., Jacksonville and Sanford (Fla.), Columbia and Orangeburg (S.C.), Birmingham and Tuskegee (Ala.), Louisville (Ky.), Macon (Miss.), and Chattanooga and Jackson (Tenn.).
Source: Adapted from data in U.S. Department of Labor, "Condition of the Negro in Various Cities," *Bulletin No. 10* (May 1897), p. 266.

only a third of the families occupied fewer than three rooms. In view of the small size of the average urban family, these data do not indicate any appreciable "overcrowding" of living quarters. But the representativeness of the data is, of course, open to question.

The Labor Department's study also recorded the sanitary conditions of the dwellings. In Nashville all relied on privies and only one family had a bathroom; in Atlanta 31 houses had flush toilets and 5 had bathrooms in a total of 282 houses investigated. In Cambridge, on the other hand, 95 of the 97 houses studied had flush toilets. The other cities sampled showed a few bathrooms and a sprinkling of flush toilets, but the dominant sanitary convenience was the privy.[53] In such a primitive means of urban waste disposal lay a menacing source of the typhoid, dysentery, and other "filth diseases" that ravaged the black population in the urban slum blocks and alleys.

Du Bois' pioneering study of Philadelphia took account of residential space and sanitation. In the Seventh Ward in 1896 he counted 9,302 rooms occupied by 2,401 families, which implied an average of 3.9 rooms per family and just over one individual per room. He judged the data to indicate "considerable overcrowding, but not nearly as much as is often the case in other cities." About 14 percent of the families had access to bathrooms and flush toilets; but "over 20 per cent and possibly 30 per cent of the Negro families of this ward lack some of the very elementary accommodations necessary to health and decency," for in many cases extensive construction of tenements had crowded out the space once reserved for privies. "These tenement abominations of Philadelphia are perhaps better than the vast tenement houses of New York," said Du Bois, "but they are bad enough, and cry for reform in housing."[54]

That many urban blacks lived in a gloomy, disease-ridden, and dangerous environment is clearly revealed in the following summary, penned by Du Bois in 1908:

The nucleus of Negro population in Southern cities is the alley. It is seen at its worst in the slums of Charleston, Savannah, Washington, and such cities. . . . Attention has lately been directed to the tenement-house abominations, but little has been said of the equally pestilential and dangerous alley. . . . In Atlanta the badly drained and dark hollows of the city are threaded with these alleys, usually unpaved and muddy, and furnishing inviting nests for questionable characters. The worst type of these homes is the one-room cabin with sidings of unfinished boards running up and down; no ceiling or plastering, no windows, no paint, an open fireplace, and the whole of this cheerless box set directly on the ground, without cellar or foundation. Next to these come two-room houses, built in the same way, but with one or two windows and still without porch, blinds, or fence. Such cabins are so crowded together that they nearly touch each other, and the sun must get high before it can be seen from these alleys. Sometimes such rooms are papered inside by the inmates. They are 14 or 15 feet square and 8 or 10 feet high. The furniture is scarce – a bed or two, a few chairs, a table, a stove or fireplace, a trunk or chest. The floor is bare, and there are no pictures. Sometimes six or eight persons live in two such rooms and pay $1.50 a month or more for rent; sometimes as much as $4.00. These houses have water outside in a well or street hydrant; the out-houses are used in common by several tenants. Probably twenty per cent of the Negro homes in Atlanta fall into this class.[55]

But even though some 20 percent of the population inhabited the squalid alleys, the great majority could still enjoy a somewhat better residential environment.

And indeed, in the cities, many blacks did acquire more comfortable and pleasant housing. As Du Bois commented, "these homes are often unnoticed because they are not distinguishable from corresponding white homes, and so are continually overlooked." At their best such houses might have seven or eight rooms, many windows with curtains and shades, electric bells and gas, bathrooms and water in the house, tiled hearths, a piano or an organ, and a full assortment of furniture – and only four to six occupants. Perhaps as many as 5 percent of the black houses were of this type in some cities by the early twentieth century.[56] Normally only the most successful teachers, merchants, and professional men acquired this quality of housing, but a much larger group comprised of craftsmen, small businessmen, and laborers with steady employment occupied comfortable and attractive dwellings. In 1913 Park described the variety of housing occupied by urban blacks as follows:

There are, particularly in every large city as well as in every small town in the South, multitudes of Negroes who live meanly and miserably. They make their homes in some neglected or abandoned quarters of the city and maintain a slovenly, irregular and unhealthy sort of existence, performing odd jobs of one kind or another. Very few colored people of the artisan class, however, live in these so-called "Negro quarters." There are always other quarters of the city, frequently in the neighborhood of some Negro school, where there will be another sort of community and in this community a large proportion of the people will be composed of Negro artisans and small tradesmen. They will live, for the most part, in little three- or four-room houses and, if they happen to own their homes, there will be a vine training over the porch, curtains in the windows, a rug or carpet on the floor. . . . There will be a few books in the front bedroom, a little garden in the rear of the house and a general air of thrift and comfort about the place.[57]

Indeed, even in New York City's Harlem district, later notorious as a black slum, housing conditions were initially quite good. As late as 1914 an Urban League report described Harlem as "a community in which Negroes as a whole are . . . better housed than in any other part of the country."[58]

Rents varied widely according to region and city. In the sprawling cities of the South, housing was relatively cheap, while in the more densely populated Northern cities like New York and Philadelphia rents might claim a major part of black incomes. In Philadelphia's Seventh Ward in 1896, 21 percent of the families paid less than $5 per month, 29 percent $5–10, 17 percent $10–15, 11 percent $15–20, 17 percent $20–30, and 4 percent $30 or more. Of course the larger rents tended to be for houses with more rooms. The average rent was $10.50 per month. By contrast in the small town of Xenia, Ohio, in 1903, black families paid an average rent of less than $4 per month. In many Southern towns rents were even lower.[59] Data in Table 5.1 above, for example, imply considerably lower rents in Atlanta.

A good deal of evidence indicates that blacks often paid higher rents than whites for equivalent housing, especially in the large Northern cities. In New York City in 1909, "real estate agents, who have handled properties during the change from white to Negro tenants, testified that Negro families upon moving in pay from $2.00 to $5.00 more per apartment. Others corroborated their statements." In Philadelphia some blacks paid 20 to 50 percent more than whites. Further, many tenants complained that their landlords would not make necessary repairs or improvements. And at times real estate agents or owners refused to rent to black tenants on any terms.[60]

Probably a part of the racial differential in rents reflected pure racial discrimination, but another part did not. As Abram Harris has observed, "the high [rental] rate may not increase the total rental income. . . . It is a premium levied for depreciation, which is both psychological and physical, and the loss and uncertainty of rent payments due to the high rate of turnover among Negro tenants." Du Bois himself had anticipated this explanation as early as 1899, when he characterized the additional rent paid by blacks as "a sort of insurance." He also confirmed that "undoubtedly certain classes of Negroes bring much deserved criticism on themselves by irregular payment or default of rent, and by the poor care they take of property."[61] He urged that landlords distinguish between good and bad tenants; but in fact the costs of making such distinctions prior to a rental transaction were probably prohibitive for most landlords in a large city. A cheaper way to protect their interest was simply to charge a rental premium to any black tenant. The resulting discrimination – logically equivalent to the racial "signaling" form of wage discrimination discussed in Chapter 4 – sprang not necessarily from racial antipathy *per se* but rather from the costs of discovering which individual tenants would be trustworthy in a group that, on the average, performed relatively poorly in that respect. All this is not to assert that such considerations account entirely for the observed racial differences in house rents but merely to emphasize that more than pure racial discrimination was involved, even in cases where blacks paid more for accommodations of equivalent quality.

Quite apart from any form of direct racial discrimination, the average urban black would have paid a relatively high house rent because of the necessity of living near his place of employment. Du Bois noted that "the nature of the Negro's work compels him to crowd into the centre of the city much more than is the case with the mass of white working people."[62] Working as laundresses, porters, drivers, waiters, and janitors, urban blacks in the North – and to a lesser degree in the South as well – could not live far from the downtown center. In this neighborhood they could obtain housing space only by paying a rental rate high enough to bid the space away from the multitude of bidders with alternative residential, commercial, or industrial uses. Competition for the use of especially valuable land near the city's center would have insured high rents in any event. That racial discrimination also occurred only exacerbated the black worker's dilemma.

Compounding the locational imperatives associated with the black employment structure was the simple fact that most blacks preferred to live near other blacks. This "social" agglomeration grew out of the desire to be near friends, churches, and organized group activities such as lodge meetings, dances, and the like. "The Negro who ventures away from the mass of his people and their organized life," said Du Bois, "finds himself alone, shunned and taunted, stared at and made uncomfortable." Mary White Ovington agreed:

[In New York City] the colored working people, like the Italians and Jews and other nationalities, have their quarter in which they live very much by themselves, paying little attention to their white neighbors. If the white people of the city have forced this upon them, they have easily accepted it. Should this 2 per cent of the population be compelled to distribute itself mathematically over the city, each ward and street having its correct quota, it would evince dissatisfaction. This is not true of the well-to-do element, but of the mass of the Negro workers.[63]

The concentration of blacks in certain urban districts, then, resulted from several interacting forces, not least of which was the voluntary attempt to locate near congenial neighbors.

In the black enclaves of the large Northern cities the density of settlement was high in part because of the prevailing system of taking in unrelated lodgers. This practice served to spread the high rents over a larger number of actual tenants. In Philadelphia's Seventh Ward in 1896, 31 percent of the families lived alone, 38 percent took in lodgers, and 31 percent were themselves subrenting. Together these families contained 7,751 individuals. The ward also housed 1,924 individuals lodging with families. In New York City in 1909, 27 percent of the blacks studied by Haynes were lodgers, and 46 percent of the 2,500 families he sampled took in lodgers. "Many of the lodgers consisted of married couples, sometimes with one or two children, and of parts of broken families."[64] By taking in lodgers, black families reduced their actual rents considerably below their apparent rents, with a corresponding sacrifice of space and privacy.

In the late nineteenth and early twentieth centuries, as increasing numbers of blacks settled in the larger cities, what has come to be called the "ghetto" became increasingly apparent, particularly in Northern cities such as New York and Chicago. The underlying causes of this locational concentration were several. As shown above, black employment structure and social voluntarism played important roles. But racial discrimination also reared its head. When individual blacks sought to move into predominantly white residential areas, they could expect – if things went well – insults and petty abuse from their new neighbors. If things went poorly, they could expect intimidation and physical violence, against which the police offered them scant protection. These conditions naturally discouraged many who desired to escape from the ghetto into more attractive residential neighborhoods.[65]

As the black population continued to grow in a given city, however, some expansion of the black-occupied area was inevitable; and attempts to prevent it sooner or later collapsed. The movement of blacks into once-fashionable Harlem provides a revealing example:

The basic cause of the collapse of all organized efforts to exclude Negroes from Harlem was the inability of any group to gain total and unified support of all white property owners in the neighborhood. Without such support it was impossible to organize a successful neighborhood-wide restrictive movement. Landlords forming associations by blocks had a difficult time keeping people on individual streets united. There also continued to be speculators, Negro and white, who, as in 1904 and 1905, sought to exploit the situation for their own profit. They bought tenements and opened them to Negroes to try to force neighbors to repurchase them at higher prices. . . . The minority of Harlem landlords who adhered to their original restrictive covenants suffered serious economic consequences. Many were unable to find white people willing to rent their apartments. To encourage white tenants already in them to remain, some were forced to reduce rents drastically. . . . The opponents of Negro settlement faced the dilemma of maintaining a "White Only" policy and probably losing everything, or renting to Negroes at higher prices and surviving. Most chose what seemed to them the lesser of two evils.[66]

Similar events took place in Chicago and elsewhere.[67] Once again – as in the efforts of Southern planters to hold down wage rates and tenant shares – white attempts to discriminate collectively broke down in the face of competition, and restrictive agreements proved unenforceable in the absence of some legally binding enforcement power. But if competitive forces ultimately triumphed, they did so only after extended periods of racial restriction and coercion.

Summary: Improvements in the level of living

A variety of evidence establishes beyond all doubt that the level of black real income per capita advanced substantially during the first half century after emancipation. The precise magnitude of the increase is uncertain, but my crude estimates – deliberately conservative estimates – indicate that between 1867–68 and the turn of the century black real income per capita probably more than doubled. The estimates imply that black incomes grew more rapidly than white incomes over the last third of the nineteenth century. An examination of budget data confirms that the average black family around 1900 did not confine its expenditures to "necessities" – food, clothing, and shelter – but allocated a significant fraction of its income to churches, lodges, consumer durables, travel, amusement, and savings. Quite obviously, the average black was then well above the subsistence level characteristic of the immediate postwar years. Improvements in diet and housing occupied a central place in the rising level of living: although many remained loyal to the three M's, many others came to consume a more varied and healthful diet; although many lived in ramshackle rural cabins and squalid urban tenements, many others came to occupy more solid, spacious, and comfortable houses. By modern standards the average black of 1914 remained desperately poor; even by comparison with the whites of his own time he was poor indeed. Perhaps because he remained relatively poor the gains in his material well-being during the period 1865–1914 have often been denied or minimized. But the evidence lends overwhelming support to a different conclusion: in fact, the first half century of black freedom witnessed major improvements in the level of living.

6

Overview and interpretation

One of the most significant things I saw in the South – and I saw it everywhere – was the way in which the white people were torn between their feeling of race prejudice and their downright economic needs.

Ray Stannard Baker, 1908

In Chapter 1 I sketched in a preliminary way how one might usefully approach the facts of black economic history in the half century after 1865. The objective there was to provide a tentative interpretive framework into which a variety of diverse facts might be fitted, to simplify the task of ordering the facts and relating them to one another in causal sequences. Within this analytical framework, Chapters 2–5 have presented numerous facts as well as several theoretical extensions and complications relevant to questions other than those posed at the outset. This final chapter returns to the initial focus, seeking to integrate the factual material and the partial models that constitute the heart of the book into an interpretive whole. To attain interpretive simplicity and still be true to the facts in all their historical diversity is, of course, impossible. The present objective is to incorporate as much genuine complexity as possible within an intelligible interpretation.

What was accomplished?

Emancipation granted the black people both very little and a great deal. With freedom came no land or other tangible resources; except for the sporadic, inconsistent, and transitory efforts of the Freedmen's Bureau and the army of occupation, no protection against the intimidation and violent abuse of Southern whites; except for the limited efforts of missionaries, philanthropists, and the bureau, no education. All that emancipation gave the blacks was, in short, themselves. No longer could they be bought and sold or offered as collateral for loans; no longer did they lack all rights white men were bound to respect. In the eyes of the law, they now held property rights over their own bodies and over such services as their bodies might produce. How well those rights would be respected and enforced depended on the erstwhile master class, on the legal authorities, and on the freedmen themselves.

The old masters being typically hostile and the legal authorities generally either weak or insincere, the blacks themselves took the initiative in asserting the reality of their freedom; and the predominant manifestation of their resolve was physical movement. From plantation to plantation, from countryside to city, from east to west the freedmen moved, establishing a precedent that would prove invaluable in keeping their freedom more than a mere legality. The Southern whites, with the legal machinery they increasingly and eventually completely controlled, sought to suppress this mobility. Through laws against vagrancy and the enticement of employees or tenants under contract, through statutes placing prohibitive taxes on emigrant labor agents and making certain indebtedness subject to criminal rather than civil prosecution, and through extralegal threats and intimidation the whites attempted to keep the black laborers and tenants in place. Although such devices no doubt had some effect on black mobility, in general they failed to achieve their objective of immobilizing the black labor force. In the annual Christmas moves of a host of plantation tenants, in the exodus from the old cotton states to the newer areas of the Mississippi Delta, Texas, and Oklahoma, and in the steady drift to the cities the blacks demonstrated conclusively that they could not be held in place against their will.

Besides confirming the reality of their freedom, black migrants reaped the gains of an important form of investment. In the western regions of the cotton kingdom, laborers and tenants earned higher incomes than in the Atlantic coast states. In the cities, black workers commanded higher wages than in the countryside – not to mention the greater security against arbitrary treatment at the hands of the whites. Everywhere the most oppressive employers experienced the greatest difficulty in hiring laborers, for the blacks quickly learned to seek employment under the more humane and honest, albeit paternalistic, white employers. Overall, the kaleidoscopic movements of the black population resulted in higher incomes, better working conditions, and greater security of person and property than would otherwise have been enjoyed. All of this is not to say, of course, that migration provided a panacea for the economic and social ills that plagued the blacks, but merely to emphasize that, even within a generally hostile environment, some opportunities were better than others, and that migration was essential for taking advantage of the best opportunities available.

While the freedmen understood that physical movement would certify the reality of their freedom, they recognized as well that their ignorance placed them in serious jeopardy, and they sought education with a determination that astounded almost everyone who witnessed those first days of freedom. No one knew the extent of literacy among the blacks of 1865; perhaps 5 percent, perhaps as many as 10 percent had some knowledge of the written word. The census of 1870, for what it is worth, reported that about 20 percent of the blacks over nine years of age could read and write. In 1910, by contrast, about 70 percent told the census takers they could read and write.[1] No doubt some made a false claim to literacy, and certainly many who claimed literacy were functionally illiterate. But even if the true literacy figure a half century after emancipation reached only 50 percent, the magnitude of the accomplishment is still striking, especially when one recalls the overwhelming obstacles blocking black educational efforts. For a large population to transform itself from virtually unlettered to more than half literate in 50 years ranks as an accomplishment seldom witnessed in human history.

The attainment of literacy had major economic consequences. It meant, in the language of the economist, the accumulation of human capital. Obviously many jobs were closed to those who could not read and write, many skills beyond the grasp of the illiterate. While literacy itself was an essential skill in the emerging industrial economy, it was also a prerequisite for a variety of job-specific training and experience. But literacy provided more than the key to better jobs or training: it supplied vital protection against being cheated. Time and again were stories told of farm laborers and tenants who could only guess whether they had received their due because the employer or the storekeeper kept the accounts and they had no way to check the honesty of his records. A little literacy went a long way in the Southern countryside. And, everywhere, the ability to read was essential if one was to learn something of the wider world and the opportunities it contained. Perhaps a significant reason for the limited migration from the South to the North was that those who stood to gain most from it – the unskilled – were the least informed about Northern opportunities. In view of all these considerations, the rise of black literates from a tiny fraction to a majority of the population had manifold consequences. Really ruthless white supremacists understood the importance of keeping the blacks intensely ignorant, but they could not do so. Although the black population of 1914 still suffered from ignorance on a wide front, it was far, far removed from the conditions of 1865. For this gain, and all that flowed from it, the blacks had themselves to thank in great part; Northern philanthropists and the grudging Southern public school systems provided the rest.

While the population grew more literate it also became more skilled and better trained in specific economic tasks. Not the least of these growing skills, though one generally overlooked, was expertise in farm

management. Many writers seem to believe that anyone could cultivate cotton and corn successfully, but such an assumption is surely
mistaken. To become a skilled farmer required instruction, example,
and most of all experience. In 1865 relatively few blacks could independently manage a farm successfully. With the passage of time, many
served apprenticeships as partially supervised sharecroppers or tenants,
gaining valuable experience in farm management. Thanks to these
learning experiences, in 1910 one black farmer in four was a wholly
independent owner operator, and many tenants farmed successfully
with little or no supervision. In the skilled trades a growing number
of workers acquired skills and experience. While some craft skills were
transmitted by those who had learned a trade under slavery, others –
like skills in plumbing, electrical work, and iron working – were almost
wholly the acquisition of the postbellum period. Professional training,
too, was almost entirely new to the black population. The doctors,
lawyers, teachers, and other professionals of 1914 had virtually no
counterparts under the slave regime. In sum, the growth of education,
training, and experience after 1865 was largely responsible for the
movement of black workers into better-paying jobs and, in many cases,
into more productive self-employment. That the stock of human capital
expanded greatly in the first half century after emancipation is in-
contestable. That this larger stock yielded correspondingly greater
returns to the efforts of the black labor force is equally evident.

The changing occupational structure of the black labor force reflected these and other influences. Not only the accumulation of skills
and experience but changing demands for labor underlay the shifting
pattern of black employment. The relative decline of agricultural employment mirrored a transformation occurring rapidly in the overall
American economy. Similarly, the relatively slow growth of employment
in domestic and personal services and the relatively rapid expansion of
jobs in trade, transportation, manufacturing, mining, and the professions reflected forces at work in the wider economy. With these sectoral
shifts went a measure of up-grading in the black labor force. Also
significant was the increasing independence from direct white supervision achieved in the expansion of owner operation in agriculture and
in the emergence of a "group economy" in the larger cities. In this respect the incipient ghettos had obvious advantages, for they promoted a
modicum of independence and physical security for growing numbers
of blacks.

Another economic trend of central importance was the growing
accumulation of property. Much of this occurred in agriculture, where
thousands of black farmers acquired land, tools, buildings, and work
stock. In the cities many blacks acquired land, business structures,

equipment, and inventories. Expanding stocks of other property, like churches, lodge halls, and household furniture, yielded satisfaction but no pecuniary return. The accumulation of residential houses yielded an implicit return when occupied by the owner, a pecuniary return when rented to tenants. Early in the twentieth century a committee of the American Economic Association estimated, largely on the basis of data from the census of 1900, the aggregate wealth of American blacks. The committee concluded that "the accumulated wealth of the Negro race in the United States in 1900 was approximately $300,000,000, and probably neither less than $250,000,000 nor more than $350,000,000." Several years later Du Bois used the wealth of Georgia blacks, documented in the state's tax records, as a basis for extrapolating the United States total to 1907. He concluded, deliberately employing the language of the earlier estimate: "The accumulated wealth of the Negro race in the United States in 1907 may be approximately $550,000,000 and possibly neither less than $500,000,000 nor more than $600,000,000."[2] Assuming in rough figures that the black population of 1910 numbered about 10 million and that their aggregate wealth reached $600 million, the implied wealth per capita of the entire population was $60. Assuming that this capital sum yielded only a 5 percent return, the yield increased annual income by $3.00 per capita. Of course, the great majority of blacks owned very little property, while a handful had amassed substantial fortunes. Of those with significant wealth, most possessed only a few hundred dollars worth of property, invested mainly in land and houses. The computation of a per capita wealth figure serves to put the estimates in more meaningful focus, but the distribution of the total must not be forgotten. Whether the sum was "large" or "small" is of course a matter of judgment, dependent on some comparative standard. Viewed in the context of its very low starting point and the serious obstacles and discouragements in the way of its increase, black property holding after 50 years of freedom appears substantial. Judged by the standards of white accumulation, it appears much less impressive.

In sum, the investments of all kinds made by blacks during the first 50 years after emancipation were substantial and, as blacks now had a legal claim to the fruits of their own labors, such investments resulted in great improvement in their economic condition. As a joint result of migration, education, training, and property accumulation the level of black income per capita in 1900 was probably more than double what it had been in the late 1860s. Further growth in the early twentieth century no doubt pushed it considerably higher. While the exact magnitude of the increase between 1865 and 1914 is open to debate, there is no doubt whatever that a large increase occurred. Evidence on black diets, housing, clothing, and other consumption shows that the level of living, on the average, had improved greatly since the early days of freedom. Some people, especially the poorest in the countryside, remained destitute. But one must remember that 50 years earlier destitution was typical rather than exceptional. Writers who have portrayed the economic condition of the blacks in the late nineteenth or early twentieth centuries as having improved only slightly are surely mistaken. Their conclusion could be reached only by comparing the worst of 1914 with the best of the late 1860s – a comparison both misleading and analytically unjustifiable. The variance of black incomes was greater in 1914 than in the late sixties, but just as surely the average stood much higher.

What was not accomplished?

Perhaps the widespread failure to recognize the genuine economic gains of the first half century of freedom springs from an exclusive concentration on certain obstacles to even greater black progress. These obstacles were largely, though not entirely, noneconomic, but all had repercussions on the economic development of the race. To catalog the major barriers blocking more rapid progress is to identify important elements of what might conceivably have been but was not accomplished. Since almost every historian of black Americans has lavished attention on these aspects of the story, the present account requires little more than a list of the major problems, with brief comments on their relation to black economic development – a relation that has not always been recognized.

The fundamental problem was the failure to achieve free and equal participation in politics: to vote, to hold office, to influence the exercise of governmental powers. During Reconstruction, of course, blacks did participate actively in politics, though almost nowhere was their political influence proportional to their numbers. But even during Reconstruction they bore great risks in attempting to exercise their newly acquired political rights. The Southern whites of the postwar era believed that, more than anything else, the black franchise must be combatted. The overriding objective of the Ku Klux Klan and a plethora of similar terrorist organizations was to eliminate the independent black voter, and they were prepared to use any means to achieve this end. In one state after another, through fraud, intimidation, and violence, the "Redeemers" wrested political control from the Reconstruction politicians, black and white, and reestablished white supremacy as the fundamental axiom of local government. Though some blacks continued to vote – the black vote never disappeared completely – and legal disfranchisement did not occur until the 1890s or later, nowhere did the black population possess appreciable political influence after 1876.

Exclusion from political influence produced both direct and indirect effects on black economic development. The direct effects sprang from their inability to influence the public allocation of resources. Perhaps the most important of the publicly supplied goods was education. Even though the public school systems created during Reconstruction remained in operation, white public school administrators made sure that the sums allocated to white education considerably exceeded the sums allocated to that of blacks. As a result, ramshackle and poorly equipped school houses, incompetent teachers, and half-taught pupils – and in many districts not even this much – characterized the blacks' portion of the public school system.[3] Even if competitive forces in the labor market assured black workers a wage commensurate with their productivity, the fact remained that illiterate, ignorant, and untrained workers were simply not very productive: a "fair" wage was still dismally low. For sending masses of young blacks into the labor market unprepared for any but the most unskilled occupations, the white-dominated Southern public school systems bore primary responsibility. Needless to say, public institutions such as hospitals, orphanages, insane asylums, or even tolerable prisons were virtually unavailable to the blacks.

The indirect effects of exclusion from governmental influence did even more damage. The foremost of these effects grew out of the discriminatory character of the laws and their administration. From vagrancy and antienticement laws enforced solely against blacks to segregation ordinances of all kinds, a massive body of public law restricted the blacks. Such laws were often evaded, ignored, or poorly enforced, so one must not emphasize the mere letter of the law unduly. Nevertheless, they stood on the statute books, ready for strict application at the command of the white authorities. A more pervasive influence than the written law was the actual day-to-day enforcement of the law – or the lack of it – by white officers. Especially in the rural South the sheriff, his deputies, and the local judge normally awaited the behest of influential whites: wealthy planters, merchants, and other powerful private individuals. One black aptly described the trial justices as men "whose judgment and decisions the 'Boss' influences as I would the movements of a devoted dog."[4] Under these circumstances the administration of the law was casual and arbitrary: at one time lax, to keep a dangerous black criminal at work in the cotton field; at another time severe, to make an example of a petty offender or an innocent victim. Needless to say, the black could expect no legal protection whatever against intimidation or violent abuse by the whites, as literally thousands of unpunished lynchings attest. His only hopes lay in securing a powerful white patron, usually his landlord or employer, who would intercede with the authorities on his behalf, and in doing his best to stay out of harm's way. Little wonder that black criminality flourished, for the black people recognized the law for what it was: a tool of hostile whites to restrain and suppress blacks. But without influence in politics blacks had no way whatever to rectify the situation. They could only appeal to the whites' sense of fair play. Although such appeals sometimes evoked a genuine response, they constituted a beggarly approach to the table of justice. There was much truth in Du Bois' charge early in the twentieth century that the South was "simply an armed camp for intimidating black folk."[5]

To survive in this environment required careful behavior from the black man. He must not attempt too much; he must not argue his own case too strongly; he must at all times assent to the white man's judgment and opinion; he must scrupulously observe the racial etiquette; above all he must never appear "uppity," for his life itself would thereby be endangered. In short, he must stay "in his place." Not only did all this take its toll in manhood and self-respect but it had important economic consequences. A farm owner might have to forego acquiring a good farm near the main road or the white church in favor of a poorer farm near the swamp or up on a distant hillside. A laborer must simply concede the earnings fraudulently withheld by a dishonest employer. To argue only added personal risk to pecuniary loss; one could only move on and hope for better treatment elsewhere. Similarly, a tenant with a grievance against his landlord was well advised to keep quiet, lest he find himself on the chain gang, the victim of a trumped-up charge, a phoney trial, and a harsh sentence.

If all this treading lightly was anything, it was the antithesis of that aggressive, pushing behavior for which economically successful Americans have been justly famous. The successful black, however, must take a circuitous route to his achievement, entering, as it were, by the back door. Without political power the black man could not enjoy well-enforced personal and property rights, and hence he could not pursue economic opportunities as the white man could. Forced to discount the future heavily, the shrewd black investor stuck to the tried and true, the well known. To remain poor, agreeable, and obsequious was, after all, a kind of life insurance. The real wonder is that so many blacks made as much progress as they did.

Initial conditions versus racial discrimination

Because of the exclusion of blacks from politics and the consequent public discrimination in education and legal treatment, black economic development proceeded more slowly than it otherwise would have done. Moreover, even though discrimination in the marketplace was much less pervasive, it too occurred, slowing progress still further. But *how much* did all these discriminatory obstacles retard black progress? To say that discrimination in all its forms slowed black progress is to utter the obvious. Further insight into the effect of discrimination requires a consideration of the magnitudes of various influences. Was the entire difference between black and white income levels in 1914, for example, ascribable to discrimination during the preceding half century of freedom? That is, even in the complete absence of racial discrimination, could the blacks have caught up with the whites after 50 years?

This is an extremely difficult question and by its very nature admits of no more than a conjectural answer, but some simple calculations can illuminate the issue. No one knows with any certainty where the black income level stood relative to the white level in 1865. For purposes of illustration assume – it is a plausible assumption – that the level of black income per capita was one-fourth the white level in 1865.[6] The white level was growing at almost 2 percent annually compounded during the period 1865–1914,[7] which means that over a half century it increased about 2.7 times. For the blacks to have achieved income equality in 1914, their income per capita would have had to have increased 10.8 times. Such an increase in 50 years implies an annual rate of growth of almost 5 percent annually compounded. That such growth could have been realized even under the most favorable circumstances is extremely unlikely. Of all the nations for which long-term growth data are available, none ever achieved such rapid growth over such a long period.[8] One can, of course, quarrel with the precise numbers employed in the example. But the point remains: quite apart from any retardation ascribable to discrimination after 1865, the very low initial level of black income made it inescapable that a very long time would elapse before the blacks caught up with the whites who, after all, were hardly standing still. Even if the blacks could have steadily raised their income per capita twice as fast as the whites (again assuming an initial white level four times greater than the black and a white growth rate of 2 percent), about 70 years would have been required to close the gap. Calculations shown in the Technical Appendix, Section 4B, suggest that the black growth rate did exceed the white rate and hence that the relative black income increased during the period from 1867–68 to 1900; but still the gap did not narrow much. Black income per capita probably did not exceed four-tenths of the white level in 1914.

Such calculations are suggestive, emphasizing as they do the awesome power of compound interest, but they are essentially lifeless, and most scholars have preferred to assess the black experience in the light of the actual development of various immigrant groups. These comparisons suggest that the blacks labored under greater constraints and disadvantages than the European immigrants, prejudice and discrimination against blacks being usually greater, and the initial levels of black literacy, skill, experience, wealth, and income generally lower. Moreover, the enduring badge of color obstructed many avenues of assimilation open to the European immigrants, or at least to their children.[9] These findings, then, do not help much in establishing how much black economic backwardness was associated with discrimination and how much with initially low endowments. They merely confirm that two burdens are heavier than one.

Perhaps a more relevant comparison, certainly one that deserves more extensive study, would be with the Oriental immigrants. These people experienced great discrimination, both public and private, and they also were readily indentified by their physical appearance. In California, where most Japanese immigrants settled, the state for a time legally prohibited their ownership of land. During the Second World War the United States government forced them into concentration camps, causing them to lose much of the property they had accumulated. Yet despite the restrictions and discriminations they experienced, by 1959 the median income of Japanese males was approximately the same as that of whites. Apparently a rapid increase in educational attainment had much to do with the success of the Japanese. Residence on the West Coast, one of the nation's highest-income regions, probably contributed something, too. That the Japanese could achieve economic parity with the whites in three generations is surely suggestive. An initially higher level of education than that possessed by blacks, a better location, and a more cohesive family structure probably made at least part of the difference between the Japanese and the blacks. Moreover, the Japanese had no heritage of slavery, with its associated white attitudes, which may help to explain why apparent prejudice against them (at least as shown in a survey in 1967) has virtually disappeared.[10] A comparison of the Japanese and the blacks leads to no unambiguous conclusions, but it does suggest that racial prejudice and physical identifiability were insufficient to preclude the rapid economic progress of at least one minority group. So many elements of the comparison diverge, however, that one may well hesitate before imposing this conclusion on the black case.

One is left, then, with the question of magnitudes still unresolved. It seems quite clear that a half century was not long enough for the blacks to close the economic gap separating them from the whites, even under the most favorable circumstances, including a complete absence of racial discrimination. To migrate, to acquire literacy, skills, and experience, and to accumulate capital all took time. Catching up with a swift competitor who has a large head start is difficult in any contest; to do so while carrying a discriminatory weight only compounds the difficulty. Just how much of the racial differential in income in 1914 was due to discrimination no one will ever know with certainty. But simply to recognize that the question involves two elements – initial levels *and* subsequent rates of growth – helps to clarify an assessment of black economic development after the Civil War.

Vicious circles?

As characterized in this book, racial discrimination constituted an additional constraint on the economic behavior of blacks. Not only did they face the usual economic constraints of a limited resource endowment, limited knowledge, and limited opportunities for transforming present endowments into greater ones in the future. In addition they faced systematic exclusion from certain opportunities and higher risks in the pursuit of others. But thus far the discussion has implicitly supposed that the economic behavior of blacks was unchanged by the imposition of discriminatory constraints except insofar as certain opportunities were ruled out and others were no longer attractive because of the risk associated with them. The assumption has been, in short, that the economic motivations of the blacks – in economist's jargon, their utility functions – were invariant with respect to discriminatory constraints. It may well be, however, that while this conceptualization plays an analytically useful role it fails to represent a historically important element: the feedback from discriminatory constraints to black motivation, attitudes, and ambition.

Such a feedback relation is difficult if not impossible to quantify and test, dealing as it does with intangible mental states and processes. This kind of relation takes on reality only for those closely connected with its operation. Perhaps as well as anyone, Du Bois was qualified to perceive and assess it. An appeal to his authority cannot settle the issue, of course, but his judgment deserves a hearing:

[T]he higher classes of white labor are continually being incorporated into the skilled trades, or clerical workers, or other higher grades of labor. Sometimes this happens with Negroes but not often. . . . Consequently we find the ranks of the laborers among Negroes filled to an unusual extent with disappointed men, with men who have lost the incentive to excel, and have become chronic grumblers and complainers, spreading this spirit further than it would naturally go. . . . Any one of these [discriminatory] things happening now and then would not be remarkable or call for especial comment; but when one group of people suffer all these little differences of treatment and discriminations and insults continually, the result is either discouragement, or bitterness, or over-sensitiveness, or recklessness. And a people feeling thus cannot do their best. . . . There are of course numerous exceptions, but the mass of the Negroes have been so often refused openings and discouraged in efforts to better their condition that many of them say, as one said, "I never apply – I know it is useless." . . . The social environment of excuse, listless despair, careless indulgence and lack of inspiration to work is the growing force that turns black boys and girls into gamblers, prostitutes and rascals. And this social environment has been built up slowly out of the disappointments of deserving men and the sloth of the unawakened.[11]

This is subjective testimony, to be sure, but it adds up to an eminently plausible assertion about human behavior: few men will persist in knocking on a door that is usually slammed in their faces.[12]

Even if one admits the existence of this feedback relation, however, its historical significance turns on its magnitude and pervasiveness. How deeply discouraged were the blacks by their hostile environment? How many of them succumbed to the pressures and gave up their efforts for material betterment? Apparently, many possessed great resilience in the face of discouragement and difficulty, for many realized notable gains despite the discriminatory constraints. Equally evident were those to whom Du Bois called attention, those who had lost virtually all hope for a better future. And perhaps the largest group, as usual, comprised those in the middle, discouraged and frustrated but still trying. To know the relative magnitudes of these three groups would be to understand more deeply the economic history of black Americans. Because it is unlikely that anyone *can* know such magnitudes, our understanding must necessarily remain incomplete.

Competition and coercion: The limits of individualism

Powerful as the forces of racial coercion were, they were not all-powerful, and one can learn much by considering where they failed and why. Clearly the whites did fail in some of their attempts at discrimination. Immediately after the emancipation the Southern whites generally believed that, although further defense of the peculiar institution was hopeless, the substance of slavery could and should be preserved: the blacks would remain confined to menial and subordinate positions, receiving only such compensation as the whites might choose to offer them, properly no more than the traditional allowance of slaves. To suppress black resistance to this virtual continuation of slavery, the whites looked to the passage and strict enforcement of repressive laws: the slave code under a new name. They would concede a few trifling rights to the blacks while retaining a firm grip on the machinery of racial control. They had the power, or they would soon get it – Congress, the Freedmen's Bureau, and the Reconstruction governments notwithstanding. But they failed to anticipate the difficulty they would have in resolving differences within their own ranks.

So often have scholars used summary expressions like "master class," "the whites," "the planters," and so forth they tend to forget an obvious fact: individuals are the actors. A man's behavior is determined by the ends *he* pursues, the means *he* commands, the constraints *he* confronts. This is not to say that men are insensitive, or indifferent to, or unaffected by the desires and actions of others. But it does suggest the possibility that individual objectives may be mutually inconsistent. What makes a master *class* is an overriding agreement on objectives and a unity of action among the individuals who comprise the class. Without this solidarity each master may become a threat to every other.

For the whites of the postbellum South the dilemma arose from what might be called a divergence of tastes: the whites valued both wealth and the practice of racial discrimination, but not everyone wished to exchange these two Good Things at the same rate. And whites with an unusually keen taste for wealth often created serious problems for those who valued racial discrimination more highly. The resolution of these antagonisms, which sometimes entailed a complete elimination of racial discrimination, was not primarily a matter between blacks and whites, as scholars have so often and so mistakenly supposed; rather, the resolution grew out of competition among the whites themselves. Only when the problem took this shape, with powerful whites pitted against each other, did discrimination fail completely. Not that the blacks stood by passively. Their willingness to bear risks and other costs in taking advantage of new opportunities was indispensable. But the existence of nondiscriminatory opportunities itself grew out of fraternal competition among the whites.

The restrictive combinations of planters to hold down wages and tenants' shares in agriculture provide a clear example. These combinations generally failed because many individual planters discovered that they could not attract laborers unless they offered greater compensation than that agreed upon by the cartel. An individual planter could choose to remain true to the agreement, which entailed a sacrifice of wealth because of his inability to cultivate all his available land, or to violate the agreement, which entailed bidding up the wage or tenant share of the black laborer. If he refused to sacrifice a potential gain in wealth and chose the latter alternative, his ability to act accordingly was constrained only by the enforcement powers of the planters' organization. The cartel had to have means both to detect violations and to coerce recalcitrant members into acting in accordance with the agreement. In both respects these combinations were ill equipped. Detection of violations was often impossible, and the organizations could usually do little more than appeal to the social importance of solidarity to enforce an individual planter's compliance. They had no legal power of enforcement. Threats and intimidation were unlikely to move a powerful planter with the ability and spirit to meet force with force and a quick resentment against his neighbors' "butting into my business." As a result, mavericks broke the solidarity of the group and set in train a pell-mell rush to attract laborers by offering them better contractual terms. Attempts to prevent the acquisition of Southern farmland by blacks or to block expansion of ghetto areas in Northern cities failed for similar reasons. In each case individual wealth maximization and adherence to a discriminatory group's objective clashed, and sooner or later discriminatory restrictions collapsed.

Clearly any analysis of these occurrences that focuses on the bargaining power of an individual black *vis-à-vis* an individual white misses the point. To reap the gains growing out of the white competition, an individual black needed no power except the ability to choose among alternative opportunities, to move from farm to farm or from job to job, from house to house in the towns. Potential mobility was central, however. That the blacks possessed this after 1865 in a way that they had not previously, made all the difference between freedom and slavery. White benevolence, needless to say, had nothing whatever to do with all this. In the abstract the whites resented the blacks' newly acquired mobility, and they attempted both legally and extralegally to suppress it. But they failed, again because individual self-serving incentives clashed with the overall objective of immobilizing the blacks. An individual planter heartily approved of immobilizing the most productive laborers on his own plantation; but he would hardly concern himself with the stability of a neighbor's labor force when his own fields lay untilled and cotton prices promised to be high. The general absence of racial discrimination in farm wage rates, rental contracts, and merchant credit terms resulted from quite selfish competition among the whites. Neither white benevolence nor black power had much to do with the attainment of these nondiscriminatory outcomes.

One must not overstate the case, however, for even within these competitive limits there remained plenty of room for racial coercion. Dishonest settlements with laborers and tenants, fraudulent accounting at the country store, and even a measure of genuine peonage all took their toll mainly from the blacks. That they did so owed something to ignorance and to the timidity inherited from slavery. But, more importantly, these problems were inextricably bound up with the blacks' inferior legal status. To sue for wages due or to challenge a storekeeper or a landlord in the courts was worse than futile. White judges and juries committed to enforcing black subordination were loath to accept the black man's word about anything when a white man disputed it; and even an instance of clearcut robbery of a black man by a white was unlikely to impress them as morally reprehensible. To appeal to the law was to seek aid in the enemy's stronghold.

Legal power or standing could be used to enforce certain discriminatory restrictions even though some whites might suffer as a result. Certain trade unions raised the price of skilled nonagricultural labor by excluding blacks from apprenticeship and employment, thus curtailing the supply of the relevant class of labor. This hurt the (white) employers of such labor, but they were typically not powerful enough to use legal force to destroy the unions or to alter their discriminatory practices. These unions could succeed because the law recognized the legitimacy of their existence and their exercise of monopoly powers in the labor market. Such cases contrast markedly with the agricultural labor markets, where discrimination in employment and wages scarcely existed. The crucial difference lay in organization. In the skilled urban trades an employer was often compelled to bargain with a block of white workers who possessed genuine monopoly power if they acted together; in agriculture an employer dealt with individual white workers without organization and often constituting a minority element in the labor market. In any context, individual attempts to extract discriminatory premiums generally failed. Real racial power required that the whites work as a unified single-minded group and such solidarity was generally attainable only where legal sanctions, either directly or indirectly, could be brought to bear against mavericks within the group.

Nowhere was this more evident than in the actions of the Southern governments, which unquestionably exerted real, unchallenged discriminatory power. In the operation of the public school systems and in the provision of legal and police protection for personal and property rights, discrimination was gross and deliberate. Indeed, the whole panoply of segregation ordinances constituted a well-enforced exclusion of blacks from an array of consumption opportunities on racial grounds alone; and these restrictions had the full weight of the law and its enforcement machinery to support them. Competitive pressures were either altogether lacking or forcefully suppressed in these areas of public discrimination. The private employer might face the prospect of foregone wealth if he discriminated in the conditions of employment he offered. But the public school administrator, the sheriff, the judge – what had they to lose from discriminatory conduct of their offices? Indeed, a greater threat to these public officials arose from the appearance of providing their services equally to both races.

To be labeled a "nigger lover," no matter how unjustly, dealt a damning blow to anyone seeking public office in the post-Reconstruction South. And although the charge was occasionally leveled, it was rarely deserved.

In sum, the white man who wished to indulge successfully his taste for discrimination was well advised to join together with his fellows of like persuasion. Only as a group would they possess the power to resist competitive forces. Where individual employers or workers attempted to extract discriminatory premiums in the market place, their efforts generally met with failure. A unified group, especially if it possessed some legally enforceable sanctions against recalcitrant members, stood a much better chance to gain from discrimination.[13] And finally, that strongest and most forceful group of all, the occupants of public office, met with little or no resistance in discriminating against blacks. Free from competitive counterpressures and strongly equipped to enforce compliance, public officials could discriminate pretty much as their pleasure or caprice might dictate. Under these circumstances it was a definite blessing for the blacks that the governments of the post-bellum South were still quite limited in the range of functions to which they attended. Such salvation as the black man found, he found in the private sector.

Summary: The nature of black economic history, 1865–1914

The starting point for the economic progress of the free black population was extremely low: largely illiterate and relatively unskilled, possessing little wealth, and earning incomes not far above subsistence, the blacks of 1865 faced an almost impossible task in their attempts to catch up with the whites economically. Certainly, even under the most favorable circumstances, a half century would not have been long enough for them to close the gap. But the circumstances they confronted were far from favorable; for the whites, hoping to preserve the substance of slavery, deliberately undertook to obstruct black economic progress in various ways.

Central to these efforts was the control of politics, and the Southern whites struggled relentlessly, using every device at their command, to regain political control of their states. When they did achieve political supremacy they quickly proceeded to exclude the blacks from effective participation in political affairs. Without political power the blacks could not influence the allocation of public resources. Discrimination by white public school administrators seriously retarded the acquisition of literacy and training by blacks. Even more importantly, discrimination by public officials, especially the legal authorities, placed the personal and property rights of the blacks in serious jeopardy. From dishonest settlements with tenants, through segregation ordinances of all kinds, to literally thousands of unimpeded and unpunished lynchings, the inferior legal status of the blacks took its toll. Though far less pervasively than in the public sector, discrimination also occurred in the marketplace. To be effective this discrimination required group action; individual attempts to extract discriminatory gains generally foundered on the rock of individual wealth-seeking behavior. Really effective discrimination, even by groups, required legal sanction or support, as in the cases of trade union discrimination or peonage restrictions. The fountainhead of effective discrimination, then, whether public or private, lay in the governments of the Southern states, counties, and cities, where the racial monopoly of politics allowed the hostile whites to treat the blacks as they pleased.

These conditions had direct and indirect effects on black opportunities and incentives to make the investments that would raise their incomes and levels of living. Directly, certain opportunities were simply ruled out by segregation ordinances and other legal barriers; indirectly, many opportunities became unattractive in view of the higher risks surrounding black investments. Never was it more evident that property is only as substantial as the property rights associated with it and that these in turn depend on the protection afforded or denied by governmental authorities. Many blacks were discouraged from investing in migration, education, training, and tangible property by the racial constraints created or sanctioned by Southern governments. Others made the investments only to discover that the expected returns could not be realized, and they gave up in despair. But still others, a legion of them, persevered in the struggle, and their efforts were responsible for the achievment of major gains. Despite all the difficulties and discouragements of a low starting point and a host of discriminatory obstacles, blacks managed to raise their incomes per capita substantially, perhaps as much as threefold during the first half century of freedom. Still relatively poor in 1914, they had much to complain of and to protest against, but they had, too, much cause for honest pride. With Frederick Douglass, they could "marvel that they have, under the circumstances, done so well."

Technical appendix

This appendix presents analytical materials too technical for inclusion in the text. These provide derivations, proofs, and econometric results that explain, support, or supplement conclusions asserted in the text.

1. The effect of urbanization on black fertility

A. This section presents the calculations that underlie the statements made in Chapter 2 concerning the strength of the association between changes in black fertility and urbanization.

In 1910, when data were compiled separately for places of 25,000 or more, the child–woman ratio in those places was about 40 percent as large as the ratio in smaller places (including the purely rural population). Suppose the urban–rural differential had remained constant in this proportion throughout the period 1880–1910.[1] Then one can treat the 1880 aggregate child–woman ratio of 760 as a weighted average of the urban and rural ratios as follows (where P_r and P_u are the proportions of the population in rural and urban places, F_r and F_u are the child–woman ratios in rural and urban places, and "urban" means places of 25,000 or more):

$$760 = P_r F_r + P_u F_u$$
$$= P_r F_r + P_u(0.4 F_r)$$

Census data for 1880 supply values for P_r and P_u that reduce the equation to a single unknown:

$$760 = 0.903 F_r + (0.097)(0.4 F_r)$$
$$= 0.942 F_r$$

Hence the solutions, $F_r = 807$ and $F_u = 323$.

Making use of these estimates and the available census data, one can calculate the separate effects of urbanization and other factors on changes in the aggregate child–woman ratio. If the urban and rural child–woman ratios had remained fixed at their estimated 1880 levels while the urban–rural distribution of the population changed, then the aggregate ratio in 1910 would have been:

$$F = P_r F_r + P_u F_u = (0.816)(807) + (0.184)(323) = 718$$

The indicated decline in the aggregate ratio (760 − 718 = 42) comes to only about 17 percent of the actual decline (760 − 519 = 241). On the other hand, if the urban–rural distribution of the population had remained fixed at the 1880 level while the urban and rural child–woman ratios fell to the observed levels of 1910, then the aggregate ratio in 1910 would have been:

$$F = P_r F_r + P_u F_u = (0.903)(596) + (0.097)(239) = 561$$

In this calculation the indicated decline in the aggregate child–woman ratio (760 − 561 = 199) comes to 83 percent of the actual decline.

Clearly the redistribution of black population in favor of the urban areas can explain only a relatively small part of the observed decline in the aggregate child–woman ratio. A different definition of "urban" might result in a slightly larger attribution of influence to urbanization. But, in any case, the bulk of the decline in black fertility must be ascribed to influences other than urbanization.

B. In this section I consider a statistical finding reported by Edward Meeker in an unpublished appendix to his paper on black health trends.[2] This finding suggests that urbanization played a significant role in the decline of black fertility but raises some difficult problems of interpretation.

Meeker's regression equation relates black child–woman ratios to corresponding levels of urbanization and illiteracy. The equation is fitted to cross-sectional data for 1900, with observations for the 32 states having at least 1,000 blacks aged 0–5 and at least half of the nonwhite population black; "urban" here means places of at least 2,500. The fitted equation is as follows, where F is the child–woman ratio, U is percent urban, I is percent illiterate, and standard errors appear in parentheses:

$$\ln F = 5.886 - 0.223 \ln U + 0.298 \ln I \qquad N = 32$$
$$\quad\;\; (0.055) \qquad\;\; (0.077) \qquad\;\; R^2 = 0.912$$

Within the functional form estimated, both urbanization and illiteracy are statistically significant at conventional test levels. The coefficients indicate that a given proportionate change in illiteracy had a slightly greater effect than a change of the same proportion in urbanization. The equation statistically explains over nine-tenths of the variance in the (transformed) dependent variable.

To employ this result to explain changes in black fertility over time, one must assume that the cross-sectional relation estimated for 1900 adequately describes the relation among variables changing over time and that the relation remained stable over the time period to which it is applied. As a test of the equation's predictive power with time-series data, one can use it to predict the decline in the aggregate black child–woman ratio after 1880. Between 1880 and 1910 the black urbanization ratio increased by 91 percent (from 0.143 to 0.273); the illiteracy ratio fell by 56 percent (from 0.700 to 0.305). Meeker's equation implies that the child–woman ratio should have fallen by about 37 percent under these circumstances. In fact, as shown above, it fell by about 32 percent. Thus the cross-sectional relation overestimates somewhat the decline in the child–woman ratio after 1880, but its prediction is still in the neighborhood of the truth.

Of the total 37 percent decline predicted by Meeker's equation, somewhat more than half (a decline of over 20 percent) is ascribable to urbanization. Does this result contradict the conclusion reached in the previous section, which ascribes a much smaller part of the decline to urbanization? Not necessarily. First, one may well question whether a cross-sectional relation for 1900, no matter how tightly it fits the cross-sectional data, adequately describes the relation among variables changing over time between 1880 and 1910. Second, even if an application of the cross-sectional relation to time-series data is considered warranted, one may question the completeness of the specification. Surely no one – and Meeker concurs in this – believes that black fertility depended solely on the levels of urbanization and illiteracy. Indeed, Meeker's own paper experiments with an equation that includes two other variables (proxies for black incomes and child death rates). These additional variables proved statistically insignificant and were dropped. Notably, dropping them raises the coefficient of the urbanization variable from −0.162 to the −0.223 figure reported above, a 38 percent increase in absolute value.

The purpose of mentioning this is not to quarrel with Meeker's dropping the specific proxy variables with which he experimented – indeed, those proxies probably contained more noise than information – but rather to make a more general point: to the extent that specification error affects the equation, the coefficients of the included variables are biased.[3] For example, if black fertility truly depended on income, the relation being negative, and if income and urbanization were positively correlated, as indeed they were, then to some extent the true explanatory power of the (left-out) income variable would increase the absolute value of the regression coefficient of the (included) urbanization variable. In this event the explanatory power of urbanization would be overestimated by the regression coefficient in the incomplete specification.

This discussion is not meant to disparage Meeker's efforts to explain black fertility differentials in a rigorous manner. His work is clearly moving in the right direction. But a satisfactory explanation of the fertility decline after 1880 will require a more complete specification. Only within the context of such a specification will one be able to attach a reliable weight to the influence of urbanization. The main difficulty in this endeavor is the lack of appropriate data. But clever econometricians have often solved that problem in the past; one hopes they will do so again in the future.

2. Race, tenure, and resource allocation in Southern agriculture

This part of the appendix presents and assesses some recent econometric work by the author dealing with racial differences in prevailing forms of farm rental contracts and in farm size, research which forms the basis for several conclusions asserted in Chapter 4.

A. This section presents regression results of a cross-sectional analysis of 11 Southern states in 1910. The question is: what determined how much of the acreage cultivated by full tenants (i.e., farmers who rent all the land they cultivate) was rented for shares? Elsewhere I have developed a model to answer this question.[4] A principal implication of the model is that share renting and yield risk are directly associated, other things being the same.

To test this hypothesis, leaving open the possibility of racial differences, several regression equations were estimated. The variables are defined as follows: M, percentage of acreage rented for shares in all acreage rented by full tenants; X_1, coefficient of variation in crop yield, defined as the ratio of the standard deviation to the mean; X_2, proportional variance in crop yield, defined as the ratio of the variance to the mean;[5] B, a dummy variable to distinguish observations according to race, equal to unity when the observation applies to blacks, zero when it applies to whites. The estimated equations are as follows, with standard errors in parentheses:

(1) Corn acreage: $\quad M = 47.83 + \underset{(54.59)}{95.02X_1} - \underset{(7.11)}{8.57B} \qquad N = 22 \\ R^2 = 0.19$

(2) Corn acreage: $\quad M = 55.47 + \underset{(5.66)}{14.60X_2} - \underset{(6.65)}{8.57B} \qquad N = 22 \\ R^2 = 0.29$

(3) Cotton acreage: $\quad M = 26.91 + \underset{(73.45)}{229.56X_1} - \underset{(6.31)}{6.71B} \qquad N = 22 \\ R^2 = 0.36$

(4) Cotton acreage: $\quad M = 47.67 + \underset{(0.97)}{2.95X_2} - \underset{(6.35)}{6.71B} \qquad N = 22 \\ R^2 = 0.35$

The estimated regression equations indicate that the relative prevalence of share-rent tenancy was indeed associated with the yield risk.

In equations (1) and (2) the risk coefficients differ significantly from zero at the 0.05 level, in equations (3) and (4) at the 0.01 level, for one-tailed tests. Evidently the relation is somewhat stronger for cotton than for corn crops. The coefficients of the race variable are uniformly negative, which implies that black tenants farmed a smaller proportion of their acreage under share contracts than did white tenants facing similar risk; however, these coefficients are too small relative to their standard errors to pass significance tests at conventional levels of confidence. In general, therefore, the data indicate that the form of the rental contract depended on the risk surrounding production but was not systematically associated with the race of the farmer. Although the data are generally consistent with the maintained hypothesis, the coefficients of determination are not so large that the question of what determined the form of the rental contract can be considered settled. But this hypothesis is very simple and the tests crude.[6] It would appear that the relation between yield risk and share tenancy deserves further investigation. Because of the possibility of aggregation biases in relations fitted to the cross section of states, further tests of the hypothesis using cross sections of counties might be particularly revealing.

B. This section presents regression results of a cross-sectional analysis of 72 counties of the Georgia cotton belt in 1900. The question is: did blacks and whites obtain systematically different forms of land rental contract? Elsewhere I have adduced evidence that risk conditions varied little within this area; and I have provided econometric tests of the hypothesis that geographic differences in the prevailing forms of rental contract within this area depended on the average size of the landholding unit.[7] Given that risk differences were negligible among the sample counties of the Georgia cotton belt, one can directly test for the existence of racial differences in contractual forms. The use of county data reduces the potential aggregation bias inherent in an analysis of state data, a danger noted in the previous section.

To test the hypothesis that systematic racial differences in the contractual mix were significant, the following regression equation was estimated. The variables are M_w and M_b, the percentage of farm rental contracts in the share-rent form for whites and blacks respectively. The standard error of the regression slope appears in parentheses.[8]

$$(5) \quad M_w = -10.47 + 0.964 M_b \qquad N = 72$$
$$(0.053) \qquad R^2 = 0.83$$

Notably, the rental mix for black tenants and the rental mix for white tenants were highly correlated across the counties of the cotton belt: in the predominantly white areas *both* black and white tenants tended to obtain share-rent contracts; in the predominantly black areas *both* black and white tenants tended to obtain fixed-rent contracts. Given the way tenants of the two races were distributed across counties with different rental mixes, the result for the aggregate of 72 cotton-belt counties was, oddly enough, racial equality: both black and white tenants operated 51 percent of their farms under share contracts. (The numbers involved were substantial, 18,168 of 35,891 white tenants and 28,290 of 55,364 black tenants farming under share-rent contracts.)

What do these facts imply about racial discrimination? On the one hand the high correlation ($r = 0.91$) of the rental mix for blacks and whites across counties suggests that discrimination did not occur. Yet it is also true that in a given county black tenants were likely to be a little more concentrated in share-rent contracts than were whites. (Equation (5) indicates an average difference of about 10.5 percentage points in the two mixes.) However, the within-county differences were small relative to the among-county variation. Moreover, the within-county differences may be associated only spuriously with race, the "true" relation arising from differences in wealth or some other unobservable variable correlated with race. In sum, these data provide no compelling support for the hypothesis that landlords systematically contracted with black tenants differently than with white tenants.

C. This section presents regression results of a cross-sectional analysis of nine Southern states in 1910. The question is: after the data are adjusted to control for the degree of land improvement, the crop mix, and the tenure status of the farm operator, do they still indicate that black farmers operated smaller farms than whites? It must be emphasized that the statistical results reported below do not pretend to test a *theory of farm size*. That task is beyond the scope of the present inquiry. In any event such a test, while interesting and important for some purposes, is unnecessary if the objective is merely to determine a fact: whether "similar" blacks and whites cultivated farms of approximately equal size.

My procedure is to estimate a multiple regression equation in which the dependent variable, A, is total acreage per farmer and the "explanatory" variables are as follows: I, the percentage of the total acreage improved; C, the percentage of the improved acreage devoted to cotton cultivation; F, a dummy variable distinguishing observations on fixed-rent tenants; S, a dummy variable distinguishing share-rent tenants; and B, a dummy variable distinguishing black farm operators. With observations on two races and three tenure classes in each of nine states, there are 54 observations in all.[9] The estimated equation is as follows:

$$(6) \quad \ln A = 7.3145 - 0.691 \ln I - 0.0014 \ln C - 0.275\, F - 0.507\, S$$
$$ (0.186) \qquad (0.0454) \qquad (0.102) \qquad (0.124)$$
$$- 0.324\, B \qquad R^2 = 0.905$$
$$(0.087) \qquad\; N = 54$$

Equation (6) statistically explains over 90 percent of the variance in (logarithmically transformed) farm size. Except for C, the concentration on cotton, every "explanatory" variable has a coefficient that differs significantly from zero at the 0.01 level. All the signs are negative. Apparently, the more improved the farm, the smaller was its total acreage, regardless of the race of the farmer or the form of his tenure. Also, tenant farms tended to be smaller than owner-operated farms, regardless of the farmer's race or the extent of the farm's improvement. Finally, black farmers tended to operate smaller farms than whites, quite apart from differences associated with the form of tenure or the extent of farm improvement.

That black farmers operated smaller farms than whites demands an explanation. The most plausible explanations appear to be that black farmers were less productive than the whites, perhaps because of relative ill-health, illiteracy, and inexperience, and that racial discrimination worked to hold down black farm size. The two explanations are not, of course, mutually exclusive, and indeed the most plausible explanation of all would seem to be a combination of them to allow for interrelations – or "vicious circles" – connecting the blacks' real productivity with racial discrimination. Some whites refused to sell land to blacks at any price, which raised the search costs of black buyers and might conceivably have held down the average farm size of black owners. More generally, the racial discrimination of Southern police and law courts weakened the private property rights of blacks and discouraged them from accumulating capital, particularly in the tangible, immobile form of land. But these considerations, if they have any force at all, apply only to owner operators. It is not clear that racially prejudiced landlords could get any satisfaction from holding the size of their tenants' plots below the economically optimal level, while it is evident that doing so would entail a sacrifice of wealth. Until some estimate of the relative productivity of black farmers is obtained, the impact of direct racial discrimination cannot be assessed with much confidence.

It should be emphasized, however, that while race might have had some direct effect, the maximum magnitude of this effect was small by comparison with that of the other effects already taken into account.

To see these magnitudes one can employ equation (6). By setting every variable in that equation equal to its mean value – except B, which takes a value of zero – one can determine that the "mean adjusted farm size" of whites was about 72 acres. Then, performing the calculation with B set equal to unity, one obtains the mean adjusted farm size of blacks, about 52 acres. The racial difference in mean adjusted farm size is 20 acres. This result may be contrasted with the unadjusted farm size figures for these nine states, which indicate a racial difference of 59 acres (102 acres for whites, 43 acres for blacks). In brief, controlling for differences in farm improvement and tenure form reduces by about two-thirds the racial difference in farm size. Of course, to the extent that the farmer's race was related to the form of his tenure or to the extent of the improvement in his farm, race would exert also an indirect effect on the determination of farm size. Such indirect racial influences remain to be tested by further research, but one thing seems clear. That blacks were disproportionately tenants rather than owners is due in some part to their relative lack of wealth. And their general poverty is surely attributable to their having been slaves until 45 years earlier. Therefore, in all probability, slavery and the propertyless emancipation account for a substantial part of the racial difference in farm size as late as 1910.[10]

3. Black participation in the merchant class

This part of the appendix presents regression results of cross-sectional analyses of some American states in 1890, 1900, and 1910. The questions are: what were the relations between the participation rate of the male labor force in merchandizing and (a) the proportion of the group population urbanized and (b) the distribution of the group population between the North and the South? Did these relations differ among blacks, immigrant whites, and native whites? Elsewhere I have developed the hypothesis that the merchant participation rate was directly related to the proportion of the population urbanized. Whether the interregional distribution would affect the merchant participation rate cannot be determined *a priori*, but tests can leave open the possibility of interregional differences. Differences among ethnic groups that remain after the imposition of controls for their demographic differences can also be identified and measured by the same test procedure.[11]

Multiple regression analysis provides a systematic means of performing these tests. The dependent variable is, of course, the merchant participation rate (merchants per 1,000 gainfully occupied males), here denoted by M. The "explanatory" variables are: the percentage of the group urbanized, U, where "urban place" is defined conventionally as an incorporated place of 2,500 or more; a regional dummy variable, S, defined as equal to unity for Southern states, zero otherwise; a group dummy variable, B, defined as equal to unity for blacks, zero otherwise; and another group dummy variable, F, defined as equal to unity for foreign-born whites, zero otherwise.[12] The groups analyzed are blacks, native whites, and foreign-born whites. Observations include every state in which each group had at least 100 retail dealers: 20 states in 1890 and 1900, 24 states in 1910, including the bulk of the national population.

The following equations are the ordinary-least-squares estimates for the pooled cross-sectional data for each of the three census years. Standard errors of the coefficients appear in parentheses.

$$M = -10.92 + 0.7844U + 45.34S - 38.33B + 36.02F \qquad (1890)$$
$$(0.3000) \quad (13.45) \quad (10.46) \quad (14.62)$$
$$N = 60, \quad SEE = 32.52, \quad R^2 = 0.65$$

$$M = -32.15 + 0.9061U + 57.34S - 35.06B + 33.50F \qquad (1900)$$
$$(0.2923) \quad (13.97) \quad (9.99) \quad (13.85)$$
$$N = 60, \quad SEE = 30.97, \quad R^2 = 0.67$$

$$M = -21.78 + 0.8037U + 55.20S - 37.86B + 47.64F \qquad (1910)$$
$$(0.2366) \quad (11.05) \quad (10.59) \quad (12.35)$$
$$N = 72, \quad SEE = 35.70, \quad R^2 = 0.65$$

The regression equations are remarkably similar. Every slope coefficient is highly significant in every equation. About two-thirds of the variance in merchant participation rates is accounted for by the "explanatory" variables employed.

From the regression analysis the following conclusions emerge. First, urbanization made a substantial contribution toward raising the participation rate: 10 percentage points more urbanization was associated on the average with 8–9 more merchants per 1,000 men gainfully occupied. Second, a Southern location was associated with substantially greater participation rates. Third, being black hurt the chances of an aspiring merchant, while being foreign born and white increased the odds that a man would keep a store. These conclusions are all subject, of course, to the *ceteris paribus* proviso.

For immigrants, entry into the merchant class was an important avenue of assimilation into the mainstream of opportunities for gain in the American economy of the late nineteenth and early twentieth centuries. For blacks, on the other hand, business opportunities played a relatively trivial role. While a host of immigrants exploited the opportunities and then passed successfully out of a group-centered business community, the blacks' hope for a "group economy," as Du Bois called it, went largely unrealized. Though these conclusions have been asserted before, quantitative evidence allows a more precise appraisal of just how great were the differences between the black and immigrant experiences.

To see the magnitude of this group differential, one can employ the regression equations presented above. For present purposes the equation for 1910 will serve; the results would be similar if other dates were considered. First, compute a hypothetical mean participation rate for the foreign-born whites by substituting into the equation the mean values of U and S for the overall sample, setting $B = 0$ and $F = 1$. The resulting participation rate is 95.38. Then, compute a corresponding estimate for blacks by setting $B = 1$ and $F = 0$. The resulting participation rate is 9.88. In brief, even if the blacks and the foreign born had been characterized by the same mean urban-regional values, their participation rates in the merchant class would have differed by a factor of 10.

4. Black income: Relative levels and growth

A. This section proves a proposition asserted in Chapter 5: in estimating average black income per capita in the agricultural sector, weighting by a lower figure for laborers results in a lower estimate of income per capita, even though this procedure involves giving relatively more weight to the (higher income) farm operators. This is true because the (positive) effect on the estimated average income of labor force participants is more than offset by the (negative) effect on the implicit participation of the agricultural population in the labor force.

To proceed, define the variables as follows, where it is understood that all apply to the agricultural sector: Y is income; P is population; L is labor force participants; and subscripts w and f denote wage laborers and farm operators respectively. By definition, total income is the product of labor force participants times their average income:

$$(7) \quad Y = L \left(\frac{Y}{L} \right)$$

By assumption, the average income is a weighted average of the average incomes of wage laborers and farm operators:

$$(8) \quad \left(\frac{Y}{L} \right) = \left(\frac{L_w}{L} \right) \left(\frac{Y_w}{L_w} \right) + \left(\frac{L_f}{L} \right) \left(\frac{Y_f}{L_f} \right)$$

Substitution of (8) into (7) and division of both sides by P yield an expression for income per capita in the agricultural sector:

$$\frac{Y}{P} = \frac{1}{P} \left[\left(\frac{L_w Y_w}{L_w} \right) + \left(\frac{L_f Y_f}{L_f} \right) \right]$$

Setting $Y/P = y$, $Y_w/L_w = y_w$, and $Y_f/L_f = y_f$, this becomes:

$$y = \frac{1}{P}\,(L_w\,y_w + L_f\,y_f)$$

From this expression one can clearly see that if all variables except L_w are fixed, then a lower estimate of L_w necessarily results in a lower estimate of y, i.e., $\delta y/\delta L_w > 0$. The estimate of agricultural income per capita is necessarily reduced by a "conservative" estimate of the number of farm laborers.

B. This section presents a crude reconciliation of the black income estimates of Chapter 5 with Robert Gallman's estimates of income in the overall economy. This reveals the internal consistency – and hence the plausibility – of statements in the text concerning relative levels and rates of growth of black income per capita in the late nineteenth century.

As a starting point one requires an estimate of income per capita for the overall economy *circa* 1867–68. Given the existing data, this figure must be interpolated. Gallman's estimates of GNP – which I have reexpressed in approximate 1900 purchasing power, using Gallman's own price index – indicate that GNP was $3.85 billion in 1859 and averaged $6.02 billion during the period 1869–78.[13] To be comparable with my estimates of black income per capita, these figures must be reduced from GNP to National Income and divided by population. I assume, in view of data from John Kendrick's study,[14] that National Income was approximately 90 percent of GNP. The total income figures are then $3.47 billion in 1859 and $5.42 billion on average during 1869–78. Because of the depressing effects of the war on national output, growth was probably considerably more rapid during the postwar period than during the years 1859–65. My guess is that total national income in 1867–68 was approximately $4.2 billion. With a total population of approximately 38 million, the implied income per capita is about $111 (in approximate 1900 purchasing power).

As total income per capita is a weighted average of its black and white components, the weights being known, one can use this estimate in conjunction with my estimate of black income per capita to determine the implied level of white income per capita. Let y be income per capita, P be population, and subscripts w and b denote white and black respectively. By definition,

$$(9)\quad y = \left(\frac{P_w}{P}\right) y_w + \left(\frac{P_b}{P}\right) y_b$$

Using census population data, Gallman's total income figure (as adjusted above), and my estimate of black income per capita derived in Chapter 5, this equation becomes

$$\$111 = 0.86y_w + (0.14)(\$30)$$

which implies $y_w = \$124$.

These estimates imply that black income per capita in 1867–68 was approximately 24 percent of the corresponding white level. This forms a basis for the assumption in Chapter 6 that the black income level in the late 1860s was about one-fourth of the white level.

My intermediate estimate of black income per capita *circa* 1900 is about $73. In conjunction with the $30 estimate for 1867–68, this implies an average rate of growth of approximately 2.7 percent annually during the last third of the nineteenth century. The $73 estimate also implies that the white income level in 1900 was about $208, as revealed by the following solution of equation (9), again employing adjusted estimates by Gallman:

$$\$192 = 0.88y_w + (0.12)(\$73)$$

Hence

$$y_w = \$208$$

The implied average rate of growth of white income per capita between 1867–68 and 1900 is about 2.0 percent annually, which is plausible. These estimates also imply that relative black income increased considerably over this period, reaching about 35 percent in 1900. This too seems plausible.

I must caution that further research may well modify these crude estimates substantially. But, in any event, they demonstrate the internal consistency – and hence the plausibility – of the black income estimates in Chapter 5 with income estimates for the overall economy. The calculations are crude and the underlying data base rather flimsy. Nevertheless, I believe the main conclusions are quite robust. The calculations were deliberately designed to yield conservative estimates of the growth in black income per capita between 1867–68 and 1900. I shall be quite surprised if more elaborate estimates overturn the conclusion that black incomes grew faster than white incomes during the last third of the nineteenth century.

Notes

Throughout these notes, references with two dates indicate first, the date of the publication cited and, second, in brackets, the original date of publication. Thus, in the reference to Du Bois' *Dusk of Dawn* below, the page cited is from the 1968 reprint, but the book originally appeared in 1940. For full publication details, see the Select bibliography, Select list of full titles.

"RACE" AND "RACIAL DISCRIMINATION": A NOTE ON USAGE

1 Winthrop D. Jordan, *White Over Black: American Attitudes toward the Negro, 1550–1812* (Chapel Hill, 1968), p. 584.

2 W. E. B. Du Bois, *Dusk of Dawn: An Essay toward an Autobiography of a Race Concept* (New York, 1968 [1940]), p. 153. Gilbert Thomas Stephenson (*Race Distinctions in American Law* [New York, 1910], p. 19) observed that "in practice one is a Negro or is classed with that race if he has the least visible trace of Negro blood in his veins, or even if it is known that there was Negro blood in any one of his progenitors." For an almost identical statement, see Wilford H. Smith, "The Negro and the Law," in Booker T. Washington and others, *The Negro Problem* (New York, 1969 [1903]), p. 133.

CHAPTER 1. APPROACHING THE FACTS

1 Should the preceding sketch be considered too extravagantly fictitious, compare the actual history of any group of European immigrants. See my "Race, Skills, and Earnings: American Immigrants in 1909," *Journal of Economic History* 31 (June 1971): 420–428.

2 For an outline of the economic theory that underlies this hypothetical sketch, with many applications to American economic history, see my *Transformation of the American Economy, 1865–1914: An Essay in Interpretation* (New York, 1971), pp. 6–17 and *passim*.

3 Kenneth M. Stampp, *The Peculiar Institution: Slavery in the Ante-Bellum South* (New York, 1956), pp. 423–425. The guilty consciences of the whites and their attempts to rationalize racial discrimination form a central theme in Gunnar Myrdal's classic work, *An American Dilemma: The Negro Problem and Modern Democracy* (New York, 1944). Historians disagree about the direction of causality in the association between slavery and racial prejudice. For discussions of this complex problem, see George M. Fred-

rickson, "Toward a Social Interpretation of the Development of American Racism," in Nathan I. Huggins, Martin Kilson, and Daniel M. Fox, eds., *Key Issues in the Afro-American Experience* (New York, 1971), I, pp. 240–254; and Winthrop D. Jordan, *White Over Black: American Attitudes toward the Negro, 1550–1812* (Chapel Hill, 1968), pp. 44–98. W. E. B. Du Bois, whose opinions always merit consideration by students of black history, was quite unequivocal on this issue: "the income-bearing value of race prejudice was the cause and not the result of theories of race inferiority; . . . particularly in the United States the income of the Cotton Kingdom based on black slavery caused the passionate belief in Negro inferiority and the determination to enforce it even by arms." See Du Bois' *Dusk of Dawn: An Essay toward an Autobiography of a Race Concept* (New York, 1968 [1940]), pp. 129–130.

4 George Fitzhugh, "What's To Be Done With the Negroes?" *DeBow's Review,* New Series 1 (June 1866): 578, 579, 581.

5 *Idem,* "Negro Agrarianism," *ibid.* 5 (Feb. 1868): 136. Before the Civil War, Fitzhugh's views were rather eccentric, being proslavery but not essentially racist. His later views, as represented in the passages quoted here, however, place him squarely within the dominant stream of white racial beliefs.

6 Gary S. Becker, *The Economics of Discrimination,* 2nd ed. (Chicago, 1971), *passim.*

7 W. E. B. Du Bois stated this point very clearly as early as 1899: "one of the great postulates of the science of economics – that men will seek their economic advantage – is in this case untrue, because in many cases men will not do this if it involves association, even in a casual and business way, with Negroes. And this fact must be taken account of in all judgments as to the Negro's economic progress." See Du Bois' *Philadelphia Negro: A Social Study* (New York, 1967 [1899]), p. 146.

8 Becker, *Economics of Discrimination,* p. 8.

9 See my articles: "Did Southern Farmers Discriminate?" *Agricultural History* 46 (April 1972): 325–328; "Race, Tenure, and Resource Allocation in Southern Agriculture, 1910," *Journal of Economic History* 33 (March 1973): 149–169; and "Patterns of Farm Rental in the Georgia Cotton Belt, 1880–1900," *ibid.* 34 (June 1974): 468–482.

10 *Senate Executive Documents,* 39th Congress, 1st Session, No. 2, p. 81.

11 Becker, *Economics of Discrimination,* pp. 7–8.

12 Lewis Cecil Gray, "Southern Agriculture, Plantation System, and the Negro Problem," *Annals of the American Academy of Political and Social Science* 40 (March 1912): 97. See also Lawrence J. Friedman, *The White Savage: Racial Fantasies in the Postbellum South* (Englewood Cliffs, N.J., 1970), *passim;* and Bertram Wilbur Doyle, *The Etiquette of Race Relations in the South: A Study in Social Control* (New York, 1971 [1937]), pp. 109–159.

13 If location is an attribute of consumption, then all forced segregation is inherently discriminatory. As the U.S. Supreme Court declared in its famous 1954 decision on school segregation, "separate but equal" is a self-contradictory prescription.

14 For a general discussion of the greater ease of discrimination in the public sector than in the market, see Milton Friedman, *Capitalism and Freedom* (Chicago, 1962), p. 109–118.

15 The importance of the blacks' being easily identified by white discriminators is emphasized, perhaps overemphasized, by Roger L. Ransom and Richard Sutch, "The Ex-Slave in the Post-Bellum South: A Study of the Economic Impact of Racism in a Market Environment," *Journal of Economic History* 33 (March 1973): 131–148. See also the critical remarks by Gavin Wright, "Comment on Papers by Reid, Ransom and Sutch, and Higgs," *ibid.*, p. 172.

16 The net present value, *P*, is given by the equation:

$$P = (R_0 - C_0)/(1 + i)^0 + (R_1 - C_1)/(1 + i)^1 + \ldots + (R_n - C_n)/(1 + i)^n$$

where R denotes returns, C denotes costs, i is the rate of interest, and subscripts indicate the number of periods elapsing before the values accrue.

CHAPTER 2. THE PEOPLE

1 Postwar conditions are vividly documented in the reports of the assistant commissioners of the Freedmen's Bureau. See *Senate Executive Documents,* 39th Congress, 1st Session, No. 27, *passim.*

2 Quoted in Vernon Lane Wharton, *The Negro in Mississippi, 1865–1890* (New York, 1965 [1947]), p. 54.

3 Quoted in John Richard Dennett, *The South As It Is, 1865–1866,* ed. Henry M. Christman (New York, 1967 [originally published in *Nation,* 1865–1866]), p. 15.

4 U.S. Bureau of the Census, *Negro Population, 1790–1915* (Washington, 1918), pp. 24–29. The census officials made their estimates by assuming that the black population of the Southern states in 1870 was the geometric mean of the reported figures for 1860 and 1880.

5 Francis A. Walker, "The Colored Race in the United States," *Forum* 11 (July 1891): 501–509; Frederick L. Hoffman, "Race Traits and Tendencies of the American Negro," American Economic Association *Publications* 11 (Aug. 1896): 1–32. For a similar but more qualified view a decade later, see Walter F. Willcox, "The Probable Increase of the Negro Race in the United States," *Quarterly Journal of Economics* 19 (Aug. 1905): 545–572. Actually, belief in the inevitable extinction of the blacks persisted within the medical profession and within certain "scientific" circles throughout the postbellum era. For discussions of this curious aberration in intellectual history, see John S. Haller, Jr., "Race, Mortality, and Life Insurance: Negro Vital Statistics in the Late Nineteenth Century," *Journal of the History of Medicine and Allied Sciences* 25 (July 1970): 247–261; and George M. Fredrickson, *The Black Image in the White Mind: The Debate on Afro-American Character and Destiny, 1817–1914* (New York, 1972), pp. 228–258.

6 U.S. Bureau of the Census, *Negro Population, 1790–1915,* p. 286.

7 Reynolds Farley, *Growth of the Black Population: A Study of Demo-*

graphic Trends (Chicago, 1970), p. 56. See also Ansley J. Coale and Nor-fleet W. Rives, Jr., "A Statistical Reconstruction of the Black Population of the United States, 1880–1970: Estimates of True Numbers by Age and Sex, Birth Rates, and Total Fertility," *Population Index* 39 (1973): 23–31.

8 For more on the economics of fertility, see Gary S. Becker, "An Economic Analysis of Fertility," in National Bureau of Economic Research, *Demographic and Economic Change in Developed Countries* (Princeton, N.J., 1960), pp. 209–240; Richard Easterlin, "The American Population," in Lance E. Davis and others, *American Economic Growth* (New York, 1972), pp. 158–168; Theodore Schultz, "The Value of Children: An Economic Perspective," *Journal of Political Economy* 81 (March/April 1973): S2-S13; Marc Nerlove, "Household and Economy: Toward a New Theory of Population and Economic Growth," *ibid.* 82 (March/April 1974): S200-S221; and Harvey Leibenstein, "An Interpretation of the Economic Theory of Fertility: Promising Path or Blind Alley," *Journal of Economic Literature* 12 (June 1974): 457–479.

9 For these calculations and a more detailed further discussion, see the Technical Appendix, Section 1.

10 Farley seems to favor the venereal disease hypothesis, though he offers no substantial evidence to support his conclusion. See his *Growth of the Black Population*, pp. 11–14, 40. For a thorough examination and rejection of the venereal disease hypothesis, see Joseph A. McFalls, Jr., "Impact of VD on the Fertility of the U.S. Black Population, 1880–1950," *Social Biology* 20 (March 1973): 2–19.

11 U.S. Bureau of the Census, *Negro Population, 1790–1915*, p. 302. See also S. L. N. Rao, "On Long-Term Mortality Trends in the United States, 1850–1968," *Demography* 10 (Aug. 1973): 409.

12 Jack Ericson Eblen, "New Estimates of the Vital Rates of the United States Black Population during the Nineteenth Century," *Demography* 11 (May 1974): 301–319.

13 *Ibid.*, p. 309. For evidence of unusually high mortality in the 1860s, see Whitelaw Reid, *After the War: A Tour of the Southern States, 1865–1866*, ed. C. Vann Woodward (New York, 1965 [1866]), pp. 326, 456; [Freedmen's Bureau], *Senate Executive Documents*, 39th Congress, 1st Session, No. 27, *passim;* Sidney Andrews, *The South Since the War* (Boston, 1971 [1866]), p. 368; Southerner [pseud.], "Agricultural Labor at the South," *Galaxy* 12 (Sept. 1871): 335; W. E. B. Du Bois, *Black Reconstruction in America* (New York, 1971 [1935]), pp. 142, 226; Bell Irvin Wiley, *Southern Negroes, 1861–1865* (New Haven, 1965 [1938]), pp. 202, 208, 211, 344; Willie Lee Rose, *Rehearsal for Reconstruction: The Port Royal Experiment* (New York, 1967), p. 322; and Constance McLaughlin Green, *The Secret City: A History of Race Relations in the Nation's Capital* (Princeton, N.J., 1967), pp. 64, 81–82.

14 Edward Meeker, "Mortality Trends of Southern Blacks, 1850–1910: Some Preliminary Findings," *Explorations in Economic History*, 13 (Jan. 1976): 13–42. This paper also offers some penetrating criticisms of Eblen's estimating procedures.

15 In a letter to the author, dated Oct. 7, 1974, Meeker assesses his own findings as follows: "While I do not put a lot of faith in the numbers themselves, I think that the trends are valid. . . . While my estimates for 1900
   and 1910 likely err on the down side, I think that they are not all that far
   from reality."

16 Meeker's "Mortality Trends" presents rather similar figures; his data imply a 30 percent reduction in the crude death rate between 1880 and 1910.

17 U.S. Bureau of the Census, *Negro Population, 1790–1915*, p. 314. See also
   Farley, *Growth of the Black Population*, pp. 61–62.

18 U.S. Bureau of the Census, *Negro Population, 1790–1915*, p. 314.

19 See the death registration data for these cities cited in George Edmund
   Haynes, "The Negro at Work in New York City," Columbia University,
   Studies in History, Economics and Public Law 49 (1912), pp. 34–37.

20 For documentation of the assertions made in this paragraph, see my "Mortality in Rural America, 1870–1920: Estimates and Conjectures," *Explorations in Economic History* 10 (Winter 1973): 177–195 and the sources cited
   therein. See also Edward Meeker, "The Improving Health of the United
   States, 1850–1915," *ibid.* 9 (Summer 1972): 367–368; *idem,* "Mortality
   Trends of Southern Blacks," *passim;* and Rene Dubos, *Man Adapting*
   (New Haven, 1965), pp. 365, 413, 450.

21 My "Mortality in Rural America," pp. 184–195; Meeker, "The Improving
   Health," pp. 367–368; *idem,* "Mortality Trends of Southern Blacks,"
   passim.

22 The active shifting of the black population was noticed by all close observers after the war. See, for example, Dennett, *The South As It Is, passim;* Reid, *After the War, passim;* Andrews, *The South Since the War,
   passim;* and J. T. Trowbridge, *The South: A Tour of Its Battlefields and
   Ruined Cities* (New York, 1969 [1866]), *passim.*

23 C. W. Howard, "Condition and Resources of Georgia," in U.S. Department of Agriculture, *Report of the Commissioner of Agriculture for the
   Year 1866* (Washington, 1867), pp. 573–574. In the nineteenth century,
   "emigration" meant any migratory departure, whether the destination was
   another state or another country.

24 Edward King, *The Great South: A Record of Journies* (Hartford, 1875),
   pp. 270–271, 300; Charles Nordhoff, *The Cotton States in the Spring and
   Summer of 1875* (New York, 1876), pp. 78, 104; U.S. Senate Committee on
   Education and Labor, *Report on Relations between Labor and Capital*
   (Washington, 1885), II, pp. 170–171; IV, pp. 51–52. Between 1870 and 1910
   the only Southern states with a majority of their nonwhite out-migrants
   going to non-Southern states were Virginia, West Virginia, and Kentucky.
   In the other Southern states the great bulk of the nonwhite out-migrants
   went to other Southern states. For the data on destination of migrants, see
   William Edward Vickery, *The Economics of the Negro Migration, 1900–
   1960* (unpublished Ph.D. dissertation, University of Chicago, 1969), p. 26.

25 For the age distributions of the migrants, see Hope T. Eldridge and Dorothy Swaine Thomas, *Population Redistribution and Economic Growth,
   United States, 1870–1950: III. Demographic Analyses and Interrelations*

(Philadelphia, 1964), pp. 142–143. See also R. R. Wright, Jr., "The Migration of Negroes to the North," *Annals of the American Academy of Political and Social Science* 27 (May 1906): 104–105; Gilbert Osofsky, *Harlem: The Making of a Ghetto* (New York, 1968), p. 18; and Allan H. Spear, *Black Chicago: The Making of a Negro Ghetto, 1890–1920* (Chicago, 1967), p. 11.

26 Eldridge and Thomas, *Population Redistribution,* p. 260.

27 Stanley Lebergott, *Manpower in Economic Growth: The American Record since 1800* (New York, 1964), p. 92.

28 For direct observations of blacks migrating to superior agricultural opportunities within the South, particularly to the Mississippi Delta region, see the contemporary sources cited in notes 23 and 24. See also Wharton, *The Negro in Mississippi,* pp. 106–116; George Brown Tindall, *South Carolina Negroes, 1877–1900* (Baton Rouge, 1966 [1952]), pp. 169–185; Joel Williamson, *After Slavery: The Negro in South Carolina during Reconstruction, 1861–1877* (Chapel Hill, 1965), pp. 108–111; Thomas Jackson Woofter, Jr., *Negro Migration: Changes in Rural Organization and Population of the Cotton Belt* (New York, 1969 [1920]), pp. 106–117.

29 U.S. Bureau of the Census, *Negro Population, 1790–1915,* p. 129.

30 An example is Gunnar Myrdal, *An American Dilemma: The Negro Problem and Modern Democracy* (New York, 1969 [1944]), pp. 182–201.

31 *Ibid.,* p. 193.

32 For contemporary descriptions and explanations of the exodus of 1879, see *Senate Reports,* 46th Congress, 2nd Session, No. 693, *passim.* Excerpts from this report and other related documents are reproduced in the *Journal of Negro History* 4 (Jan. 1919): 51–92. See also Carter G. Woodson, *A Century of Negro Migration* (Washington, 1918), pp. 135–143; John G. Van Deusen, "The Exodus of 1879," *Journal of Negro History* 21 (April 1936): 111–129; and Lawrence D. Rice, *The Negro in Texas, 1874–1900* (Baton Rouge, 1971), pp. 198–204. Myrdal was, of course, aware of the exodus, mentioning it in *An American Dilemma,* p. 186.

33 [Mississippi Migration Convention of 1879], "Proceedings," reprinted from the *Vicksburg Commercial Daily Advertiser,* May 5, 1879, in the *Journal of Negro History* 4 (Jan. 1919): 54. For an account of how one large planter dealt with the exodus, see the testimony of John C. Calhoun III, of Arkansas, in U.S. Senate, Committee on Education and Labor, *Report on Relations between Labor and Capital,* II, pp. 178–179.

34 Van Deusen, "The Exodus of 1879," pp. 128–129.

35 Nordhoff, *The Cotton States,* p. 105. The "emigration" to which Nordhoff was referring was the movement from Georgia to the Southwest.

36 Brinley Thomas has pointed out that "when immigration of foreign workers was in full spate the northward movement of Negroes was at a low ebb and vice versa." See the essay on "Negro Migration and the American Urban Dilemma" in his *Migration and Urban Development* (London, 1972), p. 142.

37 Note, too, that even those who did not migrate benefited, because emigra-

tion from an area reduced the supply of labor and raised the equilibrium price of labor services, other things being equal.

38 Spear, *Black Chicago*, p. 131, reaches a very similar conclusion. See also my Technical Appendix, Section 3A. That many blacks realized large gains from interregional migration after 1914 in no way contradicts the present conclusion. After 1914 the opportunities available to blacks in the North were vastly greater than they had been previously, mainly because of the great reduction in foreign immigration. See my paper on "The Boll Weevil, the Cotton Economy, and Black Migration, 1910–1930," *Agricultural History*, 50 (April 1976): 335–350.

39 Eldridge and Thomas, *Population Redistribution*, p. 218.

40 For direct evidence on the wage gains realized by blacks migrating to Northern cities, see Wright, "The Migration of Negroes to the North," p. 105; and Haynes, "The Negro at Work in New York City," pp. 27–28.

41 W. E. B. Du Bois, ed., *The Negro American Family* (Atlanta, 1908), p. 58. That urban blacks sometimes returned to the farm for temporary employment, especially during the cotton harvest, does not contradict Du Bois' statement. The proposition is that blacks who had lived in the city seldom returned to the countryside as permanent residents.

CHAPTER 3. THE PEOPLE AT WORK, 1865–1880

1 On the policies of the federal government with regard to the freedmen during Reconstruction, see W. E. B. Du Bois, *Black Reconstruction in America* (New York, 1971 [1935]), *passim;* Kenneth M. Stampp, *The Era of Reconstruction, 1865–1877* (New York, 1965), *passim;* Allen W. Trelease, *Reconstruction: The Great Experiment* (New York, 1971), *passim;* Martin Abbott, "Free Land, Free Labor, and the Freedmen's Bureau," *Agricultural History* 30 (Oct. 1956): 150–156; Christie Farnham Pope, "Southern Homesteads for Negroes," *ibid.* 44 (April 1970): 201–212; LaWanda Cox, "The Promise of Land for the Freedmen," *Mississippi Valley Historical Review* 45 (Dec. 1958): 413–440; George R. Bentley, *A History of the Freedmen's Bureau* (Philadelphia, 1955), *passim;* and William S. McFeely, *Yankee Stepfather: General O. O. Howard and the Freedmen* (New Haven, 1968), *passim.*

2 John Richard Dennett, *The South As It Is, 1865–1866,* ed. Henry M. Christman (New York, 1967 [originally published in *Nation,* 1865–1866]), p. 169; U.S. Congress, Joint Committee on Reconstruction, *Report of the Joint Committee on Reconstruction at the First Session Thirty-Ninth Congress* (Washington, 1866), Pt. IV, p. 125.

3 *Senate Executive Documents,* 39th Congress, 1st Session, No. 2, p. 16; Joint Committee on Reconstruction, *Report,* Pt. IV, p. 125. See also *Senate Executive Documents,* 39th Congress, 1st Session, No. 27, pp. 28, 164; Whitelaw Reid, *After the War: A Tour of the Southern States, 1865–1866,* ed. C. Vann Woodward (New York, 1965 [1866]), p. 344.

4 Actually, some slaves had been given the opportunity to earn extra in-

come and had responded readily to this pecuniary incentive. Robert Fogel and Stanley Engerman estimate that, on a sample of large plantations, slaves earned an average of $8.86 per capita per year in this way. See their *Time on the Cross: Evidence and Methods – A Supplement* (Boston, 1974), p. 159. One may well doubt the representativeness of this estimate; for if such paid employment was so common a feature of the slave regime, what accounts for the apparently almost universal belief of the whites in 1865 that the blacks would not work unless physically compelled? It will not do to assert that Schurz and Andrews gave biased reports, for virtually every postwar reporter told the same story.

5 Reid, *After the War*, p. 325.

6 *Senate Executive Documents*, 39th Congress, 1st Session, No. 27, pp. 78–79; *ibid.*, No. 2, pp. 73–74 (numerous atrocities in other areas of the South are described on pp. 47–105). See also John A. Carpenter, "Atrocities in the Reconstruction Period," *Journal of Negro History* 47 (Oct. 1962): 234–247. Some reports of atrocities, however, were fabrications, exaggerations, or mere rumors; see Bentley, *Freedmen's Bureau*, pp. 110–113.

7 *Senate Executive Documents*, 39th Congress, 1st Session, No. 43, p. 10.

8 Robert Somers, *The Southern States since the War, 1870–1871* (London, 1871), *passim;* Edward King, *The Great South: A Record of Journies* (Hartford, 1875), *passim;* Charles Nordhoff, *The Cotton States in the Spring and Summer of 1875* (New York, 1876), *passim.*

9 U.S. Bureau of the Census, *Negro Population, 1790–1915* (Washington, 1918), pp. 503–504; U.S. Census Office, *Report on Population of the United States at the Eleventh Census: 1890* (Washington, 1897), Pt. ii, p. cxiii. The census officials acknowledged that the labor force participation of white females was probably understated; still, a wide racial difference remains.

10 On the persistence of slavery and its forms, see *Senate Executive Documents*, 39th Congress, 1st Session, No. 2, pp. 15, 17, 23, 73, 78; *ibid.*, No. 27, pp. 83–85, 138; *ibid.*, No. 43, pp. 9–10; Joint Committee on Reconstruction, *Report*, Pt. ii, pp. 225–229; Pt. iii, p. 184; Pt. iv, pp. 50–83; and Charles Stearns, *The Black Man of the South, and the Rebels* (New York, 1969 [1872]), pp. 112–113. As late as May 19, 1865, a newspaper in Marshall, Texas, contained notices of large rewards for the return of fugitive slaves. See Bell Irvin Wiley, *Southern Negroes, 1861–1865* (New Haven, 1965 [1938]), p. 93.

11 Southerner [pseud.], "Agricultural Labor at the South," *Galaxy* 12 (Sept. 1871): 335. On the efforts of the Freedmen's Bureau to provide care for orphans, see C. W. Tebeau, "Some Aspects of Planter–Freedman Relations, 1865–1880," *Journal of Negro History* 21 (April 1936): 134.

12 *Senate Executive Documents*, 39th Congress, 1st Session, No. 27, pp. 164, 28.

13 Stearns, *The Black Man of the South*, p. 107. See also Bentley, *Freedmen's Bureau*, pp. 148–168. Because of the bureau's legal jurisdiction in matters pertaining to freedmen, the harsh Black Codes, enacted by the Southern states during the brief period of Presidential Reconstruction, never ob-

tained enforcement – a fact apparently overlooked by many writers when discussing the infamous Codes.

14 *Senate Executive Documents,* 39th Congress, 1st Session, No. 2, p. 40. See also *ibid.,* No. 27, p. 89; *ibid.,* No. 43, pp. 12–13; Joint Committee on Reconstruction, *Report,* Pt. IV, p. 8.

15 Recently it has become fashionable to depreciate the efforts of the bureau on behalf of the freedmen and to portray it as an agency dedicated to the forcible establishment of *de facto* slavery. See McFeely, *Yankee Stepfather, passim;* and Mary Francis Berry, *Black Resistance/White Law: A History of Constitutional Racism in America* (New York, 1971), pp. 91–92. Many instances of forcible actions can be documented, especially cases of bureau agents' compelling blacks to accept employment on plantations and remain there for the duration of the crop year. But, overall, the evidence does not sustain the characterization of the bureau as simply a means of repressing the freedmen. The Southern whites, who generally worked to rid themselves of the bureau, and the freedmen, who generally looked to it for protection of their newly acquired rights, perceived the agency as it truly was: a mediating force, imperfectly organized, financed, and staffed, but a mediating force nevertheless.

16 Dennett, *The South As It Is,* p. 97.

17 *Ibid.,* p. 282.

18 *Ibid., passim;* Reid, *After the War, passim;* U.S. Department of Agriculture, *Report of the Commissioner of Agriculture for the Year 1867* (Washington, 1868), pp. 412–428; Vernon Lane Wharton, *The Negro in Mississippi, 1865–1890* (New York, 1965 [1947]), pp. 58–73; Joel Williamson, *After Slavery: The Negro in South Carolina during Reconstruction, 1861–1877* (Chapel Hill, 1965), pp. 126–179. For other examples of early wage contracts, see Dennett, *The South As It Is,* pp. 281–282; Joint Committee on Reconstruction, *Report,* Pt. II, pp. 241–242; J. Carlyle Sitterson, "The Transition from Slave to Free Economy on the William J. Minor Plantations," *Agricultural History* 17 (Oct. 1943): 221–222; and Jessie Melville Fraser, ed., "A Free Labor Contract, 1867," *Journal of Southern History* 6 (Nov. 1940): 547–548.

19 Examples are Fred A. Shannon, *The Farmer's Last Frontier: Agriculture, 1860–1897* (New York, 1968 [1945]), pp. 87–88; and Trelease, *Reconstruction,* pp. 19–20.

20 Walter L. Fleming, "Reorganization of the Industrial System in Alabama After the Civil War," *American Journal of Sociology* 10 (Jan. 1905): 487. On the contractual preferences of the freedmen, see also Sidney Andrews, *The South Since the War* (Boston, 1971 [1866]), p. 212; J. T. Trowbridge, *The South: A Tour of Its Battlefields and Ruined Cities* (New York, 1969 [1866]), p. 362; U.S. Senate, Committee on Education and Labor, *Report on Relations between Labor and Capital* (Washington, 1885), IV, pp. 274, 555; Nordhoff, *The Cotton States,* p. 72; A. B. Hurt, "Mississippi: Its Climate, Soil, Productions, and Agricultural Capabilities," U.S. Department of Agriculture, *Miscellaneous Special Report No. 3* (Washington, 1884), p. 30; Charles H. Otken, *The Ills of the South* (New York, 1894),

pp. 36–37; and Pitt Dillingham, "Land Tenure Among the Negroes," *Yale Review* 5 (Aug. 1896): 201.

21 Dennett, *The South As It Is*, p. 83. On share tenancy in the antebellum South, see Marjorie Stratford Mendenhall, "The Rise of Southern Tenancy," *Yale Review* 27 (Sept. 1937): 110–129; on sharecropping arrangements during the war in Southern areas under federal control, see Wiley, *Southern Negroes, 1861–1865*, pp. 214–15, 231, 235–237.

22 Dennett, *The South As It Is*, pp. 282–283. For other examples of share contracts, see Joint Committee on Reconstruction, *Report*, Pt. II, pp. 241–242; Rosser H. Taylor, "Post-Bellum Southern Rental Contracts," *Agricultural History* 17 (April 1943): 122–123; Weymouth T. Jordan, "The Elisha F. King Family: Planters of the Alabama Black Belt," *ibid.* 19 (July 1945): 161–162; Lucille Griffith, ed., *Alabama: A Documentary History to 1900* (University, Ala., 1972), p. 590; Robert A. Calvert, "The Freedmen and Agricultural Prosperity," *Southwestern Historical Quarterly* 76 (April 1973): 466–468; and Joseph D. Reid, Jr., "Sharecropping As An Understandable Market Response: The Post-Bellum South," *Journal of Economic History* 33 (March 1973): 128–130.

23 Joint Committee on Reconstruction, *Report*, Pt. III, p. 9. The articles of agreement of one Alabama planters' association are reproduced in full in *DeBow's Review*, New Series 5 (Feb. 1868): 213. See also Trowbridge, *The South*, pp. 431–432; *Senate Reports*, 42nd Congress, 2nd Session, No. 41, p. 702; Fleming, "Reorganization of the Industrial System," pp. 485–486; and Bentley, *Freedmen's Bureau*, p. 80.

24 A. R. Lightfoot, "Condition and Wants of the Cotton Raising States," *DeBow's Review*, New Series 6 (Feb. 1869): 152; C. W. Howard, "Conditions of Agriculture in the Cotton States," in U.S. Department of Agriculture, *Report of the Commissioner of Agriculture for the Year 1874* (Washington, 1875), p. 224.

25 Joint Committee on Reconstruction, *Report*, Pt. III, p. 30.

26 *Southern Cultivator* as quoted in Paul S. Taylor, "Slave to Freedman," Southern Economic History Project, *Working Paper No. 7* (Berkeley, 1970), pp. 58, 60; Lightfoot, "Condition and Wants," p. 153.

27 *Senate Executive Documents*, 39th Congress, 1st Session, No. 27, pp. 65, 70, 78; *Southern Cultivator* as quoted in Taylor, "Slave to Freedman," p. 61.

28 Southerner, "Agricultural Labor at the South," p. 334.

29 Joint Committee on Reconstruction, *Report*, Pt. I, p. 100.

30 Lightfoot, "Condition and Wants," p. 153; *Senate Executive Documents*, 39th Congress, 1st Session, No. 27, p. 81; Somers, *Southern States Since the War*, pp. 128–129; Nordhoff, *The Cotton States, passim*; King, *The Great South*, pp. 273, 276, 298; Southerner, "Agricultural Labor at the South," pp. 328–340. For additional documentation of the low share ratios in the period 1865–1867, see Dennett, *The South As It Is*, pp. 51, 85, 109, 188, 194, 220, 227, 254, 259, 282; Andrews, *The South since the War*, pp. 99, 189, 322; and U.S. Department of Agriculture, *Report of the Commissioner of Agriculture for the Year 1867*, p. 417.

31 Somers, *Southern States since the War*, p. 145; Nordhoff, *The Cotton*

States, pp. 38, 72, 84, 99, 107; King, *The Great South,* p. 276; David C. Barrow, Jr., "A Georgia Plantation," *Scribner's Monthly* 21 (April 1881): 833. For a large number of statements as to the prevailing fixed rents in various parts of the South in 1880, see U.S. Census Office, *Report on Cotton Production in the United States* (Washington, 1884), *passim.*

32 For the economic analysis underlying these statements, see my articles: "Property Rights and Resource Allocation Under Alternative Land Tenure Forms: A Comment," *Oxford Economic Papers* 24 (Nov. 1972): 428–431; "Race, Tenure, and Resource Allocation in Southern Agriculture, 1910," *Journal of Economic History* 33 (March 1973): 151–156; and "Patterns of Land Rental in the Georgia Cotton Belt, 1880–1900," *ibid.* 34 (June 1974): 474–475.

33 Southerner, "Agricultural Labor at the South," p. 334. When the realized yield fell so disastrously low that the tenant could not pay the fixed rent, the landlord either carried it over to the next year as a debt or accepted partial payment as satisfactory fulfillment of the contract. The latter course of action implied that fixed-rent contracts became *de facto* share contracts when yields fell below a certain level. To my knowledge no one has ever rigorously analyzed the economics of contractual choice with such a contractual arrangement as one of the available options; but Steven Cheung's discussion of "escape clauses" in Chinese contracts is suggestive. See his *Theory of Share Tenancy* (Chicago, 1969), pp. 74–75.

34 Barrow, "A Georgia Plantation," p. 834. For other examples of fixed-rent contracts, see Taylor, "Post-Bellum Southern Rental Contracts," pp. 124–125, 127–128.

35 Barrow, "A Georgia Plantation," pp. 831–834. See also E. Merton Coulter, "A Century of a Georgia Plantation," *Agricultural History* 3 (Oct. 1929): 157–159.

36 W. E. B. Du Bois, "The Negro Landholder of Georgia," U.S. Department of Labor, *Bulletin No. 35* (Washington, 1901), p. 665; Enoch Marvin Banks, "The Economics of Land Tenure in Georgia," Columbia University, *Studies in History, Economics and Public Law* 23 (1905): 62–77, 119–122, 127–130. In 1881 Henry W. Grady stated that blacks owned 2,680,800 acres in the cotton states. The figure is plausible, but he gave no documentation for it. That anyone could have obtained such information at that time is unlikely, which suggests that Grady either invented it or somehow obtained it by extrapolation from the data for Georgia. (If one multiplies the 1880 acreage per capita of Georgia blacks times the aggregate black population of South Carolina, Georgia, Alabama, Mississippi, Louisiana, and Arkansas, the resulting figure differs by only 1 percent from Grady's figure.) See his "Cotton and Its Kingdom," *Harper's New Monthly Magazine* 63 (Oct. 1881): 725. Testifying before a Senate committee in 1883, T. Thomas Fortune asserted that "in the cotton states they [blacks] own and cultivate 2,680,000 acres." See Senate Committee on Education and Labor, *Report on Relations between Labor and Capital,* ii, p. 525. Fortune could have taken this figure from Grady's article; or perhaps both drew it from a common (unstated) source.

37 U.S. Department of Agriculture, *Report of the Commissioner of Agriculture for the Year 1876* (Washington, 1877), p. 137.

38 *Mississippi Sentinel* as quoted in *DeBow's Review*, New Series 3 (June 1867): 586; George Campbell, *White and Black: The Outcome of a Visit to the United States* (New York, 1879), pp. 153, 329; Philip A. Bruce, *The Plantation Negro As A Freeman* (New York, 1889), pp. 185, 225. See also Nordhoff, *The Cotton States*, pp. 39, 71.

39 U.S. Census Office, *Report on Cotton Production, passim.*

40 Joel Williamson concludes in his excellent study of South Carolina during Reconstruction that "the typical [black] laborer earned only enough to pay for what he had consumed during the year," but "his rate of consumption was increasing. . . . The central fact of the Negro's experience in the economic sphere is that he realized – in spite of the general and particular hazards which obstructed his progress – an appreciable improvement in his standard of living. . . . There were, of course, many Negroes who fared worse, materially, in freedom than they had in slavery. . . . Nevertheless, the great mass of freedmen registered a progressive improvement in their material situations." See Williamson's *After Slavery*, pp. 170, 176–177. Chapter 5 deals more systematically with changes in black income levels.

41 Stearns, *The Black Man of the South*, pp. 527–528. See also *ibid.*, p. 105; *Senate Executive Documents*, 39th Congress, 1st Session, No. 27, p. 121; H. W. Pierson, *A Letter to Hon. Charles Sumner, with "Statements" of Outrages Upon Freedmen in Georgia* (Freeport, New York, 1972 [1870]), p. 5; *Senate Reports*, 42nd Congress, 2nd Session, No. 41, pp. 291, 691–692, 716; Nordhoff, *The Cotton States*, p. 78; Campbell, *White and Black*, p. 310; and *Southern Cultivator* as quoted in Taylor, "Slave to Freedman," p. 56.

42 Nordhoff, *The Cotton States*, p. 102; Senate Committee on Education and Labor, *Report on Relations between Labor and Capital*, IV, pp. 273–274.

43 Campbell, *White and Black*, p. 164. See also *ibid.*, p. 297; Joint Committee on Reconstruction, *Report*, Pt. III, p. 58; Nordhoff, *The Cotton States*, p. 38.

44 U.S. Department of Agriculture, *Report of the Commissioner of Agriculture for the Year 1867*, p. 422; Taylor, "Post-Bellum Southern Rental Contracts," pp. 122–123; Nordhoff, *The Cotton States*, p. 39. See also Senate Committee on Education and Labor, *Report on Relations between Labor and Capital*, IV, p. 682.

45 Contemporary accounts of the new system include U.S. Census Office, *Report on Cotton Production, passim*; George K. Holmes, "The Peons of the South," *Annals of the American Academy of Political and Social Science* 4 (Sept. 1893): 65–74; Otken, *Ills of the South*, pp. 12–53; M. B. Hammond, "The Southern Farmer and the Cotton Question," *Political Science Quarterly* 12 (Sept. 1897): 450–475; and *idem*, "The Cotton Industry: An Essay in American Economic History," *American Economic Association Publications*, New Series (Dec. 1897): 141–165. More recent and dispassionate treatments include Thomas D. Clark, *Pills, Petticoats, and Plows: The Southern Country Store* (New York, 1944), pp. 313–336; *idem*, "The Fur-

nishing and Supply System in Southern Agriculture since 1865," *Journal of Southern History* 12 (Feb. 1946): 24–44; and Jacqueline P. Bull, "The General Merchant in the Economic History of the New South," *ibid.* 18 (Feb. 1952): 37–59.

46 U.S. Census Office, *Report on Cotton Production*, Pt. ɪɪ, p. 520. For examples of lien notes, see Hammond, "The Cotton Industry," pp. 147–149; Southerner, "Agricultural Labor at the South," p. 338; and Clark, *Pills, Petticoats, and Plows*, p. 280.

47 Clark, "The Furnishing and Supply System," p. 28. See also Bull, "The General Merchant," pp. 46–51.

48 Williamson, *After Slavery*, p. 174; Somers, *The Southern States*, p. 241.

49 South Carolina, State Board of Agriculture [Harry Hammond], *South Carolina: Resources and Population, Institutions and Industries* (Charleston, 1883), p. 661; Bruce, *Plantation Negro As A Freeman*, p. 203. See also Roger L. Ransom and Richard Sutch, "Debt Peonage in the Cotton South After the Civil War," *Journal of Economic History* 32 (Sept. 1972): 641–669; and William W. Brown and Morgan O. Reynolds, "Debt Peonage Re-examined," *ibid.* 33 (Dec. 1973): 862–871.

50 Du Bois, "The Negro Landholder of Georgia," p. 668.

51 Charles S. Mangum, Jr., *The Legal Status of the Tenant Farmer in the Southeast* (Chapel Hill, 1952), pp. 435–443. In 1907 the Supreme Court of South Carolina struck down an 1897 law on the ground that it required involuntary servitude (*Ex Parte Hollman*, 79 S. C. Reports 22). See the discussion of Tindall, *South Carolina Negroes*, p. 113.

52 Bruce, *Plantation Negro As A Freeman*, p. 199; Southerner, "Agricultural Labor at the South," p. 332. See also Nordhoff, *The Cotton States*, p. 70; and King, *The Great South*, p. 274.

53 If the relation between urbanization and labor force structure were assumed identical in 1880 and 1890, the estimate would be 31 percent nonagricultural in 1880 (20/44 = 14/31). There is, however, little reason to accept the assumption. Between 1890 and 1910 the urban share of the population increased much faster than the nonagricultural share of the labor force (see Tables 2.6 and 4.1). If this differential growth also occurred during the 1880s, then the estimate of 31 percent nonagricultural in 1880 is too low.

54 W. E. B. Du Bois, ed., *The Negro in Business* (Atlanta, 1899), p. 11.

55 Campbell, *White and Black*, p. 347; Senate Committee on Education and Labor, *Report on Relations between Labor and Capital*, ɪᴠ, pp. 622, 628, 655, 714.

CHAPTER 4. THE PEOPLE AT WORK, 1880–1914

1 U.S. Bureau of the Census, *Negro Population, 1790–1915* (Washington, 1918), pp. 166, 503–504.

2 U.S. Department of Agriculture, Division of Statistics, "Wages of Farm Labor in the United States," *Miscellaneous Series, Bulletin 22* (Washington, 1901), pp. 5–6, 17–32; and James H. Blodgett, "Wages of Farm Labor

in the United States," U.S. Department of Agriculture, Bureau of Statistics, *Miscellaneous Series, Bulletin No. 26* (Washington, 1903), pp. 7, 32–44.

3 U.S. Department of Agriculture, *Miscellaneous Series, Bulletin 22*, p. 30; U.S. Industrial Commission, *Report* (Washington, 1901), xi, p. 123.

4 U.S. Department of Agriculture, *Miscellaneous Series, Bulletin 22*, pp. 22, 17, 31.

5 My interpretation of these wage data, first published in "Did Southern Farmers Discriminate?" *Agricultural History* 46 (April 1972): 325–328, has been challenged by Charles A. Roberts, "Did Southern Farmers Discriminate? – The Evidence Re-examined," *ibid.* 49 (April 1975): 441–445. My reply to this criticism appears in "Did Southern Farmers Discriminate? – Interpretive Problems and Further Evidence," *ibid.*, pp. 445–447. The last paper also raises the possibility that the Department of Agriculture's wage data for the two races may be flawed by aggregation biases.

6 U.S. Industrial Commission, *Report*, x, pp. 71, 471, 477. See also Lawrence D. Rice, *The Negro in Texas, 1874–1900* (Baton Rouge, 1971), pp. 153, 174.

7 Frenise A. Logan, "Factors Influencing the Efficiency of Negro Farm Laborers in Post-Reconstruction North Carolina," *Agricultural History* 33 (Oct. 1959): 185. The same claim, with identical documentation, is reproduced in Logan's *The Negro in North Carolina, 1876–1894* (Chapel Hill, 1964), p. 76. See Logan's source, pp. 82–84, 120–123.

8 In the western cattle industry, where thousands of blacks were employed, "there is no clear-cut evidence that Negro cowhands were generally or seriously discriminated against in the matter of wages . . . earning $20–25 [per month]." See Kenneth W. Porter, "Negro Labor in the Western Cattle Industry, 1866–1900," *Labor History* 10 (Summer 1969): 363.

9 U.S. Industrial Commission, *Report*, x, pp. 79, 497, 823, 913; Philip A. Bruce, *The Plantation Negro As A Freeman* (New York, 1889), pp. 186–187.

10 U.S. Industrial Commission, *Report*, xi, p. 123; x, p. 446. See also *ibid.*, pp. 120, 429.

11 Roger L. Ransom and Richard Sutch, "The Ex-Slave in the Post-Bellum South: A Study of the Economic Impact of Racism in a Market Environment," *Journal of Economic History* 33 (March 1973): 147.

12 U.S. Bureau of the Census, *Negro Population, 1790–1915*, p. 572. For the series on Georgia landownership, see W. E. B. Du Bois, ed., *The Negro American Family* (Atlanta, 1909), p. 107.

13 Ransom and Sutch, "The Ex-Slave," p. 147.

14 U.S. Bureau of the Census, *Negro Population, 1790–1915*, p. 609.

15 Robert Preston Brooks, "The Agrarian Revolution in Georgia, 1865–1912," University of Wisconsin, *Bulletin No. 639*, History Series (1914): 52, 87–89; Enoch Marvin Banks, "The Economics of Land Tenure in Georgia," Columbia University, *Studies in History, Economics and Public Law* 23 (1905): 49–50, 108.

16 My "Race, Tenure, and Resource Allocation in Southern Agriculture,

1910," *Journal of Economic History* 33 (March 1973): 151–159. For the econometric tests that underlie my conclusion about risk, see the Technical Appendix, Section 2A.

17 *Ibid.;* my "Patterns of Land Rental in the Georgia Cotton Belt, 1880–1900," *ibid.* 34 (June 1974); and the Technical Appendix, Sections 2A and 2B.

18 U.S. Industrial Commission, *Report,* x, pp. 455, 434. See also U.S. Senate, Committee on Education and Labor, *Report on Relations between Labor and Capital* (Washington, 1885), IV, p. 682. Some readers may object here, and elsewhere in this book, that the testimony of white planters as to the racial equality of contractual terms is biased evidence. Of course it may be. But one should be aware that the climate of opinion was far different during the period under investigation. Southern whites seldom hesitated to express their prejudices; they had little or nothing to lose by an admission of discriminatory behavior. To call into question their testimony, one must invoke something more convincing than mere racial identity.

19 Examples include Ransom and Sutch, "The Ex-Slave," p. 142; and Gavin Wright, "Comments on Papers by Reid, Ransom and Sutch, and Higgs," *Journal of Economic History* 33 (March 1973): 175. Wright's argument makes the small farm sizes of the blacks depend upon racial discrimination only indirectly, via the effect of discrimination in reducing alternative opportunities for black tenants.

20 U.S. Industrial Commission, *Report,* x, p. 464; Walter L. Fleming, "Reorganization of the Industrial System in Alabama After the Civil War," *American Journal of Sociology* 10 (Jan. 1905): 492–493; Stephen DeCanio, "Productivity and Income Distribution in the Post-Bellum South," *Journal of Economic History* 34 (June 1974): 438; and my "Race, Tenure, and Resource Allocation," pp. 159–166. One can, of course, quarrel about what is meant by a "large" difference. See Wright, "Comments," pp. 171–172. Further discussion of this issue, with some statistical findings, is contained in the Technical Appendix, Section 2C.

21 Du Bois, ed., *The Negro American Family,* p. 107; *idem,* "The Negro Farmer," in *Twelfth Census of the United States: 1900, Special Reports, Supplementary Analysis, and Derivative Tables* (Washington, 1906), pp. 526, 537; U.S. Bureau of the Census, *Negro Population, 1790–1915,* pp. 569, 573, 576; Brooks, "The Agrarian Revolution," p. 62. See also U.S. Industrial Commission, *Report,* x, pp. 486, 498; Banks, "The Economics of Land Tenure," pp. 62–77.

22 W. E. B. Du Bois, "The Negro Landholder of Georgia," U.S. Department of Labor, *Bulletin No. 35* (Washington, 1901), p. 670.

23 Bruce, *The Plantation Negro,* p. 216; Banks, "The Economics of Land Tenure," p. 77. See also Du Bois, "The Negro Farmer," pp. 517, 526, 539.

24 U.S. Industrial Commission, *Report,* x, pp. 424, 477, 493, 504, 910; Banks, "The Economics of Land Tenure," p. 76; T. J. Woofter, Jr., *Negro Migration: Changes in Rural Organization and Population of the Cotton Belt* (New York, 1969 [1920]), p. 53. See also Bruce, *The Plantation Negro,* pp. 185, 225.

25 U.S. Bureau of the Census, *Negro Population, 1790–1915,* pp. 628–629.

26 Fred A. Shannon, *The Farmer's Last Frontier: Agriculture, 1860–1897* (New York, 1968 [1945]), p. 92. For a recent restatement of this traditional argument, see Roger L. Ransom and Richard Sutch, "Debt Peonage in the Cotton South After the Civil War," *Journal of Economic History* 32 (Sept. 1972): 655–664.

27 Jacqueline P. Bull, "The General Merchant in the Economic History of the New South," *Journal of Southern History* 18 (Feb. 1952): 41; Thomas D. Clark, "The Furnishing and Supply System in Southern Agriculture since 1865," *ibid.* 12 (Feb. 1946): 37–39; Stephen Decanio, "Cotton 'Over-production' in Late Nineteenth-Century Southern Agriculture," *Journal of Economic History* 33 (Sept. 1973): 608–633; *idem,* "Productivity and Income Distribution," pp. 437–438.

28 Ransom and Sutch, who argue for the discrimination thesis, confess: "We do not have direct evidence of discriminatory practices against blacks in the credit market." See their "Debt Peonage," p. 140.

29 Alfred Holt Stone, "The Negro in the Yazoo-Mississippi Delta," American Economic Association *Publications,* 3rd Series 3 (Feb. 1902): 252–253; Banks, "The Economics of Land Tenure," p. 77; U.S. Industrial Commission, *Report,* x, p. 121. Henderson H. Donald asserts that "the merchants sometimes discriminated against the Negroes"; see *The Negro Freedman: Life Conditions of the American Negro in the Early Years After Emancipation* (New York, 1952), p. 18. The authority for Donald's statement is the *New York Times,* Nov. 26, 1880.

30 Pitt Dillingham, "Land Tenure Among the Negroes," *Yale Review* 5 (Aug. 1896): 198; George K. Holmes, "The Peons of the South," *Annals of the American Academy of Political and Social Science* 4 (Sept. 1893): 65–74; U.S. Industrial Commission, *Report,* x, p. 419.

31 U.S. Industrial Commission, *Report,* x, p. 381.

32 *Ibid.,* p. 908.

33 Thomas J. Edwards, "The Tenant System and Some Changes since Emancipation," *Annals of the American Academy of Political and Social Science* 49 (Sept. 1913): 43.

34 See the fascinating examples discussed by Pete Daniel, *The Shadow of Slavery: Peonage in the South, 1901–1969* (Urbana, 1972), *passim.*

35 U.S. Industrial Commission, *Report,* x, p. 419; L. C. Gray, "Southern Agriculture, Plantation System, and the Negro Problem," *Annals of the American Academy of Political and Social Science* 40 (March 1912): 96. See also Senate Committee on Education and Labor, *Report on Relations between Labor and Capital,* p. 527; and William Alexander Percy, *Lanterns on the Levee: Recollections of a Planter's Son* (New York, 1941), pp. 282–283.

36 U.S. Industrial Commission, *Report,* x, pp. 821, 910; Senate Committee on Education and Labor, *Report on Relations between Labor and Capital,* ii, p. 173. See also Ray Stannard Baker, *Following the Color Line* (New York, 1908), pp. 79, 89, 103.

37 Southerner [pseud.], "Agricultural Labor at the South," *Galaxy* 12 (Sept.

1871): 337; U.S. Industrial Commission, *Report*, x, p. 379. See also Charles S. Mangum, Jr., *The Legal Status of the Tenant Farmer in the Southeast* (Chapel Hill, 1952), pp. 241–242; R. R. Wright, Jr., "The Migration of Negroes to the North," *Annals of the American Academy of Political and Social Science* 27 (May 1906): 111; and Leo Alilunas, "Statutory Means of Impeding Emigration of the Negro," *Journal of Negro History* 22 (April 1937): 148–162. Stephen DeCanio concludes on the basis of his econometric studies that "discriminatory laws or coercive practices . . . appear to have been ineffective in maintaining planters' market power over the labor force." See his "Productivity and Income Distribution," p. 444.

38 U.S. Industrial Commission, *Report*, x, p. 416.

39 Charles H. Otken, *The Ills of the South* (New York, 1894), pp. 86–89; William F. Holmes, "Whitecapping: Agrarian Violence in Mississippi, 1902–1906," *Journal of Southern History* 35 (May 1969): 165–185; *idem*, "Whitecapping in Mississippi: Agrarian Violence in the Populist Era," *Mid-America* 55 (April 1973): 134–148. See also George Brown Tindall, *South Carolina Negroes, 1877–1900* (Baton Rouge, 1966 [1952]), pp. 131, 258. Coercive activities rather similar to the whitecapping episodes were described by Baker, *Following the Color Line*, pp. 14, 71–72, 82, 250. For descriptions of other instances where whites employed raw force, and even murder, to suppress blacks explicitly to gain economic advantages, see Mary Francis Berry, *Black Resistance/White Law: A History of Constitutional Racism in America* (New York, 1971), pp. 111, 126, 134.

40 U.S. Industrial Commission, *Report*, x, p. 166. See also Edwards, "The Tenant System," p. 41; and W. E. B. Du Bois, "The Economic Future of the Negro," American Economic Association *Publications*, 3rd Series (Feb. 1906): 240.

41 Senate Committee on Education and Labor, *Report on Relations between Labor and Capital*, ii, pp. 161, 178; Stone, "The Negro in the Yazoo-Mississippi Delta," p. 272; U.S. Industrial Commission, *Report*, x, p. 476.

42 Bruce, *The Plantation Negro*, pp. 180–181.

43 A comparison of tax returns with the census data reveals that blacks owned considerably more land than the census total for owner operators showed, the discrepancy arising because a good deal of land owned by blacks was rented. See Du Bois, "The Negro Farmer," p. 526; and Woofter, *Negro Migration*, pp. 57–58.

44 For Southern land values, see Thomas J. Pressly and William N. Scofield, eds., *Farm Real Estate Values in the United States by Counties, 1850–1959* (Seattle, 1965), pp. 42–62.

45 Gary S. Becker, *The Economics of Discrimination*, 2nd ed. (Chicago, 1971), p. 137; W. E. B. Du Bois and Augustus Granville Dill, eds., *The Negro American Artisan* (Atlanta, 1912), p. 7.

46 For example, Robert Fogel and Stanley Engerman baldly assert: "The skill composition of the black labor force deteriorated [in the post-bellum era]." See their *Time on the Cross: The Economics of American Negro Slavery* (Boston, 1974), p. 261.

47 Becker, *The Economics of Discrimination*, p. 137.

48 U.S. Bureau of the Census, *Negro Population, 1790–1915,* pp. 526–527.

49 W. E. B. Du Bois, ed., *The Negro Artisan* (Atlanta, 1902), p. 97.

50 *Ibid.,* pp. 117, 119–121; Du Bois, "The Negro Landholder," p. 664; U.S. Department of Labor, "Condition of the Negro in Various Cities," *Bulletin No. 10* (May 1897), pp. 304–332; W. E. B. Du Bois, *The Philadelphia Negro: A Social Study* (New York, 1967 [1899]), pp. 133, 345–346. Emmett J. Scott (*Negro Migration during the War* [New York, 1920], p. 16) reported that in the South in 1915 "in the mills and shops the average of wages ranged from $1 to $1.50 a day. The wages of such skilled laborers as carpenters and bricklayers ranged from $2 to $3.50 a day."

51 Du Bois, ed., *The Negro Artisan,* p. 23.

52 *Ibid.,* p. 79.

53 Du Bois and Dill, eds., *The Negro American Artisan,* pp. 115–127; E. Franklin Frazier, *Black Bourgeoisie: The Rise of a New Middle Class in the United States* (New York, 1962), pp. 63–64.

54 Du Bois, ed., *The Negro Artisan,* p. 163. See also Du Bois and Dill, eds., *The Negro American Artisan,* pp. 82–114.

55 Booker T. Washington, "The Negro and the Labor Unions," *Atlantic Monthly* 111 (July 1913): 756–767; Du Bois, "The Economic Future of the Negro," p. 237. The relation of the black man to the trade union has inspired a large literature, of which the standard work is Sterling D. Spero and Abram L. Harris, *The Black Worker: The Negro and the Labor Movement* (New York, 1931). For some particularly perceptive remarks, see Du Bois, *The Philadelphia Negro,* pp. 128–129. Hubert M. Blalock, Jr., has made an interesting attempt to interpret union policies toward blacks in the light of a theory of coalition formation; see his *Toward a Theory of Minority-Group Relations* (New York, 1967), pp. 84–92.

56 Du Bois, ed., *The Negro Artisan,* p. 173.

57 Lorenzo J. Greene and Carter G. Woodson, *The Negro Wage Earner* (Washington, 1930), pp. 141–142. See also Paul B. Worthman, "Black Workers and Labor Unions in Birmingham, Alabama, 1897–1904," *Labor History* 10 (Summer 1969): 381.

58 Du Bois said: "That the average Negro laborer today is less efficient than the average European laborer is certain." See his "Economic Future of the Negro," p. 225. See also Alfred Holt Stone, "The Economic Future of the Negro: The Factor of White Competition," American Economic Association *Publications,* 3rd Series (Feb. 1906): 243–293; Du Bois, ed., *The Negro Artisan,* pp. 23, 91, 101, 188; *idem, The Philadelphia Negro,* pp. 97–98, 126–127; Mary White Ovington, *Half a Man: The Status of the Negro in New York* (New York, 1969 [1911]), pp. 56–57; Baker, *Following the Color Line,* pp. 133–134.

59 For data showing racial differences of wages paid within the same occupation, see Du Bois, ed., *The Negro Artisan,* pp. 94–95, 97, 99, 113–117, 132, 137, 146–147, 150, 163; *idem, The Philadelphia Negro,* pp. 345–346, 449; Greene and Woodson, *The Negro Wage Earner,* pp. 150, 194. Much of this evidence is suspect because the white wage was reported by the black workers, and the investigators themselves recognized that the blacks tended

to exaggerate the amount received by the whites. See Du Bois, ed., *The Negro Artisan*, p. 117.

60 Du Bois, ed., *The Negro Artisan*, pp. 115–116. For evidence that the Georgia Railroad also paid its black firemen less than the whites between 1902 and 1909, see John Michael Matthews, "The Georgia 'Race Strike' of 1909," *Journal of Southern History* 40 (Nov. 1974): 614. As a result of this wage differential, blacks gradually replaced white firemen on the Georgia Railroad after 1902. In 1909 the (white) firemen's union struck, demanding removal of all black firemen. The arbitration committee that settled the strike not only ruled against the union demand but decreed that black and white firemen thereafter receive the same wages. Afterwards the company maintained black employment at prestrike levels, which suggests that the entire prestrike wage differential represented pure wage discrimination.

61 Du Bois, ed., *The Negro Artisan*, pp. 94, 98, 99, 102–103, 112, 114, 127, 132, 137, 144, 150. For further documentation of equal pay for equal work, see *idem, The Philadelphia Negro*, pp. 113, 131, 345; *idem*, "The Negro in the Black Belt: Some Social Sketches," U.S. Department of Labor, *Bulletin No. 22* (May 1899), p. 408; Greene and Woodson, *The Negro Wage Earner*, p. 143; George T. Surface, "The Negro Mine Laborer: Central Appalachian Coal Field," *Annals of the American Academy of Political and Social Science* 33 (March 1909): 120–123; Charles B. Spahr, "The Negro as an Industrial Factor," *Outlook* 62 (May 6, 1899): 34; *Nation* 53 (July 16, 1891): 38; Baker, *Following the Color Line*, p. 138; Richard R. Wright, Jr., *The Negro in Pennsylvania: A Study in Economic History* (New York, 1969 [1912]), p. 94; Virginia Bureau of Labor and Industrial Statistics, *Fourth Annual Report, 1901* (Richmond, 1901), pp. 3–7, 13–19, 22–25, 29–37, 76–81; *idem, Thirteenth Annual Report, 1910* (Richmond, 1910), pp. 9, 12–29, 36–40, 44–54. A systematic study of this subject will be published in my article, "Firm-Specific Evidence on Racial Wage Differentials and Workforce Segregation," *American Economic Review*, forthcoming.

62 Du Bois, ed., *The Negro Artisan*, p. 188; and sources cited in footnote 58 above.

63 *Idem, The Philadelphia Negro*, pp. 323, 339. See also Ovington, *Half a Man*, pp. 53, 89.

64 Lynchings during 1882–1915 calculated from data in Walter White, *Rope and Faggot: A Biography of Judge Lynch* (New York, 1969 [1929]), p. 231.

65 W. E. B. Du Bois, ed., *The Negro in Business* (Atlanta, 1899), pp. 6–8, 19; *idem, The Philadelphia Negro*, p. 122; August Meier, *Negro Thought in America, 1880–1915: Racial Ideologies in the Age of Booker T. Washington* (Ann Arbor, 1963), pp. 139–146; George Edmund Haynes, "The Negro At Work in New York City," Columbia University, *Studies in History, Economics and Public Law* 49 (1912): 98–99, 108, 124–125; Wright, *The Negro in Pennsylvania*, pp. 82–90; Baker, *Following the Color Line*, pp. 39–44.

66 Du Bois, ed., *The Negro in Business,* p. 7. See also Meier, *Negro Thought,* p. 144.

67 The basis for these figures, along with a more detailed discussion and a comparative analysis of native-born and foreign-born whites, appears in the Technical Appendix, Section 3. For a fuller discussion, see my "Participation of Blacks and Immigrants in the American Merchant Class, 1890–1910: Some Demographic Relations," *Explorations in Economic History,* 13 (April 1976).

68 Quoted in Baker, *Following the Color Line,* p. 40.

69 Du Bois, ed., *The Negro in Business,* p. 61. See also Giles B. Jackson and D. Webster Davis, *The Industrial History of the Negro Race of the United States* (Freeport, New York, 1971 [1908]), p. 91; Meier, *Negro Thought,* p. 146; and Constance McLaughlin Green, *The Secret City: A History of Race Relations in the Nation's Capital* (Princeton, 1967), pp. 131–133.

CHAPTER 5. THE FRUITS OF THEIR LABORS

1 Calculated from data in W. E. B. Du Bois, *The Philadelphia Negro: A Social Study* (New York, 1967 [1899]), p. 170.

2 *Ibid.,* p. 164.

3 Calculated from data in W. E. B. Du Bois, "The Negro in the Black Belt: Some Social Sketches," U.S. Department of Labor, *Bulletin No. 22* (May 1899), pp. 401–417.

4 Calculated from data in W. E. B. Du Bois, "The Negro Landholder of Georgia," U.S. Department of Labor, *Bulletin No. 35* (July 1901), p. 664.

5 Calculated from data reproduced in W. E. B. Du Bois, ed., *The Negro American Family* (Atlanta, 1908), pp. 111–112.

6 A random sample of 146 Atlanta wage earners in 1896 (drawn from U.S. Department of Labor, "Condition of the Negro in Various Cities," *Bulletin No. 10* [May 1897], pp. 304–312) yielded an average of just under 48 weeks employed per worker; at only 5 days per week – a conservative estimate – this is 240 days per year. Data displayed in Chapter 4 (Table 4.7 and text) suggest that $1.00 per day is a plausible estimate of average daily earnings. The figure of 1.5 wage earners per family, in conjunction with an assumed family size of 3.6, yields a labor force participation rate of only 42 percent; in view of the great concentration of the black urban population in the ages 20–50, such a rate is certainly not unreasonable. In fact the estimate of 1.5 wage earners per family may be too low, given the high participation of black women in the urban labor force. See Du Bois, *The Philadelphia Negro,* p. 104; and Mary White Ovington, *Half a Man: The Status of the Negro in New York* (New York, 1969 [1911]), pp. 76–92.

7 Du Bois, "The Negro Landholder," p. 663.

8 The weighted average is $(150/200)(\$0.74) + (50/200)(\$1.06) = \$0.82$.

9 U.S. Industrial Commission, *Report* (Washington, 1901), x, pp. 460–461; U.S. Department of Agriculture, "Cotton Investigation," in *Report of the*

Commissioner of Agriculture for the Year 1876 (Washington, 1877), p. 135. The typical ration allowance probably changed little, if at all, between 1876 and 1900.

10 For data on black farm size in 1900, see U.S. Bureau of the Census, *Negro Population, 1790–1915* (Washington, 1918), p. 625; for yields, see U.S. Department of Agriculture, Agricultural Marketing Service, "Cotton and Cottonseed: Acreage, Yield, Production, Disposition, Price, Value; By States, 1866–1952," *Statistical Bulletin No. 164* (June 1955), p. 5; for prices, see U.S. Bureau of the Census, *Historical Statistics of the United States, Colonial Times to 1957* (Washington, 1960), p. 301. The average price received by farmers in 1900 was 9.15 cents per pound of lint. The price had been considerably lower in the 1890s but averaged about 10 cents during the decade after 1900.

11 That he might already have "eaten up" the better part – or perhaps all or even more than all – of his share in the form of "advances" from the landlord or merchant is beside the point of this calculation.

12 Robert Somers, *The Southern States since the War, 1870–1871* (London, 1871), p. 129; U.S. Census Office, *Report on Cotton Production in the United States* (Washington, 1884), Pt. ii, p. 519; J. Bradford Laws, "The Negroes of Cinclare Central Factory and Calumet Plantation, Louisiana," U.S. Department of Labor, *Bulletin No. 38* (Jan. 1902), pp. 110–111.

13 Making no allowances for off-plantation earnings or for any income in kind, Du Bois estimated the average annual income of black farmers in 1899 at a little less than $200. See Du Bois, ed., *The Negro American Family*, p. 106. In 1913 Robert E. Park estimated, again without any allowances for off-plantation earnings or income in kind, that the average black tenant had a real income of a little less than $300 in a normal year. See his "Negro Home Life and Standards of Living," *Annals of the American Academy of Political and Social Science* 49 (Sept. 1913): 151–152. He also put the average tenant's family size at six, which implies a per capita income of about $50. Just before World War I the U.S. Department of Agriculture made a number of careful farm management surveys, which reveal the incomes earned by black farmers in a number of representative areas of the South. These data suggest that either my estimate of $300 for 1900 is much too low, or vast increases in the incomes of black farmers occurred between 1900 and 1913–1914, when the surveys were made. I believe considerable income gains were realized during this period, but I also believe that the USDA evidence supports the view that $300 is a conservative estimate for 1900. See E. A. Boeger and E. A. Goldenweiser, "A Study of the Tenant Systems of Farming in the Yazoo-Mississippi Delta," USDA *Bulletin No. 337* (Jan. 13, 1916), p. 7; H. M. Dixon, "An Economic Study of Farming in Sumter County, Georgia," USDA *Bulletin No. 492* (Feb. 10, 1917), pp. 17–20; E. S. Haskell, "A Farm-Management Survey in Brooks County, Georgia," USDA *Bulletin No. 648* (May 1, 1918), p. 16; Rex E. Willard, "A Farm Management Study of Cotton Farms of Ellis County, Tex.," USDA *Bulletin No. 659* (June 17, 1918), pp. 21–22; H. W. Hawthorne, H. M. Dixon, and Frank Montgomery, "Farm

Management and Farm Organization in Sumter County, Ga.," USDA *Bulletin No. 1034* (June 28, 1922), p. 39.

14 U.S. Bureau of the Census, *Negro Population, 1790–1915,* p. 508.

15 *Ibid.*

16 The guess is conservative even though it assigns relatively more weight to the higher component of the weighted average. It is conservative in the sense that it also reduces the implicit full-time-equivalent participation in the labor force and hence leads to a lower estimate of rural income per capita. Raising the assumed number of laborers by any amount results in a higher estimate of income per capita. For the proof, see the Technical Appendix, Section 4A.

17 The weighted average is $(500,000/1,258,000)(\$200) + (758,000/1,258,000)(\$300) = \$260$.

18 The per capita income is $(\$260)(0.25) = \$65$.

19 That is, $(0.23)(\$100) + (0.77)(\$65) = \$73$.

20 William Edward Vickery has estimated the average earnings of nonwhite workers in the South for the decade 1900–1910 as $475 in 1947–1949 purchasing power. Expressed in 1905 purchasing power, this is about $140. Assuming an unadjusted labor force participation rate of 50 percent, one arrives at an estimate of $70 per capita as an income figure (ignoring property income). This is in the same neighborhood as my estimate, which may lend some support to my procedures. But one ought not to exaggerate this correspondence, since Vickery's rather roundabout procedure, which relies on predictions via regression coefficients derived from 1950 data, inspires little confidence. For Vickery's procedures and results, see *The Economics of the Negro Migration, 1900–1960* (unpublished Ph.D. dissertation, University of Chicago, 1969), pp. 61–96.

21 U.S. Department of Agriculture, *Report of the Commissioner of Agriculture for the Year 1867* (Washington, 1868), pp. 412–413.

22 That is, $(0.5)(\$150) + (0.5)(\$225) = \$188$.

23 That is, $(0.25)(\$188) = \$47$. Robert Fogel and Stanley Engerman have estimated that the income per capita of slaves on large plantations in 1860 was about $43. See their *Time on the Cross: Evidence and Methods – A Supplement* (Boston, 1974), p. 159. Note that because of changes in the price level, $43 in 1860 probably represented a higher real income than $47 in 1867–1868, other things being equal. Of course, the freedmen had more choice in allocating their incomes and in choosing leisure over work than the slaves had. Still, it is conceivable that the material level of living was lower in the late 1860s than in 1860. Such a change would be consistent with the apparent rise in mortality after the war, discussed in Chapter 2 above.

24 That is, $(0.87)(\$47) + (0.13)(1.5)(\$47) = \$50$.

25 George F. Warren and Frank A. Pearson, *Prices* (New York, 1933), p. 26.

26 Calculated from data in Robert E. Gallman, "Gross National Product in the United States, 1834–1909," in National Bureau of Economic Research, Conference on Research in Income and Wealth, *Output, Employment, and Productivity in the United States after 1800* (New York, 1966), p. 26; and U.S. Bureau of the Census, *Historical Statistics of the United States,*

p. 7. Since the whites had overwhelming weight in the national average, the national rate approximates the rate for whites. To the extent that black incomes grew more rapidly than the national average, the white rate must have fallen slightly below it.

27 For a crude reconciliation of the levels and rates of growth of black and white income per capita in the period 1867/68–1900, see the Technical Appendix, Section 4B.

28 For additional information on Atlanta's laboring population, see the descriptions in Du Bois, ed., *The Negro American Family*, pp. 148–151. See also the suggestive series on the assessed value of household and kitchen furniture owned by Georgia blacks, 1875–1907, on p. 110 of this source. Between 1876 and 1907 this value increased more than five-fold.

29 Park, "Negro Home Life and Standards of Living," p. 152; Du Bois, ed., *The Negro American Family*, pp. 115–122; George T. Surface, "The Negro Mine Laborer: Central Appalachian Coal Field," *Annals of the American Academy of Political and Social Science* 33 (March 1909): 115–116.

30 Du Bois, *The Philadelphia Negro*, pp. 173–177; *idem*, ed., *The Negro American Family*, p. 115.

31 In the large study of urban blacks conducted in 1896, people were asked how they had subsisted when unemployed; of the 408 who had been unemployed and who responded to the question, 52 percent indicated that they had lived off their savings. See U.S. Department of Labor, "Condition of the Negro in Various Cities," pp. 304–332. Probably a higher proportion of those who had not been unemployed were savers, because of their higher incomes.

32 Alfred Holt Stone, *Studies in the American Race Problem* (New York, 1908), p. 190.

33 Du Bois, *The Philadelphia Negro*, p. 178.

34 My "Mortality in Rural America, 1870–1920: Estimates and Conjectures," *Explorations in Economic History* 10 (Winter 1973): 177–195 and references cited therein.

35 Thomas D. Clark, *Pills, Petticoats and Plows: The Southern Country Store* (New York, 1944), p. 166. See also Fred A. Shannon, *The Farmer's Last Frontier: Agriculture, 1860–1897* (New York, 1968[1945]), p. 94; Rupert B. Vance, *Human Factors in Cotton Culture: A Study in the Social Geography of the American South* (Chapel Hill, 1929), pp. 248, 297–299; Jacqueline P. Bull, "The General Merchant in the Economic History of the New South," *Journal of Southern History* 18 (Feb. 1952): 55–56.

36 W. O. Atwater and Chas. D. Woods, "Dietary Studies with reference to the Food of the Negro in Alabama in 1895 and 1896," U.S. Department of Agriculture, Office of Experiment Stations, *Bulletin No. 38* (1897), pp. 20–21.

37 H. B. Frissell and Isabel Bevier, "Dietary Studies of Negroes in Eastern Virginia in 1897 and 1898," U.S. Department of Agriculture, Office of Experiment Stations, *Bulletin No. 71* (1899), p. 8.

38 Professor B. B. Ross, of the Agricultural and Mechanical College of Alabama, as quoted in Atwater and Woods, "Dietary Studies," p. 11.

39 *Ibid.*, pp. 63–64, 68.

40 Frissell and Bevier, "Dietary Studies," p. 40.

41 Vance, *Human Factors in Cotton Culture*, p. 248.

42 Du Bois, ed., *The Negro American Family*, pp. 135–142, presents data for several prosperous farm families who consumed quite varied diets.

43 *Ibid.*, pp. 150–151, sample numbers 12 (carpenter) and 19 (laborer). See also pp. 142–149.

44 My "Mortality in Rural America," pp. 189–192 and references cited therein.

45 Du Bois, ed., *The Negro American Family*, p. 48. See also pp. 45–50. For some interesting photographs of typical slave cabins, see pp. 84–85. See also Kenneth M. Stampp, *The Peculiar Institution: Slavery in the Ante-Bellum South* (New York, 1956), pp. 292–295.

46 U.S. Industrial Commission, *Report*, x, p. 821; W. E. B. Du Bois, "The Negro Farmer," in *Twelfth Census of the United States: 1900, Special Reports, Supplementary Analysis and Derivative Tables* (Washington, 1906), p. 514.

47 U.S. Industrial Commission, *Report*, x, p. 384. See also Du Bois, ed., *The Negro American Family*, pp. 50–52; Alfred Holt Stone, "The Negro in the Yazoo-Mississippi Delta," American Economic Association *Publications*, 3rd Series 3 (Feb. 1902): 250.

48 Stone, "The Negro in the Yazoo-Mississippi Delta," p. 250; U.S. Industrial Commission, *Report*, x, p. 911; Du Bois, "The Negro Farmer," p. 514. See also Ray Stannard Baker, *Following the Color Line* (New York, 1908), p. 88.

49 Du Bois, ed., *The Negro American Family*, p. 53. See also Thomas Jackson Woofter, Jr., *Negro Migration: Changes in Rural Organization and Population of the Cotton Belt* (New York, 1969 [1920]), p. 88.

50 Du Bois, ed., *The Negro American Family*, p. 54; Park, "Negro Home Life and Standards of Living," pp. 149, 153. For some interesting photographs of a variety of rural houses, see Atwater and Woods, "Dietary Studies," pp. 24, 30; Frissell and Bevier, "Dietary Studies," p. 10.

51 Du Bois, ed., *The Negro American Family*, pp. 54–58.

52 For some interesting photographs of black housing in Atlanta, see *ibid.*, pp. 86–96.

53 U.S. Department of Labor, "Condition of the Negro in Various Cities," pp. 368–369.

54 Du Bois, *The Philadelphia Negro*, pp. 292–299. For a contemporary description of conditions in New York City, see Ovington, *Half a Man*, pp. 17–28.

55 Du Bois, ed., *The Negro American Family*, pp. 58–59.

56 *Ibid.*, pp. 64–80.

57 Park, "Negro Home Life and Standards of Living," p. 156.

58 Quoted in Gilbert Osofsky, *Harlem: The Making of a Ghetto; Negro New York, 1890–1930* (New York, 1968), p. 111.

59 Du Bois, ed., *The Negro American Family*, pp. 54–64, 122–125; *idem, The Philadelphia Negro*, pp. 287–290.

60 George Edmund Haynes, "The Negro at Work in New York City: A Study

in Economic Progress," Columbia University, *Studies in History, Economics and Public Law* 49 (1912): 63; Du Bois, *The Philadelphia Negro*, pp. 347–348; *idem*, ed., *The Negro American Family*, p. 61; Osofsky, *Harlem*, pp. 13, 112.

61 Abram L. Harris, *The Negro As Capitalist: A Study of Banking and Business Among American Negroes* (New York, 1969 [1936]), p. 57; Du Bois, *The Philadelphia Negro*, p. 348.

62 Du Bois, *The Philadelphia Negro*, p. 296.

63 *Ibid.*, p. 297; Ovington, *Half a Man*, p. 27. See also Richard R. Wright, Jr., *The Negro in Pennsylvania: A Study in Economic History* (New York, 1969 [1912]), pp. 64–67.

64 Du Bois, *The Philadelphia Negro*, p. 290; Haynes, "The Negro at Work in New York City," pp. 62–63.

65 Du Bois, *The Philadelphia Negro*, pp. 295–297; Osofsky, *Harlem*, pp. 105–108; Allan H. Spear, *Black Chicago: The Making of a Ghetto, 1890–1920* (Chicago, 1967), pp. 21, 228–229.

66 Osofsky, *Harlem*, pp. 109–110.

67 Spear, *Black Chicago*, p. 21. For an interesting theoretical discussion of changing patterns of residential segregation, see Hubert M. Blalock, Jr., *Toward a Theory of Minority-Group Relations* (New York, 1967), pp. 121–126. The role of white intermediaries in making possible the acquisition of business real estate by blacks is clearly illustrated by Bettye C. Thomas, "A Nineteenth-Century Black Operated Shipyard, 1866–1884: Reflections upon Its Inception and Ownership," *Journal of Negro History* 59 (Jan. 1974): 6. "No white shipyard owner was willing to sell or lease a shipyard directly to a black group in 1866," so the blacks persuaded a white businessman "to act as an intermediary for the transaction," then subleased the property from him.

CHAPTER 6. OVERVIEW AND INTERPRETATION

1 U.S. Bureau of the Census, *Historical Statistics of the United States, Colonial Times to 1957* (Washington, 1960), p. 214.

2 W. E. B. Du Bois, ed., *The Negro American Family* (Atlanta, 1908), pp. 106–107, 111. The figure for the lower limit of Du Bois' confidence interval, $500,000,000, is given as $550,000,000 in the source, an obvious typographical error.

3 Horace Mann Bond, *Negro Education in Alabama: A Study in Cotton and Steel* (New York, 1969 [1939]), *passim;* Louis R. Harlan, *Separate and Unequal: Public School Campaigns and Racism in the Southern Seaboard States, 1901–1915* (New York, 1969 [1958]), *passim;* Henry Allen Bullock, *A History of Negro Education in the South: From 1619 to the Present* (Cambridge, Mass., 1967), pp. 1–193.

4 *New York Age,* May 16, 1885, quoted in George Brown Tindall, *South Carolina Negroes, 1877–1900* (Baton Rouge, 1966 [1952]), p. 114.

5 W. E. B. Du Bois, *The Souls of Black Folk* (New York, 1961 [1903]), p. 85. For some evidence of the widespread exclusion of blacks from service on

juries, see Gilbert Thomas Stephenson, *Race Distinctions in American Law* (New York, 1910), pp. 253–272. See also Wilford H. Smith, "The Negro and the Law," in Booker T. Washington and others, *The Negro Problem* (New York, 1969 [1903]), pp. 127–159; Tindall, *South Carolina Negroes,* pp. 264, 273; and Lawrence D. Rice, *The Negro in Texas, 1874–1900* (Baton Rouge, 1971), pp. 240–257. Lynching was insightfully examined by Ray Stannard Baker, *Following the Color Line* (New York, 1908), pp. 175–215. Baker also observed (pp. 49, 98) discriminatory sentencing in the courts at first hand. One remarkable instance involved the sentencing of a black man to six months on the chain gang or a fine of $25 for the theft of a potato valued at 5 cents.

6 The income estimates presented in Chapter 5, along with income estimates for the overall economy, imply a relative black income in the neighborhood of one-fourth the white level. See the Technical Appendix, Section 4B, for the calculations.

7 This growth rate is inferred from the growth rate for the entire population, in which the whites had predominant weight. For details see the Technical Appendix, Section 4B.

8 Simon Kuznets, *Modern Economic Growth: Rate, Structure and Spread* (New Haven, 1966), pp. 64–65.

9 W. E. B. Du Bois, *The Philadelphia Negro: A Social Study* (New York, 1967 [1899]), pp. 11, 145; my *Transformation of the American Economy, 1865–1914: An Essay in Interpretation* (New York, 1971), pp. 114–123; Allan H. Spear, *Black Chicago: The Making of a Negro Ghetto, 1890–1920* (Chicago, 1967), pp. 228–229; Nathan Glazer, "Blacks and Ethnic Groups: The Difference, and the Political Difference It Makes," in Nathan I. Huggins, Martin Kilson, and Daniel M. Fox, eds., *Key Issues in the Afro-American Experience* (New York, 1971), II, pp. 193–211; National Advisory Commission on Civil Disorders, "Comparing the Immigrant and Negro Experience," in *Report* (New York, 1968), pp. 278–282.

10 Gene N. Levine and Darrell M. Montero, "Socioeconomic Mobility among Three Generations of Japanese Americans," *Journal of Social Issues* 29 (1973): 33–48. See also Ivan H. Light, *Ethnic Enterprise in America: Business and Welfare among Chinese, Japanese, and Blacks* (Berkeley, 1972), *passim.*

11 Du Bois, *The Philadelphia Negro,* pp. 134, 325, 350–351. For similar remarks by another careful contemporary observer, see Richard R. Wright, Jr., *The Negro in Pennsylvania: A Study in Economic History* (New York, 1969 [1912]), pp. 188–191.

12 E. Franklin Frazier's statement went even further: "Living constantly under the domination and contempt of the white man, the Negro came to believe in his own inferiority, whether he ignored or accepted the values of the white man's world." See *Black Bourgeoisie: The Rise of a New Middle Class in the United States* (New York, 1962), p. 112. Ray Marshall observes that "when discrimination becomes institutionalized, as it has for blacks, overt discrimination becomes a relatively less important cause of the disadvantages of discriminatees, because inadequate education, segre-

gated labor market institutions, and other forces which deny equal access to jobs, training or information greatly reduce the probability that those discriminated against will aspire to, prepare for, or seek to enter the status occupations. In neoclassical language, institutional discrimination makes it less likely that black and white workers will be homogeneous substitutes." See "The Economics of Racial Discrimination: A Survey," *Journal of Economic Literature* 12 (Sept. 1974): 861.

13 Hubert M. Blalock, Jr., expresses a closely related idea: "If the minority's competition were numerous, then one might expect discrimination to take the form of political action and overt violence. Thus, poor whites in the South may not have been able to regulate Negro competition directly by economic means, but they succeeded in accomplishing the same by political action and intimidation." See *Toward a Theory of Minority-Group Relations* (New York, 1967), p. 150.

TECHNICAL APPENDIX

1 Data are available to test this assumption for 1900 and 1890. In 1900 the proportion was in fact 40 percent; in 1890 it was 45 percent. This difference led Walter Willcox to argue that urban fertility was falling faster than rural fertility (see "The Probable Increase of the Negro Race in the United States," *Quarterly Journal of Economics* 19 [Aug. 1905]: 555–556); but in view of the known defectiveness of the 1890 census enumeration and the likelihood that the greatest undercount was of infants and children in the countryside, the actual 1890 differential was probably smaller than the data show. Hence, the assumption of a constant urban–rural differential in child–woman ratios throughout the period 1880–1910 probably does not result in any appreciable error.

2 "Mortality Trends of Southern Blacks, 1850–1910: Some Preliminary Findings," *Explorations in Economic History,* 13 (Jan. 1976): 13–42.

3 An expression for evaluating the bias is derived in Potluri Rao and Roger LeRoy Miller, *Applied Econometrics* (Belmont, Calif., 1971), pp. 60–62. It should be mentioned that Meeker was using his equation as a predictive device, not as a basis for testing hypotheses. Therefore, bias of the coefficients mattered little for his purposes, and he did not concern himself with the possibility of specification error.

4 "Race, Tenure, and Resource Allocation in Southern Agriculture, 1910," *Journal of Economic History* 33 (March 1973): 151–156.

5 I employ two different measures of risk to guard against arbitrary results. The second measure, X_2, is equal to X_1 times the standard deviation; hence it depends on units of measurement while X_1 does not. It therefore provides an independent measure of risk and is not a simple algebraic transformation of X_1. I computed the two measures of risk using data on physical yields in the 10 years 1900–1909. For the data and their sources, see *ibid.*, p. 158.

6 For a critical discussion of the underlying model and the tests, see Gavin Wright, "Comment on Papers by Reid, Ransom and Sutch, and Higgs," *ibid.*, pp. 173–176.

7 "Patterns of Farm Rental in the Georgia Cotton Belt, 1880–1900," *ibid.* 34 (June 1974): 469–477.

8 Data are drawn from the census. For a map showing the boundaries of the sample area, see my "Patterns of Farm Rental," p. 471.

9 The data are for all Southern states with substantial cotton acreage except Texas and Oklahoma, which are excluded because the numerous large cattle ranches and wheat farms in these states render them incomparable with the other cotton states in an investigation of farm size. For the data and their sources, see my "Race, Tenure, and Resource Allocation," pp. 162–163.

10 For a critical discussion of my analysis of racial differences in farm size, see Wright, "Comment," pp. 171–172, 175.

11 "Participation of Blacks and Immigrants in the American Merchant Class, 1890–1910: Some Demographic Relations," *Explorations in Economic History*, 13 (April 1976).

12 Data are drawn from the census reports for the years indicated. States considered Southern are Maryland, Virginia, North Carolina, South Carolina, Georgia, Florida, Alabama, Mississippi, Louisiana, Texas, Arkansas, Tennessee, and Kentucky. For more detailed discussion of the data, the tests, and their interpretation, see *ibid.*

13 Robert E. Gallman, "Gross National Product in the United States, 1834–1909," in National Bureau of Economic Research, Conference on Research in Income and Wealth, *Output, Employment, and Productivity in the United States after 1800* (New York, 1966), p. 26.

14 John W. Kendrick, *Productivity Trends in the United States* (Princeton, 1961), p. 290. Kendrick's data show that the ratio of NNP to GNP during the decade 1869–1878 was about 91 percent. I believe that deduction of indirect business taxes from NNP would yield a National Income not much below 90 percent of GNP; but I have been unable to find an estimate of indirect business taxes *circa* 1867–1868 to confirm my belief. In any event my conclusions are not sensitive to the assumption of a 90 percent figure.

Select bibliography

This bibliography has two parts: in the first I discuss the more important sources I have used in my research; in the second I present a select, alphabetized list of sources consulted. References in the bibliographical essay appear in abbreviated form. For more complete publication details the reader can refer to the select list of sources. In no sense is this a comprehensive bibliography. Nevertheless, I hope that it will prove useful to students and researchers in the field of black economic history.

ESSAY ON SOURCES

The best bibliographical starting point for the student of black economic history is the carefully organized and annotated volume by James M. McPherson and others, *Blacks in America* (1971). Also useful is the bibliography edited by Elizabeth W. Miller and Mary L. Fisher, *The Negro in America* (1970). On postbellum Southern agriculture an excellent reference work is Helen H. Edwards, ed., *A List of References for the History of Agriculture in the Southern United States, 1865–1900* (1971). See also Gerald D. Nash, "Research Opportunities in the Economic History of the South after 1880," *Journal of Southern History* (1966) and James A. Gross, "Historians and the Literature of the Negro Worker," *Labor History* (1969). As the literature is growing rapidly, only a continuing perusal of current book reviews and periodical article listings can keep the researcher up to date.

Black economic history needs to be placed in the context of overall American economic history. A number of textbooks tell the story of American development. The best treatment is the collaborative work by Lance E. Davis and others, *American Economic Growth* (1972); briefer and more provocative is Douglass C. North, *Growth and Welfare in the American Past* (1974). Economic data series are conveniently compiled and annotated in U.S. Bureau of the Census, *Historical Statistics of the United States, Colonial Times to 1957* (1960) and *idem, Long Term Economic Growth, 1860–1965* (1966). A brief interpretive study of American economic development in the post-Civil War era is my *Transformation of the American Economy, 1865–1914* (1971). A useful compilation of articles is Ralph Andreano, ed., *The Economic Impact of the American Civil War* (1967). On Southern development, see Rupert B. Vance, *Human Geography of the South* (1935), an informative work with much historical perspective. A more analytical contribution is Stanley L. Engerman, "Some Economic Factors in Southern Backwardness in the Nineteenth Century," in John F. Kain and John R. Meyer, eds., *Essays in Regional Economics* (1971).

The most comprehensive study of American race relations is still Gunnar Myrdal, *An American Dilemma* (1944), a work full of historical information. But much has happened since Myrdal and his collaborators made their classic study, and it now requires supplementation at many points with more recent research findings. An indispensable theoretical contribution, tough reading for noneconomists, is Gary S. Becker, *The Economics of Discrimination* (1971). Becker's analysis is extended and applied by Finis Welch, "Labor-Market Discrimination: An Interpretation of Income Differences in the Rural South," *Journal of Political Economy* (1967). Taking issue with Becker and offering an alternative analysis is Lester C. Thurow, *Poverty and Discrimination* (1969). For a discussion that advocates no particular model of discrimination but rather the use of a variety of models, see Henry C. Wallich and William J. Dodson, "Economic Models and Black Economic Development," *Review of Black Political Economy* (1972). A recent critical survey of various theories is Ray Marshall, "The Economics of Racial Discrimination: A Survey," *Journal of Economic Literature* (1974). See also Joseph E. Stiglitz, "Approaches to the Economics of Discrimination," *American Economic Review* (1973). During the 1930s a number of social anthropologists became interested in the Southern "caste" system and conducted detailed field investigations. Two of the best such studies are Hortense Powdermaker, *After Freedom* (1939) and Allison Davis, Burleigh B. Gardner, and Mary R. Gardner, *Deep South* (1941); both contain much historical information and many insights of value to economic historians. A provocative work by a sociological theorist, less systematic but more comprehensive than Becker's treatment, is Hubert M. Blalock, Jr., *Toward a Theory of Minority-Group Relations* (1967). See also the detailed sociological study by Bertram Wilbur Doyle, *The Etiquette of Race Relations in the South* (1937).

Whether one employs economic, anthropological, or sociological theory, an essential supplement is information on the precise historical forms of the variables and constraints specified in the theory. Evidence on the Southern whites' "taste for discrimination" is available in practically every periodical and newspaper that served as an organ of white opinion. For the sentiment of the immediate postwar period, see George Fitzhugh, "What's To Be Done with the Negroes?" *De Bow's Review* (1866) and the same author's "Negro Agrarianism," *ibid.* (1868). Useful secondary works on the racial ideologies of the whites include Lawrence J. Friedman, *The White Savage* (1970) and George M. Fredrickson, *The Black Image in the White Mind* (1972). See also Fredrickson's "Toward a Social Interpretation of the Development of American Racism," in Nathan I. Huggins, Martin Kilson, and Daniel M. Fox, eds., *Key Issues in the Afro-American Experience* (1971); Joel R. Williamson, "Black Self-Assertion Before and After Emancipation," in *ibid.*; and Otey M. Scruggs, "The Economic and Racial Components of Jim Crow," in *ibid.* The comparison between blacks and immigrants is pursued by Nathan Glazer, "Blacks and Ethnic Groups: The Difference and the Political Difference It Makes," in *ibid.* Glazer concludes that although the blacks and the European immigrants had similar experiences in the North, they had very different experiences overall because of the racial peculiarities of the South, where the great majority of the blacks lived. Taking issue with Glazer's analysis of the Northern black experience is Patrick Renshaw, "The Black Ghetto, 1890–1940," *Journal of American Studies* (1974). On the European immigrants, see my "Race, Skills, and Earnings: American Immigrants in 1909," *Journal of Economic History* (1971). The intriguing case of the Japanese, who constitute a more valid comparative group than the European immigrants, is examined in Gene N. Levine and Darrell M. Montero, "Socio-economic Mobility among Three Generations of Japanese Americans," *Journal of Social*

Issues (1973). See also Ivan H. Light, *Ethnic Enterprise in America* (1972), an insightful comparative study of blacks and the Japanese and Chinese immigrants.

Quantitative evidence relevant to the study of black economic history can be found in a variety of sources. The U.S. Bureau of the Census, *Historical Statistics* (1960) contains only a few statistical series disaggregated by race. The reports of the decennial federal census are major sources of figures. A magnificent annotated compilation of census data, some of them unpublished in the original census reports, is U.S. Bureau of the Census, *Negro Population, 1790–1915* (1918); this indispensable volume presents data on population, education, labor force, agriculture, and a variety of other subjects. A revealing collection of maps, charts, and data, along with an objective narrative, is O. C. Stine and O. E. Baker, *Atlas of American Agriculture* (1918). Various bulletins of the Census Bureau, the Department of Agriculture, and the Department of Labor provide useful quantitative evidence. Extremely rich sources of figures and commentary are the annual *Atlanta University Publications,* edited by W. E. B. Du Bois between 1898 and 1914; but these volumes must be used carefully, for they contain data of very uneven reliability – some of them merely hearsay or guesses – and internal inconsistencies even within a given volume. Nevertheless, if used carefully, they provide an unequalled storehouse of information.

General histories of black Americans contain much that relates either directly or indirectly to economic history. The standard work is John Hope Franklin, *From Slavery to Freedom* (1967). A briefer, better written, and more interpretive volume is August Meier and Elliott Rudwick, *From Plantation to Ghetto* (1970). Dan Lacy, *The White Use of Blacks in America* (1972) is a provocative survey, strong on the interrelations of economic, social, and political behavior, but marred by an implicit conspiracy theory of white behavior that fails to appreciate how broad developments sometimes occurred without anyone's designing or willing them; further, the level of economic analysis is superficial, at times simply wrong. A general work on a more restricted time span is Rayford W. Logan, *The Betrayal of the Negro, from Rutherford B. Hayes to Woodrow Wilson* (1965). August Meier, *Negro Thought in America, 1880–1915* (1963) is excellent and much broader than its title suggests. See also Henderson Donald, *The Negro Freedman* (1952), which cover the late nineteenth century from the perspective of the Southern whites, a view no longer fashionable.

No one can really understand postbellum black history without an appreciation of the antebellum economy of the South. A subtle and sophisticated study of the establishment of slavery in North America is Winthrop D. Jordan, *White Over Black* (1968). The gentle racism of U. B. Phillips makes him unpopular nowadays, but his *Life and Labor in the Old South* (1929) is still well worth reading. After four decades, L. C. Gray, *History of Agriculture in the Southern United States to 1860* (1933) remains without peer. An elegant and deeply researched interpretation of the slave system is Kenneth M. Stampp, *The Peculiar Institution* (1956). Other influential works include Stanley M. Elkins, *Slavery* (1959), Eugene D. Genovese, *The Political Economy of Slavery* (1965), John W. Blassingame, *The Slave Community* (1972), and Robert S. Starobin, *Industrial Slavery in the Old South* (1970). Richard Wade, *Slavery in the Cities* (1964) offers an interpretation now seriously challenged by Claudia Dale Goldin, "Urbanization and Slavery: The Issue of Compatibility," in Leo F. Schnore, ed., *The New Urban History* (1975). By far the most controversial interpretation of the slave economy to appear in recent years is Robert William Fogel and Stanley L. Engerman, *Time on the Cross* (1974). This analysis has stirred an immense cloud of scholarly dust, and no one can predict now how the landscape of slavery studies will appear when the dust has settled. A good starting point for evaluating the controversy is Paul A. David and Peter Temin, "Slavery: The Progressive Institution?" *Journal of Economic History* (1974). See also Gavin Wright, "New and Old Views on the Economics of Slavery," *ibid.* (1973).

A number of monographs treat developments in particular states during short periods of the postbellum era in great detail. Among the best of these are Joel Williamson, *After Slavery* (1965), which contains an illuminating account of the emerging tenant systems in South Carolina during Reconstruction; Vernon Lane Wharton, *The Negro in Mississippi, 1865–1890* (1947); and George Brown Tindall, *South Carolina Negroes, 1877–1900* (1952). Somewhat less illuminating is Frenise A. Logan, *The Negro in North Carolina, 1876– 1894* (1964), which suffers from superficial economic analysis: Logan is too quick to claim racial discrimination when the evidence indicates only racial difference. Lawrence D. Rice, *The Negro in Texas, 1874–1900* (1971) has two chapters on economic matters and one on the black man's legal status. An account of the emancipated blacks on the Sea Islands of South Carolina during the Civil War is Willie Lee Rose, *Rehearsal for Reconstruction* (1964). On the late 1860s in Alabama, see Peter Kolchin, *First Freedom* (1972), which emphasizes that the blacks' postwar economic condition, with all its shortcomings, was vastly superior to slavery.

Contemporaries expressed valuable insights into the economic and social life of the blacks. Frances Butler Leigh, *Ten Years on a Georgia Plantation since the War* (1883) is the view of a Southern white woman on an island rice plantation off the coast of Georgia. Frederick Douglass, one of the most remarkable men of the nineteenth century and the first black leader of national prominence, tells his story in *Life and Times of Frederick Douglass* (1892). Booker T. Washington's views come through clearly in all his published works, including *The Future of the American Negro* (1899), the autobiographical *Up From Slavery* (1901), *The Negro in the South* (1907), and *The Story of the Negro* (1909). W. E. B. Du Bois' views are set forth in a multitude of publications, including *The Souls of Black Folk* (1903), "The Economic Future of the Negro," American Economic Association *Publications* (1906), and the autobiographical *Dusk of Dawn* (1940). For the views of an articulate Mississippi planter and student of race relations, see Alfred Holt Stone, *Studies in the American Race Problem* (1908). On the condition of blacks in New York City, as seen by a white woman who helped to found the National Association for the Advancement of Colored People, see Mary White Ovington, *Half a Man* (1911). Richard R. Wright, Jr., a black man of many talents, brought together his observations in *The Negro in Pennsylvania* (1912).

Traveling correspondents sometimes took note of the black role in the Southern economy. Among the accounts with substantial and fairly reliable comments are Robert Somers, *The Southern States since the War, 1870–71* (1871), Edward King, *The Great South* (1875), Charles Nordhoff, *The Cotton States in the Spring and Summer of 1875* (1876), and Sir George Campbell, *White and Black* (1879). A later work that belongs partly to this genre but contains some insightful analysis along with its reportorial comments is Ray Stannard Baker, *Following the Color Line* (1908).

Sophisticated work in black demography is just getting under way, and the period 1865–1914 is in some ways more difficult to analyze than the periods before and after it. Many contemporaries were obsessed by the thought that the blacks were becoming extinct. A major work published in the nineteenth century, which expressed this obsession, is Frederick L. Hoffman, "Race Traits and Tendencies of the American Negro," American Economic Association *Publications* (1896). Hoffman, an actuary, declared himself particularly well suited to study black vital rates because he did not hold any prejudices; but this declaration was either a smokescreen or a self-deception, for this study is marred throughout by prejudiced interpretations. Even so capable and scientific a demographer as Walter F. Willcox was not immune to such prejudice; see his "The Probable Increase of the Negro Race in the United States," *Quarterly Journal of Economics* (1905). Reynolds Farley, *Growth of the Black Population* (1970) has relatively little to say about the period from 1865 to 1914, and what is said is largely conjectural and historically ill informed. Jack Ericson Eblen, "New Estimates of the Vital Rates of the United States Black Population during the Nineteenth Century," *Demography* (1974) makes use of sophisticated demographic techniques but reaches implausible conclusions. More plausible estimates are provided by Edward F. Meeker, "Mortality Trends of Southern Blacks, 1850–1910: Some Preliminary Findings," *Explorations in Economic History* (1976). Of related interest are Reynolds Farley, "The Demographic Rates and Social Institutions of the Nineteenth-Century Negro Population: A Stable Population Analysis," *Demography* (1965), which is narrower in scope than its title suggests; Paul Demeny and Paul Gingrich, "A Reconsideration of Negro-White Mortality Differentials in the United States," *ibid.* (1967), which considers twentieth-century data; and Ansley J. Coale and Norfleet N. Rives, Jr., "A Statistical Reconstruction of the Black Population of the United States, 1880–1970: Estimates of True Numbers by Age and Sex, Birth Rates, and Total Fertility," *Population Index* (1973), which deals with the late nineteenth and early twentieth centuries by making some highly implausible assumptions. An article that does not deal separately with blacks and whites but raises issues central to any analysis of historical changes in black mortality is my "Mortality in Rural America, 1870–1920: Estimates and Conjectures," *Explorations in Economic History* (1973). See also S. B. Jones, "Fifty Years of Negro Public Health," *Annals of the American Academy of Political and Social Science* (1913).

Estimates of the interstate migration of blacks since 1870 are available in Hope T. Eldridge and Dorothy Swaine Thomas, *Population Redistribution and Economic Growth, United States, 1870–1950: III. Demographic Analyses and Interrelations* (1964). On the exodus of 1879, see the documents reprinted in the *Journal of Negro History* (1919) and John G. Van Deusen, "The Exodus of 1879," *ibid.* (1936). Carter G. Woodson, *A Century of Negro Migration* (1918) is almost obsolete but contains some interesting details. Thomas Jackson Woofter, Jr., *Negro Migration* (1920) is both broader and narrower than its title suggests, since it deals with much besides migration but, for the period before 1914, with migration only within Georgia. See also R. R. Wright, Jr., "The Migration of Negroes to the North," *Annals of the American Academy of Political and Social Science* (1906). Many studies of the so-called Great Migration during World War I contain valuable comments on the earlier migrations. See U.S. Department of Labor, Division of Negro Economics, *Negro Migration in 1916–17* (1919) and Emmett J. Scott, *Negro Migration during the War* (1920).

The economic conditions of urban blacks are described with a profusion of quantitative data in U.S. Department of Labor, "Condition of the Negro in Various Cities," *Bulletin No. 10* (1897). A classic – required reading for any student of black economic and social history – is W. E. B. Du Bois, *The Philadelphia Negro* (1899); its many conceptual insights, voluminous data base, and conscientious interpretation make this one of the best books ever written on black economic life. A more modest but still useful monograph is George Edmund Haynes, "The Negro at Work in New York City," Columbia University, *Studies in History, Economics and Public Law* (1912). An interesting collection of documents is Hollis R. Lynch, ed., *The Black Urban Condition* (1973). Three competent studies of black community development in Northern cities are Gilbert Osofsky, *Harlem* (1968), Allan H. Spear, *Black Chicago* (1967), and David M. Katzman, *Before the Ghetto* (1973), a study of Detroit in the nineteenth century. See also Seth M. Scheiner, *Negro Mecca* (1965), which deals with New York City blacks, 1865–1920; Constance McLaughlin Green, *The Secret City* (1967), a study of Washington, D.C.; Allan Spear, "The Origins of the Urban Ghetto, 1870–1915," in Nathan I. Huggins, Martin Kilson, and Daniel M. Fox, eds., *Key Issues in the Afro-American Experience* (1971); and John W. Blassingame, "Before the Ghetto: The Making of the Black Community in Savannah, Georgia, 1865–1880," *Journal of Social History* (1973).

The postbellum development of Southern agriculture is vividly – at times too vividly – described by Fred A. Shannon, *The Farmer's Last Frontier* (1945). See also Eugene Lerner, "Southern Output and Agricultural Income, 1860–1880," *Agricultural History* (1959) and Willard Range, *A Century of Georgia Agriculture, 1850–1950* (1954). A number of established views are challenged in the pioneering econometric studies of Stephen J. DeCanio, *Agricultural Production, Supply and Institutions in the Post-Civil War South* (1972). Carter G. Woodson, *The Rural Negro* (1930) contains a mass of historical details but the economic analysis is superficial. A study that emphasizes the burden of easy identifiability for blacks in agriculture is Roger L. Ransom and Richard Sutch, "The Ex-Slave in the Post-Bellum South: A Study of the Economic Impact of Racism in a Market Environment," *Journal of Economic History* (1973). It is unfortunate that Ransom and Sutch attempt to apply a "signaling" (costly information) model of racial discrimination to a context where it has little applicability.

During the late 1920s and the 1930s a number of sociological works dealing with the rural South were published. To the extent that the economic conditions of the interwar period resembled those prevailing earlier, these studies provide valuable insights into the Southern rural economy of the post-Civil War era. Of particular value is Rupert B. Vance, *Human Factors in Cotton Culture* (1929). Two other informative works are Charles S. Johnson, *Shadow of the Plantation* (1934) and Arthur F. Raper, *Preface to Peasantry* (1936). In using these studies, one must make careful allowance for the interests and biases of their authors. Almost without exception they were primarily interested in reform rather than mere analysis; perhaps because of this interest they focused heavily on the poorest and most hopeless people and areas. While they offered a mass of detailed evidence, the representativeness of the evidence is often suspect. Moreover, the studies conducted in the 1930s often blamed alleged structural defects in the rural economy for problems that actually grew out of the Great Depression with its collapse of farm prices and incomes.

Contemporary government reports provide a mass of information on the rural economy of the postbellum South. An informative survey of the cotton economy is contained in U.S. Department of Agriculture, *Report of the Commissioner of Agriculture for the Year 1876* (1877). The U.S. Census Office, *Report on Cotton Production in the United States* (1884) is a massive two-volume study of the cotton economy conducted in connection with the census of 1880; it contains information on all aspects of cotton cultivation, including land rents, labor and tenancy systems, marketing, and costs of production. For the testimony of many Southerners, both black and white, on their economic condition in 1883, see the four volumes of U.S. Senate, Committee on Education and Labor, *Report on Relations between Labor and Capital* (1885). Another major source of information on agricultural matters is the tenth volume of the U.S. Industrial Commission, *Report* (1901), of which some 250 pages of testimony deal with the Southern rural economy. A thorough analysis of data from the census of 1900 is W. E. B. Du Bois, "The Negro Farmer," in *Twelfth Census of the United States* (1906). The development of the cotton economy is quantitatively documented in U.S. Department of Agriculture, Agricultural Marketing Service, "Cotton and Cottonseed: Acreage, Yield, Production, Disposition, Price, Value; by States, 1866–1952," *Statistical Bulletin No. 164* (1955).

Contemporary analyses of the Southern rural economy are more useful for telling us what people believed to be the problems than for telling us what the problems actually were. A case in point is Henry W. Grady, "Cotton and Its Kingdom," *Harper's New Monthly Magazine* (1881), a superficial analysis that has had remarkable longevity in the footnotes of historical treatises. A larger work of the same sort is M. B. Hammond, "The Cotton Industry," American Economic Association *Publications* (1897). A racially prejudiced but still informative work is Philip A. Bruce, *The Plantation Negro As a Freeman* (1889). More solidly analytical contemporary works are Robert Preston Brooks, "The Agrarian Revolution in Georgia, 1865–1912," University of Wisconsin, *Bulletin No. 639* (1914) and Lewis Cecil Gray, "Southern Agriculture, Plantation System, and the Negro Problem," *Annals of the American Academy of Political and Social Science* (1912).

The first few years after emancipation are among the most intensively studied periods of black history. A well-documented summary that covers the period 1865–1868 is Oscar Zeichner, "The Transition from Slave to Free Agricultural Labor in the Southern States," *Agricultural History* (1939). Charles E. Seagrave's dissertation concludes that the real incomes of first-class agricultural laborers more than doubled between 1855 and 1867; see his abstract entitled "The Southern Negro Agricultural Worker: 1850–1870," *Journal of Economic History* (1971). The general failure of the homesteading privileges made available to blacks after the Civil War is the subject of Christie Farnham Pope, "Southern Homesteads for Negroes," *Agricultural History* (1970).

The Freedmen's Bureau played a central role in the transition from slavery to a free labor system. The standard work is George R. Bentley, *A History of the Freedmen's Bureau* (1955). More hostile toward the bureau's activities, arguing that the bureau's agents often worked more in the interests of the whites than in the interests of the freedmen, is William S. McFeely, *Yankee Stepfather* (1968). For an early reinterpretation that emphasizes the positive contributions of the bureau in assisting the ex-slaves, see W. E. B. Du Bois, "The Freedmen's Bureau," *Atlantic Monthly* (1901). See also Martin Abbott,

"Free Land, Free Labor, and the Freedmen's Bureau," *Agricultural History* (1956); Joe M. Richardson, "The Freedmen's Bureau and Negro Labor in Florida," *Florida Historical Quarterly* (1960); and William S. McFeely, "Unfinished Business: The Freedmen's Bureau and Federal Action in Race Relations," in Nathan I. Huggins, Martin Kilson, and Daniel M. Fox, eds., *Key Issues in the Afro-American Experience* (1971). Of course, the best sources of all on this topic are the reports of the bureau itself. See especially *Senate Executive Documents,* 39th Congress, 1st Session, No. 27, which makes it quite clear why different historians have been able to draw different conclusions from the same source materials. In brief, the evidence on the actions of the bureau does not point consistently toward any single conclusion.

Probably the best single description of postwar conditions in the South, though not unprejudiced by any means, is Carl Schurz's report to the President, printed in *Senate Executive Documents,* 39th Congress, 1st Session, No. 2. Benjamin C. Truman's report was more sympathetic toward the defeated rebels; see *ibid.,* No. 43. A mass of testimony is contained in U.S. Congress, Joint Committee on Reconstruction, *Report* (1866). A remarkably analytical discussion of the economics of slavery and emancipation is Daniel R. Goodloe, "Resources and Industrial Condition of the Southern States," in U.S. Department of Agriculture, *Report of the Commissioner of Agriculture for the Year 1865* (1866). An informative report sympathetic to the planters is "Southern Agriculture," in U.S. Department of Agriculture, *Report of the Commissioner of Agriculture for the Year 1867* (1868). For a solidly Southern white view, see A. R. Lightfoot, "Condition and Wants of the Cotton Raising States," *DeBow's Review* (1869). A number of Northern correspondents covered the postwar Southern scene. Four good reports, listed in descending order of their value to the economic historian, are: John Richard Dennett, *The South As It Is: 1865–1866* (articles from 1865–1866 collected and reprinted in 1965); Whitelaw Reid, *After the War* (1866); Sidney Andrews, *The South Since the War* (1866); and J. T. Trowbridge, *The South* (1866).

The market for agricultural labor in the postwar South is succinctly described by Southerner [pseud.], "Agricultural Labor at the South," *Galaxy* (1871). Though the anonymous author of this piece shared all the usual prejudices of his class, his article is a superb source of information on many aspects of the rural Southern economy, particularly valuable for its discussion of the extent and methods of competition among planters in securing the labor services of the freedmen. Another useful discussion by a Southern planter is Alfred Holt Stone, "The Negro in the Yazoo-Mississippi Delta," American Economic Association *Publications* (1902). Farm wage rates classified by race are presented in U.S. Department of Agriculture, Division of Statistics, "Wages of Farm Labor in the United States," *Miscellaneous Series, Bulletin No. 22* (1901) and James H. Blodgett, "Wages of Farm Labor in the United States: Results of Twelve Statistical Investigations, 1866–1902," U.S. Department of Agriculture, Bureau of Statistics, *Miscellaneous Series, Bulletin No. 26* (1903). Drawing upon the data of the former report, my "Did Southern Farmers Discriminate?" *Agricultural History* (1972) argues that, after adjustment for racial differences of income in kind, blacks and whites earned approximately equal real wages when employed as agricultural laborers. This proposition is disputed by Frenise A. Logan, "Factors Influencing the Efficiency of Negro Farm Laborers in Post-Reconstruction North Carolina," *Agricultural History* (1959), but Logan's documentation does not support his claims. Charles A. Roberts questions my interpretation of the USDA wage data in "Did Southern Farmers Discriminate? – The Evidence Re-Examined," *Agricultural History* (1975); and I respond to Roberts' criticism in "Did Southern Farmers Discriminate? – Interpretive Problems and Further Evidence," *ibid*. A little-known aspect of black agricultural employment is surveyed in Kenneth W. Porter, "Negro Labor in the Western Cattle Industry, 1866–1900," *Labor History* (1969). Porter estimates that about a quarter of the western cowboys were blacks; he also finds no evidence of wage discrimination against them, although they were generally excluded from positions as trail bosses.

Historians have been too quick to condemn and too slow to understand the systems of land rental that grew up in the South after the Civil War. For extending our comprehension of these systems, a pioneering and indispensable theoretical work is Steven N. S. Cheung, *The Theory of Share Tenancy* (1969). A good source to use for putting Cheung's theory into the Southern context is Harold Hoffsommer, ed., *The Social and Economic Significance of Land Tenure in the Southwestern States* (1950). Joseph D. Reid, Jr., "Sharecropping As An Understandable Market Response: The Post-Bellum South," *Journal of Economic History* (1973) takes issue with Cheung's analysis, but it appears that Reid's own model has limited utility for analyzing the postbellum South; nevertheless, his article is useful for the many extracts from share-tenant contracts that it presents. Cheung's analysis is extended and econometric tests presented in my "Race, Tenure, and Resource Allocation in Southern Agriculture, 1910," *ibid*. and my "Patterns of Farm Rental in the Georgia Cotton Belt, 1880–1900," *ibid*. (1974). For a good contemporary discussion of the shift from share-rent to fixed-rent tenancy on a typical Southern plantation, see David C. Barrow, Jr., "A Georgia Plantation," *Scribner's Monthly* (1881). Several rental contracts from South Carolina are reproduced in their entirety in Rosser H. Taylor, "Post-Bellum Southern Rental Contracts," *Agricultural History* (1943). Among the best contemporary analyses of Southern land tenure are Thomas J. Edwards, "The Tenant System and Some Changes since Emancipation," *Annals of the American Academy of Political and Social Science* (1913); W. E. B. Du Bois, "The Negro Landholder of Georgia," U.S. Department of Labor, *Bulletin No. 35* (1901); and an insightful analytical contribution by Enoch Marvin Banks, "The Economics of Land Tenure in Georgia," Columbia University, *Studies in History, Economics and Public Law* (1905). During the second and third decades of the twentieth century, the Department of Agriculture conducted a number of careful investigations of the Southern farm economy. The analytical and empirical quality of these studies is outstanding, and they shed much light on a variety of questions about the rural South. See E. A. Boeger and E. A. Goldenweiser, "A Study of the Tenant Systems of Farming in the Yazoo-Mississippi Delta," U.S. Department of Agriculture, *Bulletin No. 337* (1916); H. M. Dixon and H. W. Hawthorne, "An Economic Study of Farming in Sumter County, Georgia," *idem, Bulletin No. 492* (1917); E. S. Haskell, "A Farm-Management Survey in Brooks County, Georgia," *idem, Bulletin No. 648* (1918); Clyde R. Chambers, "Relation of Land Income to Land Value," *idem, Bulletin No. 1224* (1924); C. O. Brannen, "Relation of Land Tenure to Plantation Organization," *idem, Bulletin No. 1269* (1924); and an admirable survey of monographic proportions by L. C. Gray and others, "Farm Ownership and Tenancy," *idem, Yearbook, 1923* (1924).

The merchant credit system of the postbellum South is another institution much condemned but poorly understood. Contemporary discussions were almost invariably polemical. For example, see Charles H. Otken, *The Ills of the South* (1894) and George K. Holmes, "The Peons of the South," *Annals of the American Academy of Political and Social Science* (1893). Perhaps because of its misleading title, the latter has been often misunderstood: it deals with the merchant credit system but says nothing about actual peonage. More recent and dispassionate discussions include Thomas D. Clark, *Pills, Petticoats and Plows* (1944); *idem*, "The Furnishing and Supply System in Southern Agriculture since 1865," *Journal of Southern History* (1946); and Jacqueline P. Bull, "The General Merchant in the Economic History of the New South," *ibid.* (1952). The credit scarcity that prevailed in the postbellum South is the subject of William E. Laird and James R. Rinehart, "Deflation, Agriculture and Southern Development," *Agricultural History* (1968). For a more searching analysis of this subject, see Richard Sylla, "Federal Policy, Banking Market Structure, and Capital Mobilization in the United States, 1863–1913," *Journal of Economic History* (1969). A fascinating account of some particularly horrifying instances of peonage is Pete Daniel, *The Shadow of Slavery* (1972). These cases make it quite clear that genuine peonage resulted from the legal impotence of the peon rather than from debt *per se.* Unfortunately, Daniel's book does not provide what is really wanting here: a firm estimate of the prevalence of genuine peonage. Roger L. Ransom and Richard Sutch, "Debt Peonage in the Cotton South after the Civil War," *Journal of Economic History* (1972) pours old wine into new bottles. William W. Brown and Morgan O. Reynolds, "Debt Peonage Re-examined," *ibid.* (1973) takes issue with Ransom and Sutch, largely on *a priori* grounds.

The employment of blacks in nonagricultural jobs is documented in W. E. B. Du Bois, ed., *The Negro Artisan* (1902) and *idem, The Negro American Artisan* (1912). As noted earlier, the hodgepodge of information thrown together in these Atlanta University Publications must be used with caution. See also Kelly Miller, "Professional and Skilled Occupations," *Annals of the American Academy of Political and Social Science* (1913) and R. R. Wright, Jr., "The Negro in Unskilled Labor," *ibid.* Two general works containing a mass of historical details but marred by superficial analysis are Charles H. Wesley, *Negro Labor in the United States, 1850–1925* (1927) and Lorenzo J. Greene and Carter G. Woodson, *The Negro Wage Earner* (1930). See also Paul B. Worthman and James R. Green, "Black Workers in the New South, 1865–1915," in Nathan I. Huggins, Martin Kilson, and Daniel M. Fox, eds., *Key Issues in the Afro-American Experience* (1971), a survey that gives disproportionate attention to organized labor and therefore fails to consider the mass of black workers. For a systematic study of nonagricultural workers, see my "Firm-Specific Evidence on Racial Wage Differentials and Workforce Segregation," *American Economic Review,* forthcoming.

The relation of black workers to the organized labor movement has attracted considerable scholarly attention. The standard work is Sterling D. Spero and Abram L. Harris, *The Black Worker* (1931). Contemporary views are expressed in Mary White Ovington, "The Negro in the Trade Unions in New York," *Annals of the American Academy of Political and Social Science* (1906) and Booker T. Washington, "The Negro and the Labor Unions," *Atlantic Monthly* (1913). A more recent descriptive survey is Gerald N. Grob, "Organized Labor and the Negro Worker, 1865–1900," *Labor History* (1960). Three interesting case studies are William M. Tuttle, Jr., "Labor Conflict and Racial Violence: The Black Worker in Chicago, 1894–1919," *Labor History* (1969); Paul B. Worthman, "Black Workers and Labor Unions in Birmingham, Alabama, 1897–1904," *ibid.;* and John Michael Matthews, "The Georgia 'Race Strike' of 1909," *Journal of Southern History* (1974).

Black business enterprise is documented and analyzed in an Atlanta University Publication edited by W. E. B. Du Bois, *The Negro in Business* (1899). A useful work that focuses on black banking enterprises is Abram L. Harris, *The Negro As Capitalist* (1936). For a provocative essay that relates in part to black business, see E. Franklin Frazier, *Black Bourgeoisie* (1962). See also Walter B. Weare, *Black Business in the New South* (1973), an insightful social history of the men who organized and managed one of the most successful black firms. A comparative view of the relation between demographic variables and black business is provided by my "Participation of Blacks and Immigrants in the American Merchant Class, 1890–1910: Some Demographic Relations," *Explorations in Economic History* (1976). See also Ivan H. Light, *Ethnic Enterprise in America* (1972) for comparison of blacks with the Japanese and Chinese immigrants.

Information on the black level of living is scattered throughout a variety of sources. The best single source is W. E. B. Du Bois, ed., *The Negro American Family* (1909), a much broader work than its title suggests. The Labor Department conducted a number of illuminating studies of black communities: see especially "Condition of the Negro in Various Cities," *Bulletin No. 10* (1897); W. E. B. Du Bois, "The Negro in the Black Belt: Some Social Sketches," *Bulletin No. 22* (1899); J. Bradford Laws, "The Negroes of Cinclare Central Factory and Calumet Plantation, Louisiana," *Bulletin No. 38* (1902). A useful contemporary survey is Robert E. Park, "Negro Home Life and Standards of Living," *Annals of the American Academy of Political and Social Science* (1913). For carefully collected and analyzed data on black diets, see W. O. Atwater and Chas. D. Woods, "Dietary Studies with reference to the Food of the Negro in Alabama in 1895 and 1896," U.S. Department of Agriculture, Office of Experiment Stations, *Bulletin No. 38* (1897) and H. B. Frissell and Isabel Bevier, "Dietary Studies of Negroes in Eastern Virginia in 1897 and 1898," *idem, Bulletin No. 71* (1899).

Black educational attainment is best documented in the literacy and school attendance data of the census reports. Useful secondary sources include Horace Mann Bond, *Negro Education in Alabama* (1939), Louis R. Harlan, *Separate and Unequal* (1958), and Henry Allen Bullock, *A History of Negro Education in the South* (1967). Almost all general black histories contain substantial amounts of information on educational attainments and discrimination. (After completing my text I discovered a systematic quantitative study by Richard Kent Smith, *The Economics of Education and Discrimination in the U.S. South: 1870–1910* [unpublished Ph.D. dissertation, University of Wisconsin, 1973]. One of Smith's conclusions is that "the white taxpayers in the South were subsidizing black education until 1890. As blacks accumulated taxable property and wealth and operated farms rented from white landowners, black taxpayers bore an increasing share of the burden of education, until, by the turn of the century, black tenant farmers and property owners were subsidizing white education.")

Political developments during the crucial Reconstruction period are the subject of W. E. B. Du Bois, *Black Reconstruction in America* (1935), an unsuccessful attempt to force the facts into a Marxist mold; John Hope Franklin, *Reconstruction* (1961); Kenneth M. Stampp, *The Era of Reconstruction, 1865–1877* (1965); Robert Cruden, *The Negro in Reconstruction* (1969); and Allen W. Trelease, *Reconstruction* (1971). Later developments are traced by Paul

Lewinson, *Race, Class, and Party* (1932) and C. Vann Woodward, *Origins of the New South, 1877–1913* (1951). Woodward's book is the standard work on the overall economic, social, and political history of the South after Reconstruction, but its economic analysis is now seriously in need of up-dating. Despite his disclaimer, Woodward casts the tenancy and merchant credit systems as the villains of the play – an interpretation that recent research by economic historians will not generally sustain.

For testimony concerning the force and violence that bore so heavily on the freedmen, see *Senate Executive Documents,* 39th Congress, 1st Session, No. 27; *Senate Reports,* 42nd Congress, 2nd Session, No. 41; and Charles Stearns, *The Black Man of the South, and the Rebels* (1872). Modern articles include John A. Carpenter, "Atrocities in the Reconstruction Period," *Journal of Negro History* (1962), which draws on the records of the Freedmen's Bureau; and Herbert Shapiro, "The Ku Klux Klan during Reconstruction: The South Carolina Episode," *ibid.* (1964), which deals with a small but representative part of a much larger pattern. The coercive activities of poor white farmers known as "whitecapping" are described by William F. Holmes, "Whitecapping: Agrarian Violence in Mississippi, 1902–1906," *Journal of Southern History* (1969), and *idem,* "Whitecapping in Mississippi: Agrarian Violence in the Populist Era," *Mid-America* (1973). A work that contains a good deal of nonsense but has some provocative passages on patterns of Southern violence is W. J. Cash, *The Mind of the South* (1941). A stimulating if inconclusive recent analysis is Sheldon Hackney, "Southern Violence," *American Historical Review* (1969).

The history of legal segregation is traced by C. Vann Woodward, *The Strange Career of Jim Crow* (1966). Other aspects of the blacks' legal status are treated as well in Gilbert Thomas Stephenson, *Race Distinctions in American Law* (1910), Charles S. Mangum, Jr., *The Legal Status of the Negro* (1940), and *idem, The Legal Status of the Tenant Farmer in the Southeast* (1952). The last work contains a concise discussion of the legalities of peonage, which makes it plain that peonage grew not so much from the law itself as from the inability of blacks to obtain the equal protection of the laws. Also useful are Leo Alilunas, "Statutory Means of Impeding Emigration of the Negro," *Journal of Negro History* (1937); Oscar Zeichner, "The Legal Status of the Agricultural Laborer in the South," *Political Science Quarterly* (1940); and Mary Frances Berry, *Black Resistance/White Law* (1971).

SELECT LIST OF FULL TITLES

Abbott, Martin, "Free Land, Free Labor, and the Freedmen's Bureau," *Agricultural History* 30 (Oct. 1956): 150–156.

Abzug, Robert H., "The Black Family during Reconstruction," in Nathan I. Huggins, Martin Kilson, and Daniel Fox, eds., *Key Issues in the Afro-American Experience* (New York: Harcourt Brace Jovanovich, 1971), II, pp. 26–41.

Alilunas, Leo, "Statutory Means of Impeding Emigration of the Negro," *Journal of Negro History* 22 (April 1937): 148–162.

Andreano, Ralph, ed., *The Economic Impact of the American Civil War,* 2nd ed. (Cambridge, Mass.: Schenkman, 1967).

Andrews, Sidney, *The South since the War, as Shown by Fourteen Weeks of Travel and Observation in Georgia and the Carolinas* (Boston: Houghton Mifflin, 1971 [1866]).

Appel, John J., "American Negro and Immigrant Experience: Similarities and Differences," *American Quarterly* 18 (Spring 1966): 95–103.

Atwater, W. O., and Chas. D. Woods, "Dietary Studies with reference to the Food of the Negro in Alabama in 1895 and 1896," U.S. Department of Agriculture, Office of Experiment Stations, *Bulletin No. 38* (1897).

Baker, Ray Stannard, *Following the Color Line: American Negro Citizenship in the Progressive Era* (New York: Harper Torchbooks, 1964 [1908]).

Banks, Enoch Marvin, "The Economics of Land Tenure in Georgia," Columbia University, *Studies in History, Economics and Public Law* 23 (1905).

"Labor Supply and Labor Problems," *Annals of the American Academy of Political and Social Science* 35 (Jan. 1910): 143–149.

Barrow, David C., Jr., "A Georgia Plantation," *Scribner's Monthly* 21 (April 1881): 830–836.

Becker, Gary S., *The Economics of Discrimination*, 2nd ed. (Chicago: University of Chicago Press, 1971).

Bentley, George R., *A History of the Freedmen's Bureau* (Philadelphia: University of Pennsylvania Press, 1955).

Berry, Mary Frances, *Black Resistance/White Law: A History of Constitutional Racism in America* (New York: Appleton-Century-Crofts, 1971).

Bizzell, William Bennett, "Farm Tenantry in the United States," Texas Agricultural Experiment Station, *Bulletin No. 278* (April 1921).

Blalock, Hubert M., Jr., *Toward a Theory of Minority-Group Relations* (New York: John Wiley and Sons, 1967).

Blassingame, John W., *The Slave Community: Plantation Life in the Antebellum South* (New York: Oxford University Press, 1972).

"Before the Ghetto: The Making of the Black Community in Savannah, Georgia, 1865–1880," *Journal of Social History* 6 (Summer 1973): 463–488.

Bloch, Herman D., "Labor and the Negro, 1866–1910," *Journal of Negro History* 50 (July 1965): 163–184.

Blodgett, James H., "Wages of Farm Labor in the United States: Results of Twelve Statistical Investigations, 1866–1902," U.S. Department of Agriculture, Bureau of Statistics, *Miscellaneous Series, Bulletin No. 26* (1903).

Boeger, E. A., and E. A. Goldenweiser, "A Study of the Tenant Systems of Farming in the Yazoo-Mississippi Delta," U.S. Department of Agriculture, *Bulletin No. 337* (1916).

Bond, Horace Mann, *Negro Education in Alabama: A Study in Cotton and Steel* (New York: Atheneum, 1969 [1939]).

Brandfon, Robert L., *Cotton Kingdom of the New South: A History of the Yazoo Mississippi Delta from Reconstruction to the Twentieth Century* (Cambridge, Mass.: Harvard University Press, 1967).

Brannen, C. O., "Relation of Land Tenure to Plantation Organization," U.S. Department of Agriculture, *Bulletin No. 1269* (1924).

Branson, E. C., "Rural Life in the South," American Statistical Association, *Quarterly Publications* 13 (March 1912): 71–75.

Brooks, Robert Preston, "The Agrarian Revolution in Georgia, 1865–1912," University of Wisconsin, *Bulletin No. 639*, History Series (1914).

Brown, William W., and Morgan O. Reynolds, "Debt Peonage Re-examined," *Journal of Economic History* 33 (Dec. 1973): 862–871.

Bruce, Philip A., *The Plantation Negro As A Freeman* (New York: G. P. Putnam's Sons, 1889).

The Rise of the New South (Philadelphia: George Barrie and sons, 1905).

Bulkley, William L., "The Industrial Condition of the Negro in New York

City," *Annals of the American Academy of Political and Social Science* 27 (May 1906): 128–134.

Bull, Jacqueline P., "The General Merchant in the Economic History of the New South," *Journal of Southern History* 18 (Feb. 1952): 37–59.

Bullock, Henry Allen, *A History of Negro Education in the South: From 1619 to the Present* (Cambridge, Mass.: Harvard University Press, 1967).

Cable, George W., *The Negro Question: A Selection of Writings on Civil Rights in the South*, ed. Arlin Turner (New York: Norton, 1958).

Calvert, Robert A., "Nineteenth-Century Farmers, Cotton, and Prosperity," *Southwestern Historical Quarterly* 73 (April 1970): 509–521.

"The Freedmen and Agricultural Prosperity," *Southwestern Historical Quarterly* 76 (April 1973): 461–471.

Campbell, George, *White and Black: The Outcome of a Visit to the United States* (New York: R. Worthington, 1879).

Carpenter, John A., "Atrocities in the Reconstruction Period," *Journal of Negro History* 47 (Oct. 1962): 234–247.

Cash, W. J., *The Mind of the South* (New York: Knopf, 1941).

Chambers, Clyde R., "Relation of Land Income to Land Value," U.S. Department of Agriculture, *Bulletin No. 1224* (1924).

Cheung, Steven N. S., *The Theory of Share Tenancy* (Chicago: University of Chicago Press, 1969).

Clark, Thomas D., "Historical Aspects of Imperfect Competition: In the Southern Retail Trade after 1865," *Journal of Economic History* 3 (Dec. 1943): 38–47.

Pills, Petticoats and Plows: The Southern Country Store (Indianapolis: Bobbs-Merrill, 1944).

"The Furnishing and Supply System in Southern Agriculture since 1865," *Journal of Southern History* 12 (Feb. 1946): 24–44.

Cloud, N. B., "Cotton Culture in 1866," in U.S. Department of Agriculture, *Report of the Commissioner of Agriculture for the Year 1866* (1867), pp. 190–193.

Coale, Ansley J., and Norfleet W. Rives, Jr., "A Statistical Reconstruction of the Black Population of the United States, 1880–1970: Estimates of True Numbers by Age and Sex, Birth Rates, and Total Fertility," *Population Index* 39 (1973): 3–36.

Coleman, Kenneth, ed., "How to Run a Middle Georgia Cotton Plantation in 1885: A Document," *Agricultural History* 42 (Jan. 1968): 55–60.

Coman, Katherine, "The Negro as a Peasant Farmer," American Statistical Association *Publications* 9 (June 1904): 39–54.

Coulter, E. Merton, "A Century of a Georgia Plantation," *Agricultural History* 3 (Oct. 1929): 147–159.

Coulter, John Lee, "The Rural South," American Statistical Association, *Quarterly Publications* 13 (March 1912): 45–64.

Cox, Lawanda Fenlason, "Tenancy in the United States, 1865–1900: A Consideration of the Validity of the Agricultural Ladder Hypothesis," *Agricultural History* 18 (July 1944): 97–105.

"The Promise of Land for the Freedmen," *Mississippi Valley Historical Review* 45 (Dec. 1958): 413–440.

Cox, Lawanda Fenlason, and John H. Cox, eds., *Reconstruction, the Negro, and the New South* (Columbia, S.C.: University of South Carolina Press, 1973).

Cruden, Robert, *The Negro in Reconstruction* (Englewood Cliffs, N.J.: Prentice-Hall, 1969).

Current, Richard N., ed., *Reconstruction [1865–1877]* (Englewood Cliffs, N.J.: Prentice-Hall, 1965).

Daniel, Pete, *The Shadow of Slavery: Peonage in the South, 1901–1969* (Urbana: University of Illinois Press, 1972).

David, Paul A., and Peter Temin, "Slavery: The Progressive Institution?" *Journal of Economic History* 34 (Sept. 1974): 739–783.

Davis, Allison, "Caste, Economy, and Violence," *American Journal of Sociology* 51 (July 1945): 7–15.

    Burleigh B. Gardner, and Mary R. Gardner, *Deep South: A Social Anthropological Study of Caste and Class* (Chicago: University of Chicago Press, 1965 [1941]).

Davis, Lance E., and others, *American Economic Growth: An Economist's History of the United States* (New York: Harper and Row, 1972).

DeCanio, Stephen J., *Agricultural Production, Supply and Institutions in the Post-Civil War South* (unpublished Ph.D. dissertation, Massachusetts Institute of Technology, 1972).

    "Agricultural Production, Supply, and Institutions in the Post-Civil War South," *Journal of Economic History* 32 (March 1972): 396–398.

    "Cotton 'Overproduction' in Late Nineteenth-Century Southern Agriculture," *Journal of Economic History* 33 (Sept. 1973): 608–633.

    "Productivity and Income Distribution in the Post-Bellum South," *Journal of Economic History* 34 (June 1974): 422–446.

Demeny, Paul, and Paul Gingrich, "A Reconsideration of Negro-White Mortality Differentials in the United States," *Demography* 4 (1967): 820–837.

De Mond, Albert Lawrence, "Certain Aspects of the Economic Development of the American Negro, 1865–1900," Catholic University of America, *Studies in Economics* 18 (1945).

Dennett, John Richard, *The South As It Is: 1865–1866,* ed. Henry M. Christman (New York: Viking Press, 1965 [1865–1866]).

Dillingham, Pitt, "Land Tenure Among the Negroes," *Yale Review* 5 (Aug. 1896): 190–206.

Dixon, H. M., and H. W. Hawthorne, "An Economic Study of Farming in Sumter County, Georgia," U.S. Department of Agriculture, *Bulletin No. 492* (1917).

Donald, Henderson, *The Negro Freedman: Life Conditions of the American Negro in the Early Years after Emancipation* (New York: Henry Schuman, 1952).

Douglass, Frederick, *Life and Times of Frederick Douglass* (New York: Collier Books, 1962 [1892]).

Dowd, Douglas F., "A Comparative Analysis of Economic Development in the American West and South," *Journal of Economic History* 16 (Dec. 1956): 558–574.

Doyle, Bertram Wilbur, *The Etiquette of Race Relations in the South: A Study in Social Control* (New York: Schocken Books, 1971 [1937]).

Du Bois, W. E. B., *The Philadelphia Negro: A Social Study* (New York: Schocken Books, 1967 [1899]).

    ed., *The Negro in Business* (Atlanta: Atlanta University Press, 1899).

    "The Negro in the Black Belt: Some Social Sketches," U.S. Department of Labor, *Bulletin No. 22* (1899).

"The Freedmen's Bureau," *Atlantic Monthly* 87 (March 1901): 354–365.

"The Negro Landholder of Georgia," U.S. Department of Labor, *Bulletin No. 35* (1901).

ed., *The Negro Artisan* (Atlanta: Atlanta University Press, 1902).

The Souls of Black Folk: Essays and Sketches (Greenwich, Conn.: Fawcett, 1961 [1903]).

"The Negro Farmer," in *Twelfth Census of the United States: 1900, Special Reports, Supplementary Analysis and Derivative Tables* (1906), pp. 511–579.

"The Economic Future of the Negro," American Economic Association *Publications,* 3rd Series (Feb. 1906): 219–242.

ed., *The Negro American Family* (Atlanta: Atlanta University Press, 1909).

"The Rural South," American Statistical Association, *Quarterly Publications* 13 (March 1912): 80–84.

Black Reconstruction in America: An Essay Toward a History of the Part Which Black Folk Played in the Attempt to Reconstruct Democracy in America, 1860–1880 (New York: Atheneum, 1971 [1935]).

Dusk of Dawn: An Essay toward an Autobiography of a Race Concept (New York: Schocken Books, 1968 [1940]).

Du Bois, W. E. B., and Augustus Granville Dill, eds., *The Negro American Artisan* (Atlanta: Atlanta University Press, 1912).

Eblen, Jack Ericson, "New Estimates of the Vital Rates of the United States Black Population during the Nineteenth Century," *Demography* 11 (May 1974): 301–319.

Eckert, Edward K., "Contract Labor in Florida during Reconstruction," *Florida Historical Quarterly* 47 (July 1968): 34–50.

Edwards, Helen H., ed., *A List of References for the History of Agriculture in the Southern United States, 1865–1900* (Davis, Calif.: Agricultural History Center, 1971).

Edwards, Thomas J., "The Tenant System and Some Changes since Emancipation," *Annals of the American Academy of Political and Social Science* 49 (Sept. 1913): 38–46.

Eldridge, Hope T., and Dorothy Swaine Thomas, *Population Redistribution and Economic Growth, United States, 1870–1950: III. Demographic Analyses and Interrelations* (Philadelphia: American Philosophical Society, 1964).

Elkins, Stanley M., *Slavery: A Problem in American Institutional and Intellectual Life* (Chicago: University of Chicago Press, 1959).

Engerman, Stanley L., "Some Economic Factors in Southern Backwardness in the Nineteenth Century," in John F. Kain and John R. Meyer, eds., *Essays in Regional Economics* (Cambridge, Mass.: Harvard University Press, 1971), pp. 279–306.

Evans, Robert, "Some Notes on Coerced Labor," *Journal of Economic History* 30 (Dec. 1970): 861–866.

Farley, Reynolds, "The Demographic Rates and Social Institutions of the Nineteenth-Century Negro Population: A Stable Population Analysis," *Demography* 2 (1965): 386–398.

"The Urbanization of Negroes in the United States," *Journal of Social History* 1 (Spring 1968): 241–258.

Growth of the Black Population: A Study of Demographic Trends (Chicago: Markham, 1970).

Fitzhugh, George, "What's To Be Done With the Negroes?" *DeBow's Review,* New Series 1 (June 1866): 577–581.

"Negro Agrarianism," *DeBow's Review,* New Series 5 (Feb. 1868): 134–138.

Fleming, H. S., "In Our Cotton Belt," *Cosmopolitan* 14 (March 1893): 539–548.

Fleming, Walter L., "Reorganization of the Industrial System in Alabama after the Civil War," *American Journal of Sociology* 10 (Jan. 1905): 473–500.

Fogel, Robert William, and Stanley L. Engerman, *Time on the Cross: The Economics of American Negro Slavery* (Boston: Little, Brown and Company, 1974).

Time on the Cross: Evidence and Methods – A Supplement (Boston: Little, Brown and Company, 1974).

Franklin, John Hope, *From Slavery to Freedom: A History of Negro Americans,* 3rd ed. (New York: Knopf, 1967).

Reconstruction: After the Civil War (Chicago: University of Chicago Press, 1961).

Fraser, Jessie Melville, ed., "A Free Labor Contract, 1867," *Journal of Southern History* 6 (Nov. 1940): 546–548.

Frazier, E. Franklin, *The Negro Family in the United States,* rev. ed. (Chicago: University of Chicago Press, 1966 [1948]).

Black Bourgeoisie: The Rise of a New Middle Class in the United States (New York: Collier Books, 1962).

Fredrickson, George M., "Toward a Social Interpretation of the Development of American Racism," in Nathan I. Huggins, Martin Kilson, and Daniel M. Fox, eds., *Key Issues in the Afro-American Experience* (New York: Harcourt Brace Jovanovich, 1971), I, pp. 240–254.

The Black Image in the White Mind: The Debate on Afro-American Character and Destiny, 1817–1914 (New York: Harper Torchbooks, 1972).

[Freedmen's Bureau], *Senate Executive Documents,* 39th Congress, 1st Session, No. 27 (1866).

Freeman, Richard B., "Black–White Economic Differences: Why Did They Last So Long?" paper presented to the Cliometrics Conference, Madison, Wisconsin, April 1972.

Friedman, Lawrence J., *The White Savage: Racial Fantasies in the Postbellum South* (Englewood Cliffs, N.J.: Prentice-Hall, 1970).

Frissell, N. B., "Southern Agriculture and the Negro Farmer," American Statistical Association, *Quarterly Publications* 13 (March 1912): 65–70.

Frissell, N. B., and Isabel Bevier, "Dietary Studies of Negroes in Eastern Virginia in 1897 and 1898," U.S. Department of Agriculture, Office of Experiment Stations, *Bulletin No. 71* (1899).

Genovese, Eugene D., *The Political Economy of Slavery: Studies in the Economy and Society of the Slave South* (New York: Vintage Books, 1965).

Glasson, William H., "Rural Conditions in the South," American Statistical Association, *Quarterly Publications* 13 (March 1912): 76–79.

Glazer, Nathan, "Blacks and Ethnic Groups: The Difference, and the Political Difference It Makes," in Nathan I. Huggins, Martin Kilson, and Daniel M. Fox, eds., *Key Issues in the Afro-American Experience* (New York: Harcourt Brace Jovanovich, 1971), II, pp. 193–211.

Goldin, Claudia Dale, "The Economics of Emancipation," *Journal of Economic History* 33 (March 1973): 66–85.

"Urbanization and Slavery: The Issue of Compatibility," in Leo F. Schnore, ed., *The New Urban History* (Princeton, N.J.: Princeton University Press, 1975), pp. 231–246.

Goodloe, Daniel R., "Resources and Industrial Condition of the Southern States," in U.S. Department of Agriculture, *Report of the Commissioner of Agriculture for the Year 1865* (1866), pp. 102–136.

Grady, Henry W., "Cotton and Its Kingdom," *Harper's New Monthly Magazine* 63 (Oct. 1881): 719–734.

Gray, Lewis Cecil, "Southern Agriculture, Plantation System, and the Negro Problem," *Annals of the American Academy of Political and Social Science* 40 (March 1912): 90–99.

History of Agriculture in the Southern United States to 1860 (Washington, D.C.: Carnegie Institution, 1933).

Gray, Lewis Cecil, and others, "Farm Ownership and Tenancy," in U.S. Department of Agriculture, *Yearbook, 1923* (1924), pp. 507–600.

Green, Constance McLaughlin, *The Secret City: A History of Race Relations in the Nation's Capital* (Princeton, N. J.: Princeton University Press, 1967).

Greene, Lorenzo J., and Carter G. Woodson, *The Negro Wage Earner* (Washington, D.C.: Association for the Study of Negro Life and History, 1930).

Griffin, Richard W., "Problems of the Southern Cotton Planters after the Civil War," *Georgia Historical Quarterly* 39 (June 1955): 103–117.

Griffith, Lucille, ed., *Alabama: A Documentary History to 1900* (University, Ala.: University of Alabama Press, 1972).

Grob, Gerald N., "Organized Labor and the Negro Worker, 1865–1900," *Labor History* 1 (Spring 1960): 164–176.

Gross, James A., "Historians and the Literature of the Negro Worker," *Labor History* 10 (Summer 1969): 536–546.

Hackney, Sheldon, "Southern Violence," *American Historical Review* 74 (Feb. 1969): 906–925.

Haller, John S., Jr., "Race, Mortality, and Life Insurance: Negro Vital Statistics in the Late Nineteenth Century," *Journal of the History of Medicine and Allied Sciences* 25 (July 1970): 247–261.

Hammond, Harry, "Culture of Cotton," in U.S. Department of Agriculture, Office of Experiment Stations, *Bulletin No. 33* (1896), pp. 225–270.

Hammond, M. B., "The Southern Farmer and the Cotton Question," *Political Science Quarterly* 12 (Sept. 1897): 450–475.

"The Cotton Industry: An Essay in American Economic History," American Economic Association *Publications*, New Series (Dec. 1897).

Harlan, Louis R., *Separate and Unequal: Public School Campaigns and Racism in the Southern Seaboard States, 1901–1915* (New York: Atheneum, 1969 [1958]).

Harmon, J. H., Jr., Arnett G. Lindsay, and Carter G. Woodson, *The Negro as a Business Man* (College Park, Md.: McGrath, 1969 [1929]).

Harris, Abram L., *The Negro as Capitalist: A Study of Banking and Business among American Negroes* (New York: Negro Universities Press, 1969 [1936]).

Haskell, E. S., "A Farm-Management Survey in Brooks County, Georgia," U.S. Department of Agriculture, *Bulletin No. 648* (1918).

Hawkins, Homer C., "Trends in Black Migration from 1863 to 1960," *Phylon* 34 (June 1973): 140–152.

Haynes, George Edmund, "The Negro at Work in New York City," Columbia

University, *Studies in History, Economics and Public Law* 49 (1912).
"Conditions among Negroes in the Cities," *Annals of the American Academy of Political and Social Science* 49 (Sept. 1913): 105–119.

Hibbard, Benjamin H., "Tenancy in the Southern States," *Quarterly Journal of Economics* 27 (May 1913): 482–496.

Higgs, Robert, *The Transformation of the American Economy, 1865–1914: An Essay in Interpretation* (New York: John Wiley and Sons, 1971).

"Race, Skills, and Earnings: American Immigrants in 1909," *Journal of Economic History* 31 (June 1971): 420–428.

"Did Southern Farmers Discriminate?" *Agricultural History* 46 (April 1972): 325–328.

"Property Rights and Resource Allocation under Alternative Land Tenure Forms: A Comment," *Oxford Economic Papers* 24 (Nov. 1972): 428–431.

"Race, Tenure, and Resource Allocation in Southern Agriculture, 1910," *Journal of Economic History* 33 (March 1973): 149–169 [see the Editor's Notes, *ibid.* 33 (Sept. 1973): 668, for correction of a printer's error in this article].

"Mortality in Rural America, 1970–1920: Estimates and Conjectures," *Explorations in Economic History* 10 (Winter 1973): 177–195.

"Patterns of Farm Rental in the Georgia Cotton Belt, 1880–1900," *Journal of Economic History* 34 (June 1974): 468–482.

"Did Southern Farmers Discriminate? – Interpretive Problems and Further Evidence," *Agricultural History* 49 (April 1975): 445–447.

"Participation of Blacks and Immigrants in the American Merchant Class, 1890–1910: Some Demographic Relations," *Explorations in Economic History,* 13 (April 1976).

"The Boll Weevil, the Cotton Economy, and Black Migration, 1910–1930," *Agricultural History,* 50 (April 1976): 335–350.

"Firm-Specific Evidence on Racial Wage Differentials and Workforce Segregation," *American Economic Review,* forthcoming.

Hoffman, Frederick L., "Race Traits and Tendencies of the American Negro," American Economic Association *Publications* 11 (Aug. 1896).

Hoffsommer, Harold, ed., *The Social and Economic Significance of Land Tenure in the Southwestern States* (Chapel Hill: University of North Carolina Press, 1950).

Holmes, George K., "The Peons of the South," *Annals of the American Academy of Political and Social Science* 4 (Sept. 1893): 65–74.

Holmes, William F., "Whitecapping: Agrarian Violence in Mississippi, 1902–1906," *Journal of Southern History* 35 (May 1969): 165–185.

"Whitecapping in Mississippi: Agrarian Violence in the Populist Era," *Mid-America* 55 (April 1973): 134–148.

House, Albert V., Jr., "A Reconstruction Share-Cropper Contract on a Georgia Rice Plantation," *Georgia Historical Quarterly* 26 (June 1942): 156–165.

Howard, C. W., "Condition and Resources of Georgia," in U.S. Department of Agriculture, *Report of the Commissioner of Agriculture for the Year 1866* (1867), pp. 567–580.

"Conditions of Agriculture in the Cotton States," in U.S. Department of Agriculture, *Report of the Commissioner of Agriculture for the Year 1874* (1875), pp. 215–238.

Hurt, A. B., "Mississippi: Its Climate, Soil, Productions, and Agricultural Capabilities," U.S. Department of Agriculture, *Miscellaneous Special Report No. 3* (1884).

Jackson, Giles B., and D. Webster Davis, *The Industrial History of the Negro Race of the United States* (Freeport, N.Y.: Books for Libraries Press, 1971 [1908]).
Johnson, Charles S., *Shadow of the Plantation* (Chicago: University of Chicago Press, 1934).
Jones, S. B., "Fifty Years of Negro Public Health," *Annals of the American Academy of Political and Social Science* 49 (Sept. 1913): 138–146.
Jones, Thomas Jesse, "Negro Population in the United States," *Annals of the American Academy of Political and Social Science* 49 (Sept. 1913): 1–9.
Jordan, Weymouth T., "The Elisha F. King Family, Planters of the Alabama Black Belt," *Agricultural History* 19 (July 1945): 152–162.
Jordan, Winthrop D., *White Over Black: American Attitudes toward the Negro, 1550–1812* (Chapel Hill: University of North Carolina Press, 1968).
Katzman, David M., *Before the Ghetto: Black Detroit in the Nineteenth Century* (Urbana: University of Illinois Press, 1973).
Kelsey, Carl, "The Evolution of Negro Labor," *Annals of the American Academy of Political and Social Science* 21 (Jan. 1903): 55–76.
King, Edward, *The Great South: A Record of Journeys* (Hartford, Conn.: American Publishing Co., 1875).
Kloosterboer, W., *Involuntary Labour since the Abolition of Slavery: A Survey of Compulsory Labour throughout the World* (Leiden: E. J. Brill, 1960).
Kolchin, Peter, *First Freedom: The Responses of Alabama's Blacks to Emancipation and Reconstruction* (Westport, Conn.: Greenwood Press, 1972).
Kristol, Irving, "The Negro Today Is Like the Immigrant Yesterday," *New York Times Magazine* (Sept. 11, 1966), Pt. I, pp. 50–51 ff.
[Ku-Klux Hearings], *Senate Reports*, 42nd Congress, 2nd Session, No. 41 (1872).
Lacy, Dan, *The White Use of Blacks in America: 350 Years of Law and Violence, Attitudes and Etiquette, Politics and Change* (New York: McGraw-Hill, 1972).
Laird, William E., and James R. Rinehart, "Deflation, Agriculture and Southern Development," *Agricultural History* 42 (April 1968): 115–124.
Lane, Frederic C., "Economic Consequences of Organized Violence," *Journal of Economic History* 18 (Dec. 1958): 401–417.
Laws, J. Bradford, "The Negroes of Cinclare Central Factory and Calumet Plantation, Louisiana," U.S. Department of Labor, *Bulletin No. 38* (1902).
Leigh, Frances Butler, *Ten Years on a Georgia Plantation since the War* (London: Richard Bentley and Son, 1883).
Lerner, Eugene, "Southern Output and Agricultural Income, 1860–1880," *Agricultural History* 33 (July 1959): 117–125.
Levine, Gene N., and Darrell M. Montero, "Socioeconomic Mobility among Three Generations of Japanese Americans," *Journal of Social Issues* 29 (1973): 33–48.
Lewinson, Paul, *Race, Class, and Party: A History of Negro Suffrage and White Politics in the South* (New York: Grosset and Dunlap, 1965 [1932]).
Light, Ivan H., *Ethnic Enterprise in America: Business and Welfare among Chinese, Japanese, and Blacks* (Berkeley: University of California Press, 1972).
Lightfoot, A. R., "Condition and Wants of the Cotton Raising States," *DeBow's Review*, New Series 6 (Feb. 1869): 151–154.
Logan, Frenise A., "Factors Influencing the Efficiency of Negro Farm

Laborers in Post-Reconstruction North Carolina," *Agricultural History* 33 (Oct. 1959): 185–189.

The Negro in North Carolina, 1876–1894 (Chapel Hill: University of North Carolina Press, 1964).

Logan, Rayford W., *The Betrayal of the Negro, from Rutherford B. Hayes to Woodrow Wilson* (New York: Collier Books, 1965).

Lynch, Hollis R., ed., *The Black Urban Condition: A Documentary History, 1866–1971* (New York: Thomas Y. Crowell Co., 1973).

McFalls, Joseph A., Jr., "Impact of VD on the Fertility of the U.S. Black Population, 1880–1950," *Social Biology* 20 (March 1973): 2–19.

McFeely, William S., *Yankee Stepfather: General O. O. Howard and the Freedmen* (New Haven: Yale University Press, 1968).

"Unfinished Business: The Freedmen's Bureau and Federal Action in Race Relations," in Nathan I. Huggins, Martin Kilson, and Daniel M. Fox, eds., *Key Issues in the Afro-American Experience* (New York: Harcourt Brace Jovanovich, 1971), ii, pp. 5–25.

McPherson, James M., *The Negro's Civil War: How American Negroes Felt and Acted during the War for the Union* (New York: Vintage Books, 1965).

McPherson, James M., and others, *Blacks in America: Bibliographical Essays* (Garden City, N.Y.: Anchor Books, 1971).

Mandle, R., "The Re-Establishment of the Plantation Economy in the South, 1865–1910," *Review of Black Political Economy* 3 (Winter 1973): 68–88.

"The Plantation States as a Sub-Region of the Post-Bellum Siuth," *Journal of Economic History* 34 (Sept. 1974): 732–738.

Mangum, Charles S., Jr., *The Legal Status of the Negro* (Chapel Hill: University of North Carolina Press, 1940).

The Legal Status of the Tenant Farmer in the Southeast (Chapel Hill: University of North Carolina Press, 1952).

Marshall, Ray, "Industrialisation and Race Relations in the Southern United States," in Guy Hunter, ed., *Industrialisation and Race Relations* (London: Oxford University Press, 1965), pp. 61–81.

"The Economics of Racial Discrimination: A Survey," *Journal of Economic Literature* 12 (Sept. 1974): 849–871.

Matthews, John Michael, "The Georgia 'Race Strike' of 1909," *Journal of Southern History* 40 (Nov. 1974): 613–630.

Meeker, Edward, "The Improving Health of the United States, 1850–1915," *Explorations in Economic History* 9 (Summer 1972): 353–374.

"Mortality Trends of Southern Blacks, 1850–1910: Some Preliminary Findings," *Explorations in Economic History,* 13 (Jan. 1976): 13–42.

"An Economic Model of Fertility," unpublished paper, 1974.

Meeker, Edward, and James Kau, "Occupational Discrimination in 1910: Some Preliminary Results," paper presented to the Eastern Economic Association, Albany, N.Y., Oct. 25–27, 1974.

Meier, August, *Negro Thought in America, 1880–1915: Racial Ideologies in the Age of Booker T. Washington* (Ann Arbor: University of Michigan Press, 1963).

Meier, August, and Elliott Rudwick, *From Plantation to Ghetto,* rev. ed. (New York: Hill and Wang, 1970).

Mendenhall, Marjorie Stratford, "The Rise of Southern Tenancy," *Yale Review* 27 (Sept. 1937): 110–129.

Meredith, H. L., "Agrarian Socialism and the Negro in Oklahoma, 1900–1918," *Labor History* 11 (Summer 1970): 277–284.

Meyers, John B., "The Alabama Freedmen and the Economic Adjustments During Presidential Reconstruction, 1865–1867," *Alabama Review* 26 (Oct. 1973): 252–266.

Miller, Elizabeth W., and Mary L. Fisher, *The Negro in America: A Bibliography* (Cambridge, Mass.: Harvard University Press, 1970).

Miller, Kelly, "The Economic Handicap of the Negro in the North," *Annals of the American Academy of Political and Social Science* 27 (May 1906): 81–88.

"Professional and Skilled Occupations," *Annals of the American Academy of Political and Social Science* 49 (Sept. 1913): 10–18.

Miller, Zane L., "Urban Blacks in the South, 1865–1920: The Richmond, Savannah, New Orleans, Louisville, and Birmingham Experience," in Leo F. Schnore, ed., *The New Urban History* (Princeton, N.J.: Princeton University Press, 1975), pp. 184–204.

[Mississippi Migration Convention of 1879], "Proceedings," reprinted from the *Vicksburg Commercial Daily Advertiser,* May 5, 1879, in *Journal of Negro History* 4 (Jan. 1919): 51–54.

Moore, Frederick W., "The Condition of the Southern Farmer," *Yale Review* 3 (May 1894): 56–67.

Morrill, Richard, and O. F. Donaldson, "Geographical Perspectives on the History of Black America," *Economic Geography* 48 (Jan. 1972): 1–23.

Myrdal, Gunnar, *An American Dilemma: The Negro Problem and Modern Democracy* (New York: Harper Torchbooks, 1969 [1944]).

Nash, Gerald D., "Research Opportunities in the Economic History of the South After 1880," *Journal of Southern History* 32 (Aug. 1966): 308–324.

Nordhoff, Charles, *The Cotton States in the Spring and Summer of 1875* (New York: Appleton, 1876).

North, Douglass C., *Growth and Welfare in the American Past: A New Economic History,* 2nd ed. (Englewood Cliffs, N.J.: Prentice-Hall, 1974).

Osofsky, Gilbert, *Harlem: The Making of a Ghetto, Negro New York, 1890–1930* (New York: Harper Torchbooks, 1968).

Otken, Charles H., *The Ills of the South, or Related Causes Hostile to the General Prosperity of the Southern People* (New York: G. P. Putnam's Sons, 1894).

Ovington, Mary White, "The Negro in the Trades Unions in New York," *Annals of the American Academy of Political and Social Science* 27 (May 1906): 89–96.

Half A Man: The Status of the Negro in New York (New York: Hill and Wang, 1969 [1911]).

Park, Robert E., "Negro Home Life and Standards of Living," *Annals of the American Academy of Political and Social Science* 49 (Sept. 1913): 147–163.

Percy, William Alexander, *Lanterns on the Levee: Recollections of a Planter's Son* (New York: Knopf, 1941).

Phillips, Ulrich B., "The Decadence of the Plantation System," *Annals of the American Academy of Political and Social Science* 35 (Jan. 1910): 37–41.

"Plantations with Slave Labor and Free," *American Historical Review* 30 (July 1925): 738–753.

Life and Labor in the Old South (Boston: Little, Brown and Company, 1929).

Pierson, H. W., *A Letter to Hon. Charles Sumner, with "Statements" of Outrages upon Freedmen in Georgia, and an Account of My Expulsion from Andersonville, Ga., by the Ku-Klux Klan* (Freeport, N.Y.: Books for Libraries Press, 1972 [1870]).

Pope, Christie Farnham, "Southern Homesteads for Negroes," *Agricultural History* 44 (April 1970): 201–212.

Porter, Kenneth W., "Negro Labor in the Western Cattle Industry, 1866–1900," *Labor History* 10 (Summer 1969): 346–374.

Powdermaker, Hortense, *After Freedom: A Cultural Study in the Deep South* (New York: Atheneum, 1968 [1939]).

Prunty, Merle, Jr., "The Renaissance of the Southern Plantation," *Geographical Review* 45 (Oct. 1955): 459–491.

"The Census on Multiple-Units and Plantations in the South," *Professional Geographer* 8 (Sept. 1956): 2–5.

Ransom, Roger L., and Richard Sutch, "Debt Peonage in the Cotton South after the Civil War," *Journal of Economic History* 32 (Sept. 1972): 641–669.

"The Ex-Slave in the Post-Bellum South: A Study of the Economic Impact of Racism in a Market Environment," *Journal of Economic History* 33 (March 1973): 131–148.

Rao, S. L. N., "On Long-Term Mortality Trends in the United States, 1850–1968," *Demography* 10 (Aug. 1973): 405–419.

Raper, Arthur F., *Preface to Peasantry: A Tale of Two Black Belt Counties* (New York: Atheneum, 1968 [1936]).

Reid, Joseph D., "Sharecropping As An Understandable Market Response: The Post-Bellum South," *Journal of Economic History* 33 (March 1973): 106–130.

Reid, Whitelaw, *After the War: A Tour of the Southern States, 1865–1866,* ed. C. Vann Woodward (New York: Harper Torchbooks, 1965 [1866]).

Renshaw, Patrick, "The Black Ghetto, 1890–1940," *Journal of American Studies* 8 (April 1974): 41–59.

Rice, Lawrence D., *The Negro in Texas, 1874–1900* (Baton Rouge: Louisiana State University Press, 1971).

Richardson, Joe M., "The Freedmen's Bureau and Negro Labor in Florida," *Florida Historical Quarterly* 39 (Oct. 1960): 167–174.

Ripley, W. Z., "Colored Population of African Descent," in American Economic Association, *The Federal Census: Critical Essays* (New York: Macmillan, 1899), pp. 38–48.

Roberts, Charles A., "Did Southern Farmers Discriminate? – The Evidence Re-Examined," *Agricultural History* 49 (April 1975): 441–445.

Rogers, William Warren, "Negro Knights of Labor in Arkansas: A Case Study of the 'Miscellaneous' Strike," *Labor History* 10 (Summer 1969): 498–505.

Rose, Willie Lee, *Rehearsal for Reconstruction: The Port Royal Experiment* (New York: Vintage Books, 1967 [1964]).

Saloutos, Theodore, "Southern Agriculture and the Problems of Readjustment: 1865–1877," *Agricultural History* 30 (April 1956): 58–76.

Scheiner, Seth M., *Negro Mecca: A History of the Negro in New York City, 1865–1920* (New York: New York University Press, 1965).

[Schurz, Carl], *Senate Executive Documents,* 39th Congress, 1st Session, No. 2 (1866).

Scott, Emmett J., *Negro Migration during the War* (New York: Oxford University Press, 1920).

Scruggs, Otey M., "The Economic and Racial Components of Jim Crow," in Nathan I. Huggins, Martin Kilson, and Daniel M. Fox, eds., *Key Issues in the Afro-American Experience* (New York: Harcourt Brace Jovanovich, 1971), II, pp. 70–87.

Seagrave, Charles E., "The Southern Negro Agricultural Worker: 1850–1870," *Journal of Economic History* 31 (March 1971): 279–280.

Sellers, James L., "The Economic Incidence of the Civil War in the South," *Mississippi Valley Historical Review* 14 (Sept. 1927): 179–191.

Shannon, Fred A., *The Farmer's Last Frontier: Agriculture, 1860–1897* (New York: Harper Torchbooks, 1968 [1945]).

Shapiro, Herbert, "The Ku Klux Klan during Reconstruction: The South Carolina Episode," *Journal of Negro History* 49 (Jan. 1964): 34–55.

Shofner, Jerrell H., "A Merchant Planter in the Reconstruction South," *Agricultural History* 46 (April 1972): 291–296.

Shugg, Roger Wallace, "Survival of the Plantation System in Louisiana," *Journal of Southern History* 3 (Aug. 1937): 311–325.

Simkins, Francis B., "The Problems of South Carolina Agriculture after the Civil War," *North Carolina Historical Review* 7 (Jan. 1930): 46–77.

"The Solution of Post-Bellum Agricultural Problems in South Carolina," *North Carolina Historical Review* 7 (April 1930): 192–219.

Sinclair, William A., *The Aftermath of Slavery* (New York: Arno Press, 1969 [1905]).

Sisk, Glenn N., "Agricultural Diversification in the Alabama Black Belt," *Agricultural History* 26 (April 1952): 42–45.

"Rural Merchandising in the Alabama Black Belt, 1875–1917," *Journal of Farm Economics* 37 (Nov. 1955): 705–715.

"The Wholesale Commission Business in the Alabama Black Belt, 1875–1917," *Journal of Farm Economics* 38 (Aug. 1956): 799–802.

Sitterson, J. Carlyle, "The McCollams: A Planter Family of the Old and New South," *Journal of Southern History* 6 (Aug. 1940): 347–367.

"The Transition from Slave to Free Economy on the William J. Minor Plantations," *Agricultural History* 17 (Oct. 1943): 216–224.

Smith, Richard Kent, *The Economics of Education and Discrimination in the U.S. South: 1870–1910* (unpublished Ph.D. dissertation, University of Wisconsin, 1973).

Smith, R. L., "The Elevation of Negro Farm Life," *Independent* 52 (Aug. 30, 1900): 2103–2106.

Somers, Robert, *The Southern States since the War, 1870–71* (London: Macmillan, 1871).

South Carolina, State Board of Agriculture [Harry Hammond], *South Carolina: Resources and Population, Institutions and Industries* (Charleston: State Board of Agriculture, 1883).

Southerner [pseud.], "Agricultural Labor at the South," *Galaxy* 12 (Sept. 1871): 328–340.

Spahr, Charles B., "The Negro as an Industrial Factor," *Outlook* 62 (May 6, 1899): 31–37.

Spear, Allan H., *Black Chicago: The Making of a Negro Ghetto, 1890–1920* (Chicago: University of Chicago Press, 1967).

"The Origins of the Urban Ghetto, 1870–1915," in Nathan I. Huggins, Martin Kilson, and Daniel M. Fox, eds., *Key Issues in the Afro-American Experience* (New York: Harcourt Brace Jovanovich, 1971), II, pp. 153–166.

Spero, Sterling D., and Abram L. Harris, *The Black Worker: The Negro and the Labor Movement* (New York: Columbia University Press, 1931).

Stampp, Kenneth M., *The Peculiar Institution: Slavery in the Ante-Bellum South* (New York: Vintage Books, 1956).

The Era of Reconstruction, 1865–1877 (New York: Knopf, 1965).

Starobin, Robert S., *Industrial Slavery in the Old South* (New York: Oxford University Press, 1970).

Stearns, Charles, *The Black Man of the South, and the Rebels; or, The Characteristics of the Former, and the Recent Outrages of the Latter* (New York: Negro Universities Press, 1969 [1872]).

Stephenson, Gilbert Thomas, *Race Distinctions in American Law* (New York: Appleton, 1910).

Stiglitz, Joseph, "Approaches to the Economics of Discrimination," *American Economic Review* 63 (May 1973): 287–295.

Stine, O. C., and O. E. Baker, *Atlas of American Agriculture: Pt. V, The Crops; Section A, Cotton,* U.S. Department of Agriculture, Office of Farm Management, 1918.

Stone, Alfred Holt, "The Negro in the Yazoo-Mississippi Delta," American Economic Association *Publications,* 3rd Series 3 (Feb. 1902): 233–272.

"The Economic Future of the Negro: The Factor of White Competition," American Economic Association *Publications,* 3rd Series (Feb. 1906): 243–294.

Studies in the American Race Problem (New York: Doubleday, Page and Co., 1908).

"Negro Labor and the Boll Weevil," *Annals of the American Academy of Political and Social Science* 33 (March 1909): 167–174.

"The Negro and Agricultural Development," *Annals of the American Academy of Political and Social Science* 35 (Jan. 1910): 8–15.

Sylla, Richard, "Federal Policy, Banking Market Structure, and Capital Mobilization in the United States, 1863–1913," *Journal of Economic History* 29 (Dec. 1969): 657–686.

Tang, Anthony M., "Economic Development and Changing Consequences of Race Discrimination in Southern Agriculture," *Journal of Farm Economics* 41 (Dec. 1959): 1113–1126.

Taylor, Paul S., "Slave to Freedman," Southern Economic History Project, *Working Paper No. 7* (Berkeley, Calif.: Jan. 1970).

Taylor, Rosser H., "Post-Bellum Southern Rental Contracts," *Agricultural History* 17 (April 1943): 121–128.

"The Sale and Application of Commercial Fertilizers in the South Atlantic States to 1900," *Agricultural History* 21 (Jan. 1947): 46–52.

Tebeau, C. W., "Some Aspects of Planter-Freedman Relations, 1865–1880," *Journal of Negro History* 21 (April 1936): 130–150.

Thomas, Bettye C., "A Nineteenth Century Black Operated Shipyard, 1866–1884: Reflections upon Its Inception and Ownership," *Journal of Negro History* 59 (Jan. 1974): 1–12.

Thomas, Brinley, "Negro Migration and the American Urban Dilemma," in *Migration and Urban Development* (London: Methuen, 1972), pp. 140–169.

Thurow, Lester C., *Poverty and Discrimination* (Washington, D.C.: Brookings, 1969).

Tillinghast, Joseph Alexander, "The Negro in Africa and America," American Economic Association *Publications,* 3rd Series 3 (May 1902).

Tindall, George Brown, *South Carolina Negroes, 1877–1900* (Baton Rouge: Louisiana State University Press, 1966 [1952]).

Trelease, Allen W., *Reconstruction: The Great Experiment* (New York: Harper Torchbooks, 1971).

Trowbridge, J. T., *The South: A Tour of Its Battle-Fields and Ruined Cities* (Hartford, Conn.: L. Stebbins, 1866).

[Truman, Benjamin C.], *Senate Executive Documents*, 39th Congress, 1st Session, No. 43 (1866).

Tuttle, William M., Jr., "Labor Conflict and Racial Violence: The Black Worker in Chicago, 1894–1919," *Labor History* 10 (Summer 1969): 408–432.

U.S. Bureau of the Census, "Plantations in the South," in *Agriculture, 1909 and 1910* (1913), v, pp. 877–889.

Plantation Farming in the United States (1916).

Negro Population, 1790–1915 (1918).

Historical Statistics of the United States, Colonial Times to 1957 (1960).

Long Term Economic Growth, 1860–1965 (1966).

U.S. Census Office, *Report on Cotton Production in the United States* (1884).

"Ownership of Rented Farms," in *Agriculture, Part I* (1902), v, pp. lxxxv–xciii, 309–316.

U.S. Congress, Joint Committee on Reconstruction, *Report of the Joint Committee on Reconstruction at the First Session Thirty-Ninth Congress* (1866).

U.S. Department of Agriculture, *Report of the Commissioner of Agriculture for the Year 1866* (1867).

"Southern Agriculture," in *Report of the Commissioner of Agriculture for the Year 1867* (1868), pp. 412–428.

"Cotton Investigation," in *Report of the Commissioner of Agriculture for the Year 1876* (1877), pp. 114–152.

Agricultural Marketing Service, "Cotton and Cottonseed: Acreage, Yield, Production, Disposition, Price, Value, by States, 1866–1952," *Statistical Bulletin No. 164* (1955).

Bureau of Agricultural Economics, "Statistics on Cotton and Related Data," *Statistical Bulletin No. 99* (1951).

Division of Statistics, "Wages of Farm Labor in the United States," *Miscellaneous Series, Bulletin No. 22* (1901).

U.S. Department of Labor, "Condition of the Negro in Various Cities," *Bulletin No. 10* (May 1897).

Division of Negro Economics, *Negro Migration in 1916–17* (1919).

U.S. Industrial Commission, *Report* (1901), x, xi.

U.S. Senate, "Report on the Exodus of 1879," reprinted in *Journal of Negro History* 4 (Jan. 1919): 57–92.

Committee on Agriculture and Forestry, "Report on Condition of Cotton Growers in the United States, the Present Prices of Cotton, and the Remedy; and on Cotton Consumption and Production," *Senate Reports*, 53rd Congress, 3rd Session, No. 986, Pt. ı (1895).

Committee on Education and Labor, *Report on Relations between Labor and Capital* (1885).

Vance, Rupert B., *Human Factors in Cotton Culture: A Study in the Social Geography of the American South* (Chapel Hill: University of North Carolina Press, 1929).

Human Geography of the South (New York: Russell and Russell, 1968 [1935]).

Van Deusen, John G., "The Exodus of 1879," *Journal of Negro History* 21 (April 1936): 111–129.

Vandiver, Joseph S., "The Changing Realm of King Cotton," in Raymond W. Mack, ed., *The Changing South* (Chicago: Aldine, 1970), pp. 21–35.

Vickery, William Edward, *The Economics of the Negro Migration, 1900–1960* (unpublished Ph.D. dissertation, University of Chicago, 1969).

Virginia, Bureau of Labor and Industrial Statistics, *Fourth Annual Report, 1901* (Richmond: J. H. O'Bannon, 1901).

Thirteenth Annual Report, 1910 (Richmond: Davis Bottom, 1910).

Wade, Richard C., *Slavery in the Cities: The South, 1820–1860* (New York: Oxford University Press, 1964).

Wagstaff, Thomas, "Call Your Old Master – 'Master': Southern Political Leaders and Negro Labor during Presidential Reconstruction," *Labor History* 10 (Summer 1969): 323–345.

Walker, Francis A., "The Colored Race in the United States," *Forum* 11 (July 1891): 501–509.

Wallich, Henry C., and William J. Dodson, "Economic Models and Black Economic Development," *Review of Black Political Economy* 3 (Fall 1972): 74–86.

Washington, Booker T., *The Future of the American Negro* (Boston: Small, Maynard and Co., 1899).

Up From Slavery: An Autobiography (London: Oxford University Press, 1945 [1901]).

"The Negro in Business," *Gunton's Magazine* 20 (March 1901): 209–219.

The Story of the Negro: The Rise of the Race from Slavery (New York: Doubleday, Page and Co., 1909).

"The Negro's Part in Southern Development," *Annals of the American Academy of Political and Social Science* 35 (Jan. 1910): 124–133.

"Durham, North Carolina, a City of Negro Enterprises," *Independent* 70 (March 30, 1911): 642–650.

"The Negro and the Labor Unions," *Atlantic Monthly* 111 (June 1913): 756–767.

"Industrial Education and the Public Schools," *Annals of the American Academy of Political and Social Science* 49 (Sept. 1913): 219–232.

Washington, Booker T., and others, *The Negro Problem* (New York: Arno Press, 1969 [1903]).

Washington, Booker T., and W. E. B. Du Bois, *The Negro in the South: His Economic Progress in Relation to His Moral and Religious Development* (New York: Citadel Press, 1970 [1907]).

Weare, Walter B., *Black Business in the New South: A Social History of the North Carolina Mutual Life Insurance Company* (Urbana: University of Illinois Press, 1973).

Weatherford, W. D., *Negro Life in the South: Present Conditions and Needs*, rev. ed. (New York: Association Press, 1911).

Welch, Finis, "Labor-Market Discrimination: An Interpretation of Income Differences in the Rural South," *Journal of Political Economy* 75 (June 1967): 225–240.

Wesley, Charles H., *Negro Labor in the United States, 1850–1925* (New York: Vanguard, 1927).

Wharton, Vernon Lane, *The Negro in Mississippi, 1865–1890* (New York: Harper Torchbooks, 1965 [1947]).

White, Walter, *Rope and Faggot: A Biography of Judge Lynch* (New York: Arno Press, 1969 [1929]).

Wilcox, E. V., "Lease Contracts Used in Renting Farms on Shares," U.S. Department of Agriculture, *Bulletin No. 650* (1918).

Wiley, B. I., "Vicissitudes of Early Reconstruction Farming in the Lower Mississippi Valley," *Journal of Southern History* 3 (Nov. 1937): 441–452.

  Southern Negroes, 1861–1865 (New Haven: Yale Univeristy Press, 1965 [1938]).

  "Salient Changes in Southern Agriculture since the Civil War," *Agricultural History* 13 (April 1939): 65–76.

Willcox, Walter F., "The Probable Increase of the Negro Race in the United States," *Quarterly Journal of Economics* 19 (Aug. 1905): 545–572.

Willey, D. Allen, "The Negro and the Soil," *Arena* 23 (May 1900): 553–560.

Williamson, Joel, *After Slavery: The Negro in South Carolina during Reconstruction, 1861–1877* (Chapel Hill: University of North Carolina Press, 1965).

  "Black Self-Assertion Before and After Emancipation," in Nathan I. Huggins, Martin Kilson, and Daniel M. Fox, eds., *Key Issues in the Afro-American Experience* (New York: Harcourt Brace Jovanovich, 1971), I, pp. 213–239.

Wish, Harvey, ed., *Reconstruction in the South, 1865–1877: First-hand Accounts of the American Southland after the Civil War, by Northerners and Southerners* (New York: Noonday Press, 1965).

Woodson, Carter G., *A Century of Negro Migration* (Washington, D.C.: Association for the Study of Negro Life and History, 1918).

  The Rural Negro (Washington, D.C.: Association for the Study of Negro Life and History, 1930).

Woodward, C. Vann, *Origins of the New South, 1877–1913* ([Baton Rouge]: Louisiana State University Press, 1951).

  The Strange Career of Jim Crow, rev. ed. (New York: Oxford University Press, 1966).

Woofter, Thomas Jackson, Jr., *Negro Migration: Changes in Rural Organization and Population of the Cotton Belt* (New York: Negro Universities Press, 1969 [1920]).

Worthman, Paul B., "Black Workers and Labor Unions in Birmingham, Alabama, 1897–1904," *Labor History* 10 (Summer 1969): 375–407.

Worthman, Paul B., and James R. Green, "Black Workers in the New South, 1865–1915," in Nathan I. Huggins, Martin Kilson, and Daniel M. Fox, eds., *Key Issues in the Afro-American Experience* (New York: Harcourt Brace Jovanovich, 1971), II, pp. 47–69.

Wright, Gavin, "Comment on Papers by Reid, Ransom and Sutch, and Higgs," *Journal of Economic History* 33 (March 1973): 170–176.

  "New and Old Views on the Economics of Slavery," *Journal of Economic History* 33 (June 1973): 452–456.

  "Cotton Competition and the Post-Bellum Recovery of the American South," *Journal of Economic History* 34 (Sept. 1974): 610–635.

Wright, R. R., Jr., "The Migration of Negroes to the North," *Annals of the American Academy of Political and Social Science* 27 (May 1906): 97–116.

The Negro in Pennsylvania: A Study in Economic History (New York: Arno Press, 1969 [1912]).

"The Negro in Unskilled Labor," *Annals of the American Academy of Political and Social Science* 49 (Sept. 1913): 19–27.

Zeichner, Oscar, "The Transition from Slave to Free Agricultural Labor in the Southern States," *Agricultural History* 13 (Jan. 1939): 22–32.

"The Legal Status of the Agricultural Laborer in the South," *Political Science Quarterly* 55 (Sept. 1940): 412–428.

Index